Great Thinkers in Economics

Series Editor
A. P. Thirlwall
School of Economics
University of Kent
Canterbury, UK

The famous historian, E. H. Carr once said that in order to understand history it is necessary to understand the historian writing it. The same could be said of economics. Famous economists often remark that specific episodes in their lives, or particular events that took place in their formative years attracted them to economics. Great Thinkers in Economics is designed to illuminate the economics of some of the great historical and contemporary economists by exploring the interaction between their lives and work, and the events surrounding them.

More information about this series at
http://www.palgrave.com/gp/series/15026

David Reisman

Thomas Robert Malthus

palgrave
macmillan

David Reisman
Nanyang Technological University
Singapore, Singapore

Great Thinkers in Economics
ISBN 978-3-030-01955-6 ISBN 978-3-030-01956-3 (eBook)
https://doi.org/10.1007/978-3-030-01956-3

Library of Congress Control Number: 2018957684

Cover credit: GL Archive/Alamy Stock Photo

This Palgrave Macmillan imprint is published by the registered company Springer Nature Switzerland AG
The registered company address is: Gewerbestrasse 11, 6330 Cham, Switzerland

Also by David Reisman

Adam Smith's Sociological Economics
Alfred Marshall: Progress and Politics
Alfred Marshall's Mission
Anthony Crosland: The Mixed Economy
Conservative Capitalism: The Social Economy
Crosland's Future: Opportunity and Outcome
Democracy and Exchange: Schumpeter, Galbraith, T. H. Marshall, Titmuss and Adam Smith
The Economics of Alfred Marshall
Galbraith and Market Capitalism
Health Care and Public Policy
Health Policy: Choice, Equality and Cost
Health Tourism: Social Welfare through International Trade
The Institutional Economy: Demand and Supply
James Buchanan
James Edward Meade
Market and Health
The Political Economy of Health Care
The Political Economy of James Buchanan

Richard Titmuss: Welfare and Society
Schumpeter's Market: Enterprise and Evolution
The Social Economics of Thorstein Veblen
Social Policy in an Ageing Society: Age and Health in Singapore
State and Trade: Authority and Exchange in a Global Age
State and Welfare: Tawney, Galbraith and Adam Smith
Theories of Collective Action: Downs, Olson and Hirsch
Trade in Health: Ethics, Economics and Public Policy

Contents

1
Introduction

Keynes said that economics had backed the wrong horse: 'If only Malthus, instead of Ricardo, had been the parent stem from which nineteenth-century economics proceeded, what a much wiser and richer place the world would be to-day' (Keynes 1933 [1972]: 100–101). Malthus was practical and pragmatic. Ricardo was abstract and arid. Malthus had his ear to the ground. Ricardo had his head in the clouds. It should have been Malthus. Instead, it was Ricardo's 'more fascinating intellectual construction which was victorious' (Keynes 1933 [1972]: 87). Path dependence became dependent on the wrong path. The choices made in the interregnum following the death of Adam Smith 'constrained the subject to a full hundred years in an artificial groove' (Keynes 1933 [1972]: 87). History had backed the wrong horse. History's mistake had been 'a disaster to the progress of economics' (Keynes 1933 [1972]: 98).

It had been Ricardo. It should have been Malthus. Malthus was, Keynes proclaimed, 'the first of the Cambridge economists' (Keynes 1933 [1972]: 101). Pure theory should be applied to present-day problems. Value is determined subjectively by supply and demand. Saving diverges from investment in the absence of counter-cyclical public

D. Reisman, *Thomas Robert Malthus*, Great Thinkers in Economics,
https://doi.org/10.1007/978-3-030-01956-3_1

policy. Unstable velocity drives a coach and horses through the quantity theory of money. Free trade is only effective where it is multilateral and fair. Spendthrift welfare leads to indolence and procreation. Tight-fisted welfare deprives the destitute of essential food and shelter. It is all in Malthus.

Above all else, there is the sense of purpose. Malthus was a public-spirited utilitarian who declared that he looked to economics 'to improve the condition and increase the happiness of the lower classes of society' (SE II 251). As we produce commodities, so we produce institutions. It is important to get the economic basis right. James Bonar thinks that Malthus's economics was all a matter of doing good: 'To Malthus the discovery of truth was less important than the improvement of society. When an economical truth could not be made the means of improvement, he seems to have lost interest in it' (Bonar 1885 [1924]: 213).

Malthus, never actually a Cambridge don, was the 'first of the Cambridge economists'. Later Cambridge economists such as Alfred Marshall, John Maynard Keynes and James Meade would be in agreement that their science was more than a game for graduates. It is not just in Cambridge but across the world that Malthus's call for teleology and progress will inevitably exercise a strong appeal to the earnest and the socially minded. That sense of commitment and mission will in turn have a feedback effect on the kind of economics that they study and teach. Malthus said: 'The science of political economy bears a nearer resemblance to the science of morals and politics than to that of mathematics' (PR 2, 518). Malthus's *Principles* and Ricardo's *Principles* are not the same.

1.1 From Theology to Political Economy

Thomas Robert Malthus was born on 13 February 1766 and died on 29 December 1834. He is buried in Bath Abbey. He was the sixth child (of eight) and second son of Daniel Malthus, a country gentleman with a small estate near Albury, Surrey, and a strong interest in philosophy, botany and current affairs. He was a believer with William Godwin in human perfectibility and a friend of Hume and Rousseau. He corresponded with Voltaire. Daniel Malthus died in 1800, two years after the publication of his son's first *Essay on Population.*

T. R. Malthus was educated privately (occasionally in the spirit of Rousseau's *Emile*) and then at the nonconformist Dissenting Academy in Warrington. He was influenced by the radical and anti-monarchist sympathies of his teacher, the Unitarian Minister Gilbert Wakefield, subsequently imprisoned for his seditious opinions in the white terror that followed 1789. Warrington, located in Lancashire, was in the thick of the British industrial revolution. It was a side of life that he would not have seen in rural Surrey.

From 1785 to 1788, Malthus was a student at Jesus College, Cambridge. His tutor was William Frend. Frend had been a pupil of William Paley, the Christian utilitarian, 'ecclesiastic Benthamite' (Petersen 1979: 52), Cambridge Fellow and Archdeacon of Carlisle. Malthus's contemporary and lifelong friend was William Otter, later Bishop of Chichester. Otter recalls that Malthus was 'actuated more by the love of excellence than by the desire of excelling' (Otter 1836 [1964]: xxxiii). It was not just knowledge for knowledge's sake. Malthus told Otter that he was always 'wishing to see the use and application of what I read' (quoted in Otter 1836 [1964]: xxvii).

His principal subject was mathematics. It was an unexpected choice for an instinctual inductivist, soon complaining that the Cambridge course was 'too much confined to speculation' (quoted in Otter 1836 [1964]: xxvii). Malthus might have felt more at home with physics or history. According to his colleague William Empson, he 'had no notion of theory being any thing but science grounded upon and amenable to experience' (Empson 1837 [1963]: 240).

In a letter to his father, Malthus said that 'I am rather remarked in college for talking of what actually exists in nature, or may be put to real practical use' (quoted in Empson 1837 [1963]: 240). He was already under the influence of 'the grand and consistent theory' and 'the immortal mind' (FE 126, 205) of Sir Isaac Newton, whose *Mathematical Principles of Natural Philosophy*—the *Principia*—he read in Latin in Cambridge. Only occasionally in his later work is there a glimpse of the pure mathematics he had learned.

Malthus obtained a first class honours degree in mathematics in 1788. He was the Ninth Wrangler, the ninth-ranked First, in his year. Later he was a non-resident fellow of Jesus College from 1793 to 1804. Also, in 1788, the final (sixth) volume of Edward Gibbon's *History of the Decline and Fall of the Roman Empire* was published. Malthus liked the historical approach and found Gibbon's work 'very entertaining': 'His style is sometimes really sublime' (KG I 53). Three years earlier, in Malthus's first year at Jesus, there had been Paley's *Principles of Political and Moral Philosophy* (1785), then called the *Principles of Morality and Politics.* Malthus's Cambridge years were framed by these two great intellectual influences.

Despite his impaired speech due to a cleft palate, Malthus took holy orders in 1789 and became a curate at Okewood, in Surrey. It was, in his words, a 'retired living in the country' (quoted in Bonar 1885 [1924]: 409), held under local patronage. Although the evidence is unclear, he may have resigned in 1805 when he joined the East India College. In 1824, he was given the title of perpetual curate at Okewood.

From 1803 until his death, he was (non-resident) rector at Walesby, Lincolnshire. A rector earned four times as much as a curate. As at Okewood, it was a rural attachment. Both in his writings and in his personal life, Malthus always had serious reservations about the towns. While he regarded the dark, satanic mills as an economic necessity, he was at one with romantics like Wordsworth, Coleridge and Ruskin in deploring the ugliness and the crowding that were debasing the quality of life. A 'retired living' was more to his taste. Life in the country (although he did not have access to a reference library) gave him the leisure to think and the tranquillity to study.

By the age of 30, the would-be curate was becoming convinced that the answers he sought were to found not just in the Bible but in Adam Smith's *Wealth of Nations.* The new science of political economy had the key to the alleviation and elimination of poverty. Like Ricardo, Malthus learned his economics from the classics like the Physiocrats and Steuart, his contemporaries like Bailey, Say and Sismondi. At Okewood, he wrote a pamphlet in 1796 on *The Crisis, a View of the Present Interesting State of Great Britain by a Friend to the Constitution*. It was rejected for publication and is now only available in fragments cited by Empson and Otter. It would probably not have been well received in his Church.

The Crisis shows that he was already interested in population, about which he wrote: 'I cannot agree with Archdeacon Paley, who says, that the quantity of happiness in any country is best measured by the number of people. Increasing population is the most certain possible sign of the happiness and prosperity of a state; but the actual population may be only a sign of the happiness that is past' (quoted in Empson 1837 [1963]: 244). Prosperous people have more children. Demand for labour does not keep pace with supply. Happiness past is misery present. That is the law of nature.

The Crisis proclaimed itself to be a defence of 'true Whig principles' and the 'middle classes of society' against the backward-looking Tories and the landed aristocracy: 'In the country gentleman of 1796, it is impossible to recognise that old and noble character, the jealous guardian of British freedom' (quoted in Empson 1837 [1963]: 241). *The Crisis* foreshadows Malthus's later discussion of agricultural protection, the law of primogeniture and the social underpinnings of the political order.

Malthus in 1796 proposed greater tolerance for dissenters. He called them, historically, 'among the firmest friends of the constitution' (quoted in Empson 1837 [1963]: 243). Three decades later, as a Church of England clergyman, he was to extend the same support for plurality within Christianity to Catholic Emancipation. Although in Ireland 'every year the proportion of the Catholics to the Protestants is rapidly augmenting' (1808 [1963]: 46), nonetheless he was opposed to the 'bigotry and littleness' that leads to 'the inhuman cry of no popery' (1809 [1963]: 69). Politics played a part. Wartime distress in Ireland was already leading to outright rebellion. As with bigotry and littleness, so with race. Malthus expressed his strong opposition to the slave trade (SE II 231n). There were moral limits even to demand and supply.

The Crisis devoted serious attention to the relief of poverty. Committed to universal well-being, Malthus said that the nation should unquestioningly spring to the defence of the dependent poor: 'It is the duty of society to maintain such of its members as are absolutely unable to maintain themselves' (cited in Otter 1836 [1964]: xxxv). While less leniency might be shown to the able-bodied, there must always be a safety net for the blameless widows, the faultless orphans and the dead-end residuum.

Otter says that Malthus always wanted to put the poor first. He was 'the most humane and considerate of men': his 'sole motive and tendency' was to help the needy, 'to increase their comforts, and to raise their moral and intellectual condition' (Otter 1836 [1964]: xlv).

Two years after *The Crisis*, there was the *Essay on Population*. Malthus was then 32 and had been a curate for two years. The first *Essay* in 1798 had 'dark tints' and a 'melancholy hue' (FE 62). It was published anonymously. The 'passion between the two sexes' was a borderline text for a pastor in holy orders. The 'possession of a beautiful woman' was obviously not suitable for a Sunday sermon. There was also the ambiguous theodicy of an omnipotent God who had created vice and misery when he could equally well have created happiness and abundance.

The full title of Malthus's first *Essay* is *An Essay on the Principle of Population as It Affects the Future Improvement of Society, with Remarks on the Speculations of Mr. Godwin, M. Condorcet and Other Writers.* Hume and Smith had said that a growing population is the cause and effect of the wealth of nations. Godwin and Condorcet had confirmed that more is better provided that the institutional inequities can be put right. Malthus took a more sombre view. Nature itself was the 'principal difficulty' (FE 62), the ultimate roadblock. The optimism of the Enlightenment *philosophers* had run its course. It was the Hobbesian *bellum* again.

The 1798 *Essay* arose out of discussions between Malthus and his father (who encouraged him to publish) concerning the utopian egalitarianism that had been espoused by the libertarian anarchist William Godwin (Otter 1836 [1964]: 22). Godwin's *Enquiry Concerning Political Justice* had just been published, in 1793. His chapter 'On Avarice and Profusion' was central to their discussions (Bonar 1924: 14). Malthus was playing real-world Aristotle to his father's communitarian Plato. He was telling his father that the invisible hand was not bringing prosperity and full employment but rather overpopulation and radical scarcity.

William Pitt as Prime Minister had in 1796 tabled a bill to pay a shilling a week to every family with three or more children. Pitt, influenced by Smith and Paley, had believed that more children meant greater felicity. Disturbed by Godwin, Malthus was anxious about Pitt as well when he wrote his first *Essay* to warn that misconceived generosity would unintentionally exacerbate the hardships of the poor. Empson attributes Malthus's first *Essay* 'mainly to his benevolence' (Empson 1837 [1963]: 244).

The first *Essay* ran to 50,000 words. It was accessible to an educated readership. It seemed straightforward. It avoided formal abstraction. It cited real-world evidence where scarce facts could be found. It was well written and interesting. It built on the authority of the great names who had pointed to a latent imbalance. It was also in the right place at the right time. The debate on overpopulation and subsistence had already begun. There was a perceived need for a book that would bring Adam Smith on demography up to date.

Initially seen more as a tract for the times than as a breakthrough in scholarship, what is clear is that the first *Essay* catalysed a trickle of controversy into a flood. Few books have had so immediate an impact on the popular imagination or influenced so greatly the direction of the social narrative. Pitt as early as 1800 withdrew his proposal to link child allowances to family size. It was in deference to the views of 'those whose opinions he was bound to respect' (Bonar 1885 [1924]: 43). Prominent among them were Bentham and Malthus. Malthus, still anonymous, was not a household name and Okewood not a prestigious affiliation. It is hard to see why Pitt felt bound to respect his opinion.

In 1799, Malthus made a six-month study trip to Norway, Sweden, Finland and Russia (together with Otter and two other friends) to collect facts and study customs. It was the first time he had been abroad. His travel diaries, never intended for publication, reveal that he was particularly concerned with prices, wages, extent of tillage, size of farm, clearing of forests, division of labour, agricultural technique and the willingness to work. Ethnic Danes, he recorded, were especially indolent. Even 'a good Drinkgelt could not rouse them from their lethargy': 'If you meant to describe all the ill qualities that a man could possess, it was sufficient to say he was a Danois' (TD 52).

Surprisingly for the author who had just written the *Essay*, his notebooks show only a secondary interest in population. Among the Swedes, he observed, 'the prodigal use of brandy' had been a 'cause of the slow increase of popn' (TD 61). Among the Norwegians, conscription, 'a kind of preventive check,.... accounts for their increasing so slowly'

(TD 59, 89). In general, however, there is more about excess salt in food than about excess mouths to feed. Ethnographic material abounds including the little-known fact that Norwegian women are inveterate trencher-persons: 'We were rather hungry….but some of the ladies beat us hollow' (TD 92). Already revising his book, Malthus did focus more narrowly on marriage and childbearing when in 1802 he undertook a second journey. Taking advantage of the Peace of Amiens, he travelled for five months in France and Switzerland.

Five years after the first *Essay,* there was a second edition. Malthus called the 1803 *Essay* 'a new work' (SE I 2). Large sections of the original book were carried over and so was the utilitarian maximand. The main title remained the same. The subtitle, however, had become more moderate: *A View of Its Past and Present Effects on Human Happiness, with an Inquiry into Our Prospects respecting the Future Removal or Mitigation of the Evils which It Occasions.* Population still had a tendency to increase. Britain's first census in 1801 had documented it. What was new was the 'mitigation' and the 'removal'.

Out went Chapters 18 and 19 on God and evil. In came moral restraint which could limit the pressure on food and agricultural improvement which could multiply the yields. The 1798 *Essay* had had no choice but to rely on logic to support its conclusion that the tendency to pauperism was a natural law. The second *Essay* was able to draw on comparative data to show that the race between the tortoise and the hare might not end badly after all. Malthus II may or may not have proven that Malthus I was wrong. The important thing is the popular perception. That did not change.

The 1803 edition was followed by further editions in 1806, 1807, 1817 (ten years later) and 1826 (nine years after that). In some cases, the revisions were minor, confined principally to the insertion of new statistics. In other cases, as in 1817 (when the book reached 250,000 words), whole new chapters were added. The critique of Godwin was amplified to include further radicals like Paine and Owen. The sections on the abolition of the Poor Laws became more insistent. In 1807, in a tract entitled *A Letter to Samuel Whitbread,* Malthus warned Parliament that welfare in forms like outdoor relief or public housing would only magnify the misery that it sought to suppress.

Malthus married a cousin, Harriet Eckersall, in 1804 when he was 38 and she was 27. The degree of consanguinity was not perceived to be a problem. Before that he was a 'man of liberal education' (FE 90) and, still single, living at home. Malthus and his wife were to have three children.

In 1805, Malthus became Professor of General History, Politics, Commerce and Finance, shortened to Professor of History and Political Economy, at the East India College. The College had been established by the East India Company to educate its servants for a career in commerce and governance in Asia. Although by temperament a free trader, Malthus was in effect employed for almost 30 years by a mercantilist monopoly that had been censured by Adam Smith. The College did, of course, have close links with leading philosophic radicals like Bentham and Mill.

The College was based first in Hertford Castle and then purpose-built at Haileybury, in the countryside just outside London. Accommodation was provided. College became his family home. Malthus remained at Haileybury until his death. His closest friend at the College was William Empson, Professor of General Polity and the Laws of England. Malthus's successor was the historical economist Richard Jones.

Boarders were between 16 and 20 years old. They remained in the College for two years before they left for India. Haileybury boys were believed to be rowdy. Malthus concedes that they had on occasion surrendered to 'riot, disorder, and irregularity' culminating in 'a total disregard of the rules and regulations' (1817 [1986]: 127, 146). Regular demands were made for the College to be closed. There was also the charge that the unique nature of the institution (neither public school nor university) was turning out a class of organisation men who resembled nothing so much as an Indian-like caste.

Their very Britishness was being called into question. Lord Grenville had asserted in the House of Lords that the pupils were too distant from English manners and values. Malthus's reply came in the form of two pamphlets, *Letter to Lord Grenville on the East India College* (1813) and *Statements Respecting the East India College* (1817). He said that his pupils, their education being delivered in English in their homeland, were 'not likely to lose the habits and feelings of British citizens', let alone the 'spirit of British justice' which filled a cultural void in the eastern Empire (1813 [1986]: 82, 92).

Political economy itself was not universally regarded as the equal of long-established subjects like Sanskrit and history. Malthus insisted that economics was not 'too difficult or too dull' (1813 [1986]: 80) for his adolescent pupils. As for its academic status, the new subject already had its own great book: 'The treatise which we already possess is still of the very highest value' (PR 5). Malthus 'apparently believed that a thorough grounding in the ideas of Adam Smith was an essential part of an education in political economy' (Pullen 1981: 800). Ricardo's *Principles* or even his own were secondary to the detailed exegesis of the *Wealth of Nations.* In his teaching, Malthus emphasised population to such an extent (he told the boys to stop at three) that they took to calling him 'Old Pop'. His colleagues called him 'Bob'.

Educated people in the early nineteenth century exchanged economic and political ideas not just through books but through influential journals such as the Whigs' *Edinburgh Review* (founded in 1802) and the Tories' *Quarterly Review* (from 1809). Frank Fetter calls the *Edinburgh Review*, 'for its day and generation, a "Reader's Digest" of economic literature' (Fetter 1953: 234). It was sympathetic to Malthus's population theory. Although authors remained anonymous until 1912, Fetter has established that Malthus contributed at least five extended pieces to the *Review* between 1808 and 1821 (Fetter 1953: 246–247). He wrote reviews of Newenham on Ireland, Godwin on Malthus and, in 1811, the bullionists and the anti-bullionists on the causes of inflation. One of the pamphlets he reviewed, *The High Price of Bullion*, was by a young stockbroker named David Ricardo.

When the *Review* under the influence of John Ramsay McCulloch became increasingly favourable to Ricardo's ideas on free trade, capital and rent, Malthus had to transfer his loyalties to its more conservative rival. For the *Quarterly Review*, he wrote two long book reviews, first of Thomas Tooke and then of McCulloch. His style as a reviewer is uniquely his own. The books he is reviewing play second-fiddle to his own opinions, set out at length.

Malthus, consistently a Whig, was acceptable to the *Quarterly Review* because of his surprising support for agricultural protection and the landed interest. He expressed his views on land in four widely read pamphlets from 1800 (*The Present High Price of Provisions*) to 1815 (*The Policy of Restricting the Importation of Foreign Corn*). Malthus's *Nature and Progress of Rent* and Ricardo's *Essay on Profits*, both dealing with the same topic of rent and capital, appeared simultaneously in 1815. Malthus, the leading British political economist in the period from the *Essay* in 1798 to Ricardo's *Principles* in 1817, was increasingly becoming a part of a wider professional net.

After the *Edinburgh Review* paper on the monetary controversies, Malthus initiated a correspondence with Ricardo as an alternative to debating their shared interests in print. Not intended for publication but collected in 1951 in the *Works and Correspondence of David Ricardo*, there are 73 letters from Ricardo to Malthus and 61 from Malthus to Ricardo. It is 'the most important literary correspondence in the whole development of Political Economy' (Keynes 1933 [1972]: 96), 'a perfect model of benevolent and enlightened controversy' (Otter 1836 [1964]: lii). Their friendship continued until Ricardo's death in 1823. Malthus was only one of three people outside the immediate family to have received a share in Ricardo's will. Ricardo said: 'I never knew a man more earnest on any subject than Mr. Malthus is on Political Economy' (letter from Ricardo to McCulloch, 1821, in Ricardo VIII: 336).

Stockbroker, Member of Parliament, landowner, Ricardo like Malthus did not write economics with a view to his personal stake: 'It is somewhat singular that Mr. Ricardo, a considerable receiver of rents, should have so much underrated their national importance; while I, who never received, nor expected to receive any, shall probably be accused of overrating their importance' (PR 238). What brought them together was their commitment to advancing the state of economic knowledge. Malthus said 'I never loved anybody out of my own family so much..... The object after which we were both enquiring was so entirely the truth, and nothing else' (cited in Empson 1837 [1963]: 261).

Malthus and Ricardo in 1821 were among the 20 founder-members of the Political Economy Club. It met monthly from December to June to discuss the central topics of a new research area in which there were no university courses and all the practitioners were self-taught. Malthus in 1833 was a founder-member, with Babbage and others, of the Statistical Section of the British Association for the Advancement of Science (itself founded in 1831). In 1834, he was involved in the formation of the Statistical Society of London (later the Royal Statistical Society). He was active in the Bible Society (where he advocated cooperation with religious dissenters) and in Joseph Lancaster's British and Foreign School Society. He was elected to the Royal Society in 1818 and the Royal Society of Literature in 1823. He was a member of The Athenaeum and a Foreign Member of the French Institute and the Royal Academy in Berlin. The *Essay* was translated into German in 1807 and into French in 1809.

Malthus had wanted to publish an annotated edition of the *Wealth of Nations*. Few thinkers have been closer to Smith or drawn so heavily on Smith's economic and social theories. When his idea was preempted by David Buchanan in 1814, he moved on to his second great work. *The Principles of Political Economy* appeared in 1820 when the author was 54. Its subtitle is 'Considered with a view to their practical application'. No work of disembodied abstraction, its mission statement was explicitly 'to prepare the general rules of political economy for practical application' (PR 21), to render them of direct utility to 'the common business of human life' (PR 12). It was essential for this to be done: 'There are few branches of human knowledge where false views may do more harm, or just views more good' (PR 12). Common business of life or common life of business, its subtitle looks forward to Alfred Marshall (Reisman 1987: Chaps. 2 and 3). In economics as in religion, we are all missionaries nowadays.

Malthus's *Principles of Economics* proceeds topic by topic through the definition of wealth, its distribution into rent, wages and profits and finally the relationship of value added to sustained growth and development. Its sections on effective demand are a major advance in macroeconomic awareness at a time when only a small minority were prepared to question the validity of Say's Law that supply, properly understood, is at once demand. Its final section on progress is over 40% of the whole. It shows that, as in the *Wealth of Nations*, it is restless dynamics and not complacent equilibrium that slots the disparate pieces into a unified whole.

The *Principles* resembles a series of essays. Some of the content is likely to have been taken from the author's lecture notes. The inclusion of lengthy sections from the *Inquiry on Rent*, as well as the neglect of key topics like money and taxation, may suggest that Malthus never intended his *Principles* to be a comprehensive guide. Yet first impressions can deceive. Malthus took care to include a 70-page summary of his book at the end. It shows how the narrative is being built up step by step. There is also the concluding section on social and economic improvement which reveals the underlying purpose. Readers who want to understand Malthus's *Principles* would be well advised to read his argument from back to front.

Malthus in 1823 published *The Measure of Value*. A short book but a difficult one, in it he attempted to reconcile Smith's labour embodied, Smith's labour commanded, a commodity standard like gold bullion and the free marketeer's Supreme Court of supply and demand. It was followed in 1827 by *Definitions in Political Economy, Preceded by an Inquiry into the Rules Which Ought to Guide Political Economists in the Definition and Use of Their Terms; with Remarks on the Deviation from These Rules in Their Writings*. The length of the title flags up the enormity of the problem. Malthus reflected that 'the differences of opinion among political economists have of late been a frequent subject of complaint' and that one of the main reasons has been 'the different meanings in which the same terms have been used by different writers' (DEF iii). Keynes called it 'a minor work of no great interest' (Keynes 1933 [1972]: 92n). It is not the *Essay* or the *Principles*. Any work which says that economists must 'use the same terms in the same senses' (letter from Malthus to Whewell, 1833, in de Marchi and Sturges, 1973: 393) if they are to communicate their meaning cannot, however, be regarded as entirely minor.

Malthus in the 1820s gave evidence before two Select Committees of the House of Commons: the Select Committee on Artisans and Machinery (1824) and the Select Committee on Emigration (1827).

Testifying on international factor mobility, he said that legislation to restrict trade in means of production and embedded technology was sometimes inefficient and always unfair: 'I see no evil likely to arise from the exportation of machinery' (1824: 598). The French were too far behind for effective catch-up: 'The efficiency of labour in France is less than in England, and this is one of the principal causes why the money price of labour is lower in France than in England.... I do not apprehend that they would be able to undersell us' (1824: 599, 600). Exceptions should be made where private interest was at variance with the national good. England was so far ahead that few exceptions would be required.

Malthus in the 1820s was simultaneously revising his *Principles* for a second edition. It was finally published in 1836. Uncompleted at his death in 1834, it was edited anonymously by, it is believed, John Cazenove (Pullen 1989: lvi–lxiv). Cazenove's additions are clearly marked as 'Ed.' but he may have made other changes as well. The second *Principles* is preceded by an unsigned biographical tribute known to have been the work of Malthus's lifelong friend Otter (Empson 1837 [1963]: 234).

Some of the revisions are significant (notably the weakening of support for the Corn Laws) but many are no more than the change of a word or two. The alterations in the earlier sections are more extensive than in the later ones. John Pullen, who edited the 1986 variorum, says the reason may have been that Malthus was revising in sequence 'but did not have time to complete the alterations before his death. If this interpretation is correct it would mean that the views expressed in the later, less-corrected part of the *Principles* are not necessarily Malthus' final views' (Pullen 1989: lxv). Pullen's assessment is supported by the manuscript corrections Malthus made in his personal copy of the first edition, now kept in the Cambridge University Library.

Publication was delayed by the *Measure* and the *Definitions*, the testimony to the Royal Commissions and the Haileybury controversies. The publisher did not push for a second edition because the first edition had not sold well. It was also held up by Malthus's own ambivalence towards a new edition that would improve on the old one: 'If I am to alter any thing, I can do little more than alter the language' (quoted in Empson 1837 [1963]: 234).

There was, in addition, the Ricardo factor. The death of Ricardo in 1823 made it less pressing for Malthus to clarify his own ideas on topics such as rent where he is likely to have been moving towards a more Ricardian position (Hollander 1997: 846–856). Malthus knew that until his differences with the greatly respected Ricardo and, after 1823, the Ricardian succession had been resolved, he could not feel confident that his first *Principles* was definitive.

Ricardo in 1820 had begun to write notes on the first *Principles*. Malthus had corresponded with him and tried to answer his critique. In the event, the corrections Malthus made to his second *Principles* in the light of Ricardo's notes were modest: 'The changes in this edition are extensive, but in general they do not appear to be carried out with a view to meeting Ricardo's criticisms' (Sraffa and Dobb 1951–1955: xiii). Ricardo had wanted his notes and Malthus's detailed replies to be published. In fact, they only reached the public domain more than a century later in an edition edited by Jacob Hollander and T. E. Gregory in 1928. They were republished in 1951 in Volume II of *The Works and Correspondence of David Ricardo*.

1.2 Enemies and Friends

It was a lifetime of achievement. There were total demand and unproductive labour, public works and import substitution, social stratification and individual betterment, the Christian Bible and the law of nature. There was also population. Malthus was an inveterate intellectual and a bookish polymath who was determined to satisfy his own curiosity. It is never safe to range too widely. Subtlety and sophistication yield to stereotypes and catchphrases because the popular imagination does not cut corners on one-word answers. Adam Smith is the Invisible Hand. Keynesian economics is Depression Economics. Parson Malthus is Population Malthus. It is as if the other eight symphonies had never been written.

The popular imagination had absorbed the checks and ignored the balances. The result was that Population Malthus in his own lifetime was 'egregiously misinterpreted and misunderstood' (Otter 1836 [1964]: xiv). He was called a 'cold and heartless, if not an impious man' (Otter 1836 [1964]: xvii). He was visited with 'calumny' and 'unqualified abuse' (Otter 1836 [1964]: xvii, liv).

The popular perception of the *Essay on Population* became a cultural artefact in its own right: 'Of all books that ever exercised any thing like its influence, none has been so little read, or so frequently misunderstood, as Mr. Malthus's celebrated essay….There are found persons who still persist that Mr. Malthus must be a friend to the small-pox, the plague, the slave-trade, and to every species of misery and vice. He is charged with having lost sight of the interests of the poor, while looking only to wealth' (Empson 1837 [1963]: 253). A little knowledge is a dangerous thing. In the case of the *Essay*, it was a very little knowledge indeed.

Hazlitt objected to the 'truisms', 'the nonsense', the 'dull, dogged, voluminous repetition of an absurdity' that was 'alarming the imaginations and confounding the understandings' (Hazlitt 1819: 403, 422). Malthus, Hazlitt said, was condoning the starvation of the poor while at the same time making it just as much a law of nature for the rich to 'maintain their dogs and horses. &tc., out of their ostentatious superfluities' (Hazlitt 1819: 426).

Percy Bysshe Shelley took up the cry that the children of the needy were as deserving as the puppy dogs of the privileged. Shelley complained of 'exploded superstitions' and 'sophisms like those of Mr. Malthus': they were, he said, 'calculated to lull the oppressors of mankind into a security of everlasting triumph' (Shelley 1817: x, xi). The radical William Cobbett called him an 'impudent and illiterate Parson', 'a political pimp', 'a monster in human shape': 'He is the weazel, he is the indigestion, he is the nightmare, he is the deadly malady of the ministry' (quoted in Huzel 2006: 105, 106). Cobbett did not rate him very highly. Nor did Robert Southey: 'As a political philosopher, the farthing candle of his fame must stink and go out' (quoted in Huzel 2006: 27).

Lord Byron's Don Juan had learned from Malthus's book that propagation at a 'desperate rate' had been the 'sad result of passions and potatoes'. He concluded that 'Certes it conducts to live ascetic/Or turning marriage into arithmetic' (Byron 1837: Canto XV). So had Thomas Love Peacock, whose Mr. Fax in the novel *Melincourt* warns that 'more men than corn is a fearful pre-eminence': 'Bachelors and spinsters I decidedly venerate. The world is overstocked with featherless bipeds' (Peacock 1817: 100–101). Sadler saw clearly that Malthus was a turncoat apostate who had no love for his church: 'The insults the theory of Malthus levels at God, and the injuries it meditates inflicting upon man, will be endured by neither' (Sadler 1830: I 15). It is not certain that Hazlitt, Shelley, Byron or Sadler had actually wrestled with the complexities of Malthus's book. The ill repute of the author would have been enough.

William Taylor Coleridge at least had devoted quality time to Malthus's text. The annotations on his own copy of the 1803 *Essay*, now in the British Library, reveal what he thought of a clergyman who should have stayed in his pew. On Malthus's use of the 'facts', Coleridge writes that 'a pop-gun would batter down the impregnable Fortress'. Then, there is 'Ass!', 'more Heads than Brains', 'verbiage and endless repetition', 'silly blunder', 'an entertaining farrago of quotations from books of travels', '350 pages to prove an axiom! To illustrate a self-evident truth! It is neither more nor less than Book-making' (Coleridge, n.d.).

Coleridge is just as outspoken in print. In *Table Talk,* he accuses Malthus of substituting individual for collective responsibility: 'The entire tendency of the modern or Malthusian political economy is to denationalize. It would dig up the charcoal foundations of the temple of Ephesus to burn as fuel for a steam-engine' (Coleridge 1835: II 327). Malthus's polemic is 'humbug', 'a lie in morals', 'a practical lie' (Coleridge 1835: II 88, 129). Only the Roman Catholics have got things so wrong: 'Like the Popish doctrines, it is so vicious a tenet, so flattering to the cruelty, the avarice, and sordid selfishness of most men, that I hardly know what to think of the result' (Coleridge 1835: II 88).

Coleridge deplored the fact that 'the monstrous practical sophism of Malthus', 'lamentable' in every respect, had poisoned 'the leading men of the kingdom' (Coleridge 1835: II 88). The *Essay*, he warned in *Literary Remains*, can only do harm: 'Behold this mighty nation, its rulers and its wise men, listening - to Paley and to - Malthus! It is mournful, mournful' (Coleridge 1836: II 348).

Karl Marx also found it 'mournful'. Malthus's *Essay*, he said, was 'nothing but a schoolboyish, superficial plagiary': it did not contain 'a single sentence thought out by himself' (quoted in Meek 1953: 83). 'A sin against science', a 'libel on the human race', his theories made him de facto the 'bought advocate of the landed classes' (quoted in Meek 1953: 122–123). When Malthus seemed to be on the side of the industrial bourgeoisie, it was only because he was trying to create 'a broader and more convenient material basis for the "old" society' (quoted in Meek 1953: 157). Malthus, Marx was saying, was superficially a liberal but secretly a reactionary. He wanted to preserve a social order that had had its day.

Not to be outdone, Engels declared that Malthus's 'chimerical', 'infamous' and 'repulsive blasphemy against man and nature' had revealed him to be not just 'a *plagiarist* by profession' but 'a professional sycophant of the landed aristocracy' (quoted in Meek 1953: 60, 116, 117, emphasis in original). Marx and Engels viewed Malthus as an apologist for land in a world where capital was in the ascendant. Malthus's defence of entailed estates, unproductive services and the Corn Laws, his rejection of the Physiocrats' single tax on land showed clearly that he was a partisan of a class that the less sentimental Ricardo rightly viewed with disdain: 'The interest of the landlord is always opposed to the interest of every other class in the community' (Ricardo 1815 [1951–1955], in Ricardo IV: 21). McCulloch described Malthus's *Principles* as 'the textbook – the very gospel indeed – of a few landowners who have read it in order to….defend their factitious system' (letter from McCulloch to Ricardo, 1821, in Ricardo VIII: 313). Even Francis Horner, friend and fellow utilitarian, described Malthus as 'the most important convert…. the landowners have got' (Horner 1843 [1853]: I 434).

Some of the critics homed in on Malthus's approach to the deprived and the post-feudal. Others focused not on the message but on the medium. They expressed the view that Malthus was not an easy read. Horner, who praised him for his 'ingenious turn for speculation' and his 'distinct perspicuity', conceded that he suffered from 'a want of precision in the statement of his principles' (Horner 1843 [1853]: I 433, 464). Robert Torrens, admiring him for 'a spirit of candour, and the love of truth', added pointedly that Malthus used 'very inaccurate and unphilosophical language' (Torrens 1815: xi, xin) that loses his readers in 'a chaos of original but unconnected elements' (Torrens 1821: v): 'In the leading questions of economical science, Mr. Malthus scarcely ever embraced a principle, which he did not subsequently abandon' (Torrens 1815: ix).

Torrens said he was a weathervane. Thomas De Quincey said he was simply confused. De Quincey (reviewing *The Measure of Value* under the alias 'X.Y.Z.') observed that 'logical perplexity is shockingly contagious' and that too much time spent with Malthus can be bad for the health: 'Of all the men of talents, whose writings I have read up to this hour, Mr. Malthus has the most perplexed understanding. He is not only confused himself, but is the cause that confusion is in other men' (De Quincey 1823: 587). McCulloch, reporting to Ricardo on the *Principles*, complained that it was easy to lose one's way in the repetition and the loquacity: 'Malthus is taking to his old trick of bookmaking.... His book instead of being lengthened ought to have been curtailed one third' (letter from McCulloch to Ricardo, 1821, in Ricardo VIII: 341).

Malthus had his critics but he also had his admirers. Ricardo said of him that 'a more candid or better man nowhere exists' (letter from Ricardo to Brown, 1819, in Ricardo VIII: 101). Harriet Martineau recalls that he was 'so truly good, so sensible and gentle' (quoted in James 1979: 187). Maria Edgeworth remembers him as 'a perfectly unaffected amiable, gentlemanlike man, who really *converses*; that is, listens, as well as talks' (quoted in James 1979: 226).

William Empson calls him 'a perfect gentleman', 'the best man and truest philosopher we ever were acquainted with': 'Mr. Malthus possessed in their utmost perfection the two great philosophical qualities of single-mindedness and patience. He could not contemplate any subject in the spirit of a partisan' (Empson 1837 [1963]: 233, 266, 268). Bishop Otter describes him as 'mild and placid', 'sagacious and patient', 'earnest and serious', 'moderate and contented', 'impassive to abuse' (Otter 1836 [1964]: xvi, xxix, xxxv, xlix).

William Petersen, admitting that Malthus was frequently putting 'ideas that other men had expressed into a larger framework', insists that the *Essay* is nonetheless 'the beginning of modern population theory' (Petersen 1979: 61). Malthus has had a major influence on development economics in poorer countries. He also had a major influence on Charles Darwin, who found in the *Essay* the logical basis for natural selection in the *Origin of Species*: 'Here, then, I had at last got a theory by which to work' (Darwin 1958: 121). Malthus was one of the first economists to recognise that, as Marshall was later to put it, 'the Mecca of the economist lies in economic biology' (Marshall 1890 [1949]: xii) and that evolution is organic, continuous and gradual: 'Natura non facit saltum' (Darwin 1859: 460). Kenneth Boulding, inspired by the symbiosis with biology, has carried forward Malthus's vision of the economy as a living ecosystem that does not lend itself to Walrasian mechanics (Boulding 1981: 17, 84).

At the end of the day, however, Malthus was Population Malthus. Detached and scholarly though he was, Malthus knew what people were making of him. He knew that he had been misunderstood: 'No work has been so much talked of by persons who do not seem to have read it' (SV 221). Malthus never altered his underlying thesis on the geometrical increase in population and the arithmetical increase in food: the argument in the *Essay* was 'incontrovertible' (SE II 227). What he did regret was that his theory had been so widely mistaken, so widely taken as the proof that mass poverty was inevitable: 'It is an utter misconception of my argument to infer that I am an enemy to population. I am only an enemy to vice and misery' (SE II 205).

In the Appendix to the 1806 *Essay*, Malthus expressed the hope that 'those who have not had leisure to read the whole work....may not, from the partial and incorrect statements which they have heard, mistake the import of some of my opinions, and attribute to me others which I have never held' (SE II 204). Writing in 1830 to Macvey Napier, then editing the *Encyclopedia Britannica*, he said there was a need for a 'short and *cheap* account' of the principle of population 'in order that the great mass who talk about it, may have easy means of getting better information on the subject than they appear to have at present' (letter from Malthus to Macvey Napier, 1830, in Macvey Napier Papers, ff.276, emphasis in original). His short final paper was intended to set the record straight.

A Summary View of the Principle of Population was published in 1830 when its author was 64. The bulk of the text was carried forward from his article on 'Population' in the *Supplement to the Encyclopedia Britannica* in 1824. It was clear and concise because an *Encyclopedia* entry does not afford much space for debate. Malthus as always avoided 'a controversial air' (PR 22): 'Mr. Malthus was not fond of storms, as the petrel is said to be, for their own sake' (Empson 1837 [1963]: 258). The *Summary View* was no more than a simplified restatement of his highly nuanced case. It did not make a great deal of difference. In the popular perception, he was still Population Malthus.

1.3 An Underdeveloped Country

Agriculture had long been the leading sector in the economy. Malthus's Britain was moving up the value chain. Malthus, living in the workshop of the world at the hub of international trade, saw correctly that the economic basis was experiencing an unprecedented transition. In 1803, he wrote that 'about the middle of the last century we were genuinely….an agricultural nation'; but that nowadays 'the commercial system clearly predominates' (SE I 400).

Britain in Malthus's time was passing through the world's first industrial revolution. The steam engine, the threshing machine, the spinning jenny, the factory system, the drift to the towns, the application of science to technology, the expansion of home and foreign trade, the construction of canals, all-weather roads and later the railways were creating a new economic geography and a new convection of national wealth. A new class structure was emerging in which the merchants and manufacturers were challenging the landed aristocracy for political influence.

The Corn Laws, frequently revised, had since 1660 protected home-grown grain-growers on a sliding scale against cheap imports. The extension of the suffrage that led to the Reform Act of 1832 was the political manifestation of a factor-based class struggle on which a political economist like Malthus had no choice but to express an opinion. He said that, joining the landowners but not displacing them, a middle class presence would put Parliament on 'a much broader and more solid base than ever' (PR II 454n). Bounties were eliminated in 1814 in the false peace between Elba and Waterloo. The Corn Laws were abolished in 1846 in the 'Hungry Forties'. The balance of power was shifting away from land.

Rent was a political issue. Even liberals were landowners. The Physiocrats and their followers had made the natural surplus a core element in economic growth. There was the example of America where rapid expansion was being powered by an unlimited supply of unappropriated land. In Britain, Coke of Holkham, Bakewell of Leicester and even the King—'Farmer George'—were employing capital, technology and knowledge-based 'high farming' to improve the productivity of tillage. A green revolution was taking place. Rising incomes and the income-elastic demand for meat were continuing the enclosure of common land that in turn drove peasants on traditional tenures to seek employment in the towns. The pull of higher wages reinforced the push of landlessness. Migration was creating a national market for labour in line with the law of one price.

At the bottom of the social hierarchy, there were the urban operatives. Lacking land or capital, dwelling in slums without a hygienic water supply, washing in rivers which doubled as sewers, exposed to epidemics like cholera in 1831, the detribalised Englishman was experiencing the rootlessness and powerlessness of the internal migrant. The Gordon Riots in 1780 had shown that the masses could take their dissatisfaction to the streets. The Luddites and the machine-wreckers between 1811 and 1816 demonstrated that rebellion and even revolution were a serious alternative to drunkenness and debauchery when popular frustrations were ignored, trades unions banned until 1824 and the first Factory Acts only introduced in 1833. In 1820, there was the Cato Street Conspiracy to murder the Prime Minister and the Cabinet. A year before that, in 1819, Henry Hunt had addressed a rally of 60,000 at St. Peter's Fields, Manchester. It became Peterloo when the military charged the crowd. Fifteen people were killed and 600 injured.

The new market economy was replacing the old networks of community support and mutual aid. Decennial cycles, short-term fluctuations, interruptions in foreign trade, harvest failures, high food prices, exclusionary tariffs were all contributing to poverty and joblessness among the lower classes, urban and rural. The Poor Laws, locally funded, provided parish relief for the needy at the cost of shame and stigma. In 1834, the Poor Law Amendment Act specified that paupers' living standards were to be 'less eligible' than those of the self-reliant and that outdoor relief was to be replaced by the workhouse. Chadwick and Senior, driving forward the reforms, knew that Malthus since 1798 had been calling for the abolition of the Poor Laws. The folk memory of what he was believed to have said made a contribution of its own to the hardening of hearts.

The folk memory was that irresponsible childbearing had been at the root of deprivation. Children are highly visible in a poor country where high birth rates and high death rates skew the median age down. Less attention was paid to indigence among the urban elderly despite the lengthening life-expectancy in a new industrial economy without a retirement age, a pension pot or an extended family. It is possible that as much as half of the British population was under 20 in the year of the first *Essay*. Even allowing for unregulated child labour, there was a considerable burden of young-age dependency. The precise figures were not known. The first census was only conducted in 1801. The Registrar General's Office to assure the mandatory reporting of births, marriages and deaths was only established in 1837.

Children were a drain. Yet, there was something else. Britain was at war with France, with brief interruptions, from 1793 to 1815. Malthus in 1817 recalled that so long as the conflict lasted there had been 'an extraordinary demand for men, and very little disposition to suppose the possibility of any evil resulting from the redundancy of population' (SE I 6). The 1798 *Essay* appeared when Britain was experiencing an extraordinary demand for cannon fodder. It all changed in 1815 when the peace dividend turned out to be a sustained recession. The fall in purchasing power meant that there were insufficient jobs for the demobilised military and the natural increase. Even those normally in favour of self-interest and competition were pragmatic enough to contemplate state intervention. Keynes's *General Theory* was written in the Great Depression of the 1930s. Malthus's *Principles* was written in the post-1815 slump.

The war had created a demand for men but it also had disrupted the flow of trade. Malthus wanted to see the early restoration of 'peace in our time': 'It would be wise to give up Belgium, if peace could be purchased by it' (quoted in James 1979: 226). Napoleon's 'Continental System' imposed a blockade on British exports that prevented even the world's strongest economy from fully utilising its capacity. The threat to grain imports lent urgency to the argument that the Corn Laws were essential for food security. The suspension of cash payments in 1797 had been followed by inflation and a deteriorating rate of exchange. *Post hoc* might have been *propter hoc*. Passions ran high. They always do when people do not know.

Napoleon's coup in 1798 had put political leadership back on the agenda. Adam Smith in 1776 had been recommending that 'every man, as long as he does not violate the rules of justice', should be 'left perfectly free to pursue his own interest his own way' (Smith 1776 [1961]: II 208). After 1776, there had, however, been 1789. Natural justice could no longer be taken on trust. The French Revolution, the execution of the monarch, the reign of terror and Jacobin intolerance had led even conviction liberals to argue for coercion and the Sedition Laws lest 'liberty, equality and fraternity' become its own nemesis.

America at least had not devoured its own children. Malthus never mentions the American Revolution or the nation-building which followed it. America had resolved its internal differences by means of Montesquieu, John Locke, Thomas Jefferson and Alexander Hamilton. There had been the constitution, the checks and balances and the Bill of Rights. More attuned to the economics than the politics of the American experiment, Malthus sourced his answer to Continental radicalism in good British stock. Magna Carta, Habeas Corpus and the House of Lords were the British bedrock at a time when laissez-faire to some bore a family resemblance to the chaos and disarray only twenty miles from Dover.

The Enlightenment, nature, deism and individual self-determination were under assault. Edmund Burke's *Reflections on the Revolution in France* in 1790 had evoked the spectre of mob rule and radical upheaval, of 'fury, outrage, and insult', of 'laws overturned', 'industry without vigour', 'blood and tumult', even before the Terror in 1793 and Babeuf's Conspiracy in 1796 had confirmed his worst fears (Burke 1790 [1968]: 126). Thomas Paine in *The Rights of Man* had said that 'government is nothing more than a national association acting on the principles of society', forever dependent on the people's 'common consent' for its mandate to do that for which citizens as individuals are 'not conveniently competent' (Paine 1792 [2000]: 178, 181). The street was not convinced that the butcher, the brewer and the baker would ever do enough for the excluded. The invisible hand was for the haves. The have-nots wanted levelling down and redistribution of privileges in order to concentrate resources more directly on the alleviation of distress.

It was the best of times and the worst of times. Malthus lived in the shadow of *where* and *when*. Different clocks tell different stories. Different places have different needs. One view would be that Malthus today is only of relevance to underdeveloped countries, time-warped into population explosion and early industrialisation. That is one view. It is not, however, the only view.

References

By T. R. Malthus

(1798 [1970]). (abbreviated as FE), *Essay on the Principle of Population, as It Affects the Future Improvement of Society, with Remarks on the Speculations of Mr. Godwin, M. Condorcet, and Other Writers*, ed. by A. Flew. Harmondsworth: Penguin.

(1803 et seq. [1989]). *An Essay on the Principle of Population: Or a View of Its Past and Present Effects on Human Happiness, with an Inquiry into Our Prospects Respecting the Removal of the Evils Which It Occasions* (2nd edition, 1803; further editions in 1806, 1807, 1817, 1826) (abbreviated as SE I and SE II), 2 vols., ed. by P. James. Cambridge: Cambridge University Press.

(1808 [1963]). Review of Thomas Newenham's *A Statistical and Historical Inquiry into the Progress and Magnitude of the Population of Ireland, Edinburgh Review*, 24, reprinted in *Occasional Papers of T.R. Malthus,* ed. by B. Semmel. New York: Bert Franklin, 33–52.

(1809 [1963]). Review of Thomas Newenham's *A View of the Natural, Political and Commercial Circumstances of Ireland, Edinburgh Review*, 27, 1809, reprinted in *Occasional Papers of T.R. Malthus,* ed. by B. Semmel. New York: Bert Franklin, 52–71.

(1813 [1986]). *A Letter to the Rt. Hon. Lord Grenville Occasioned by Some Observations of His Lordship on the East India Company's Establishment for the Education of Their Civil Servants,* reprinted in *The Works of Thomas Robert Malthus,* ed. by E. A. Wrigley and D. Souden. London: Pickering and Chatto, 4, 73–92.

(1817 [1986]). *Statements Respecting the East-India College with an Appeal to Facts in Refutation of the Charges Lately Brought Against It in the Court of Proprietors,* reprinted in *The Works of Thomas Robert Malthus,* ed. by E. A. Wrigley and D. Souden. London: Pickering and Chatto, 4, 97–156.

(1820 [1989]). *The Principles of Political Economy* (abbreviated as PR), ed. by J. Pullen. Cambridge: Cambridge University Press.

(1824). Evidence to the Select Committee on Artizans and Machinery (Sixth Report), in *Parliamentary Papers*. London: House of Commons, 5, 598–601.

(1827 [1986]). *Definitions in Political Economy, Preceded by an Inquiry into the Rules Which Ought to Guide Political Economists in the Definition and Use of Their Terms, with Remarks on the Deviation from These Rules in Their Writings* (abbreviated as DEF), reprinted in *The Works of Thomas Robert Malthus*, ed. by E. A. Wrigley and D. Souden. London: Pickering and Chatto, 8.

(1830). *A Summary View of the Principle of Population* (abbreviated as SV), in FE, supra, 219–272.

(1836 [1989]). *The Principles of Political Economy: The Alterations to the First Edition* (abbreviated as PR II), ed. by J. Pullen. Cambridge: Cambridge University Press.

Macvey Napier Papers, British Library, Additional Manuscript Collection, 34.614.

The Travel Diaries of T.R. Malthus (abbreviated as TD), ed. by P. James. Cambridge: Cambridge University Press, 1966.

T.R. Malthus: Unpublished Papers in the Collection of Kanto Gakuen University, Vols. I (1997) and II (2004), (abbreviated as KG), ed. by J. Pullen and T. Hughes Parry. Cambridge: Cambridge University Press.

Secondary Literature

Bonar, J. (1885 [1924]). *Malthus and His Work* (2nd ed.). London: Macmillan.

Boulding, K. E. (1981). *Evolutionary Economics*. London: Sage.

Burke, E. (1790 [1968]). *Reflections on the Revolution in France* (C. C. O'Brien, Ed.). Harmondsworth: Penguin Books.

Byron, L. (1837). *Don Juan*. Halifax: Milner and Sowerby.

Coleridge, S. T. (1835). *Specimens of the Table Talk of the Late Samuel Taylor Coleridge* (H. N. Coleridge, Ed.). London: J. Murray.

Coleridge, S. T. (1836). *The Literary Remains of Samuel Taylor Coleridge* (H. N. Coleridge, Ed., 3 vols.). London: Pickering.

Coleridge, S. T. (n.d.). Manuscript Notes on Malthus's *Essay on Population* (1803), in British Library (Restricted Collection).

Darwin, C. (1859). *The Origin of Species*. London: John Murray.

Darwin, C. (1958). *The Autobiography of Charles Darwin* (N. Barlow, Ed.). London: Collins.
de Marchi, N. B., & Sturges, R. P. (1973). Malthus and Ricardo's Inductivist Critics: Four Letters to William Whewell. *Economica, 40,* 379–393.
De Quincey, T. (1823). Measure of Value. *London Magazine, 8,* 586–588.
Empson, W. (1837 [1963]). Life, Writings, and Character of Mr. Malthus. *Edinburgh Review,* 64 (Reprinted in *Occasional Papers of T.R. Malthus,* pp. 231–268, by B. Semmel, Ed., New York: Bert Franklin).
Fetter, F. W. (1953). The Authorship of Economic Articles in the *Edinburgh Review,* 1802–47. *Journal of Political Economy, 61,* 232–259.
Hazlitt, W. (1819). *Political Essays, with Sketches of Public Characters.* London: William Hone.
Hollander, S. (1997). *The Economics of Thomas Robert Malthus.* Toronto: University of Toronto Press.
Horner, L. (Ed.). (1843 [1853]). *Memoirs and Correspondence of Francis Horner, M.P.* (2nd ed., Vols. I & II). London: J. Murray.
Huzel, J. P. (2006). *The Popularization of Malthus in Early Nineteenth-Century England: Martineau, Cobbett and the Pauper Press.* Aldershot: Ashgate.
James, P. (1979). *Population Malthus: His Life and Times.* London: Routledge and Kegan Paul.
Keynes, J. M. (1933 [1972]). Thomas Robert Malthus. In *Essays in Biography* (Reprinted in *The Collected Writings of John Maynard Keynes,* Vol. 10, pp. 71–108, by D. Moggridge, Ed., London: Macmillan).
Marshall, A. (1890 [1949]). *Principles of Economics.* London: Macmillan.
Meek, R. L. (Ed.). (1953). *Marx and Engels on Malthus.* London: Lawrence and Wishart.
Otter, W. (1836 [1964]). Memoir of Robert Malthus. In T. R. Malthus (Ed.), *Principles of Political Economy* (2nd ed., pp. xiii–liv). New York: Augustus M. Kelley.
Paine, T. (1792 [2000]). The Rights of Man. In T. Benn (Ed.), *Common Sense and the Rights of Man.* London: Phoenix Press.
Peacock, T. L. (1817). *Melincourt.* London: T. Hookham.
Petersen, W. (1979). *Malthus.* London: Heinemann.
Pullen, J. (1989). Introduction to the Variorum Edition. In J. Pullen (Ed.), *The Principles of Political Economy* (abbreviated as PR) (pp. xv–lxix). Cambridge: Cambridge University Press.
Pullen, J. R. (1981). Notes from Malthus: The Inverarity Manuscript. *History of Political Economy, 13,* 794–811.
Reisman, D. (1987). *Alfred Marshall: Progress and Politics.* Basingstoke: Macmillan.

Ricardo, D. (1815 [1951–1955]). *An Essay on the Influence of a Low Price of Corn on the Profits of Stock*, in Ricardo, infra, IV, 9–41.
Ricardo, D. (1951–1955). *The Works and Correspondence of David Ricardo* (abbreviated as Ricardo) (P. Sraffa with M. Dobb, Eds., 11 vols.). Cambridge: Cambridge University Press.
Sadler, M. (1830). *The Law of Population* (2 vols.). London: John Murray.
Shelley, P. B. (1817). *The Revolt of Islam*. London: C. and J. Ollier.
Smith, A. (1776 [1961]). *The Wealth of Nations* (E. Cannan, Ed., 2 vols.). London: Methuen.
Sraffa, P., & Dobb, M. (1951–1955). Introduction, in Ricardo, supra, II vii–viii.
Torrens, R. (1815). *An Essay on the External Corn Trade*. London: J. Hatchard.
Torrens, R. (1821). *An Essay on the Production of Wealth; with an Appendix in Which the Principles of Political Economy Are Applied to the Actual Circumstances of the Country*. London: Longman, Hurst, Rees, Orme and Brown.

2

Induction and Deduction

Adam Smith's great *Wealth of Nations* was published in 1776. His influential synthesis coincided with the accelerated transfer of the economic hegemony from land to capital. New classes were asking new questions. A self-defined community of practitioners was emerging that wanted to systematise the art of buying and selling into a scientific discipline like physics or dentistry.

The pioneer generation had to teach itself political economy from Adam Smith's great book and the smoking chimneys of the factory towns. Ricardo was a stockbroker, self-tutored in economics. J. R. McCulloch was a journalist who had studied philosophy at Edinburgh. It was to change. Malthus in 1805 became the first British professor of a sunrise subject that was figuring prominently in national debates on tariffs, bounties, poverty, population and currency. Nassau Senior, appointed Drummond Professor at Oxford in 1825, was the second. Adam Smith had been Professor of Moral Philosophy. He was never a Professor of Political Economy.

An embryonic professional body, the Political Economy Club, came into being in 1821. There was no dedicated journal in Britain before the establishment of Marshall's *Economic Journal* in 1890. The *Edinburgh Review*, the *Westminster Review* and the *Quarterly Review*

D. Reisman, *Thomas Robert Malthus*, Great Thinkers in Economics,
https://doi.org/10.1007/978-3-030-01956-3_2

were the channels that allowed the invisible college to exchange ideas within an open-bordered republic disproportionately populated by gentleman amateurs with an interest, and often a stake, in current affairs.

Political economy in its foundry years was drawn into an *ad hoc* dialogue with the news. The first generation knew that it had to do something more than talk if its circumscribed territory was to acquire the status of a science. Appropriate problems had to be identified. Procedural rules had to be laid down. Standard definitions had to be adopted. Common paradigms had to be agreed. A new trail was being blazed. In this Malthus was one of the most prominent among the classical mould-makers. So, however, was David Ricardo.

The broad philosophical issue was whether the analytical schema should precede the mining of the facts or whether the explanations should be drawn out *post festum* from repeated associations. Malthus's *Principles* in 1820 responded to Ricardo's *Principles* of 1817 with the warning that logical reasoning, however impeccable in itself, can obscure external reality behind a veil of pre-judgment and over-confidence: 'The principal cause of error, and of the differences which prevail at present among the scientific writers on political economy, appears to me to be a precipitate attempt to simplify and generalize' (PR 5–6). Ricardo was too quick to simplify and generalise. He should have complemented his deduction with open-minded induction in order to follow nature rather than to lead it.

Malthus wanted mix-and-match and Ricardo wanted *a priori*. In the event, it was Ricardo and not Malthus who 'conquered England as completely as the Holy Inquisition conquered Spain' (Keynes 1936 [1973]: 32). Single-valued dogma is always more accessible than perpetual reappraisal. Malthus respected Ricardo to such an extent that his challenge on value or gluts was never less than muted and deferential. Much of the debate was concealed in private correspondence in which Malthus the wordsmith had the comparative advantage. Whatever the reasons, it is nonetheless the pseudo-arithmetical certainties of Ricardo rather than the 'vaguer intuition of Malthus' (Keynes 1933 [1972]: 88) that animate the modern undergraduate text. Later generations would arguably have had a better understanding of consumption, production, distribution and exchange if Malthus had been able to convince the nascent discipline that abstract speculation was not enough.

2.1 The Mixed Methodology

Ricardo was a logician who jumped directly to the final point of rest. Writing to Malthus in the year of his *Principles*, he stated that his focus was on endstate equilibrium and not on endless *tâtonnement*: 'It appears to me that the one great cause of our difference in opinion….is that you have always in your mind the immediate and temporary effects of particular changes – whereas I put these immediate and temporary effects quite aside, and fix my whole attention on the permanent state of things which will result from them' (letter from Ricardo to Malthus, 1817, in Ricardo VII: 120).

Ricardo said that his approach was comparative statics whereas Malthus treated political economy as an ongoing process. Malthus agreed that Ricardo had probably got the blue water right: 'I really think that the progress of society consists of irregular movements, and that to omit the consideration of causes which for eight or ten years will give a great *stimulus* to production and population, or a great *check* to them, is to omit the causes of the wealth and poverty of nations – the grand object of all enquiries in Political Economy' (letter from Malthus to Ricardo, 1817, in Ricardo VII: 122, emphasis in original). Malthus said that Ricardo 'had in general kept his attention…steadily fixed on permanent and final results' whereas he himself had treated economic development as evolutionary, time-dominated and, of necessity, 'very slow' (PR 231). The journey and not the destination would have to be the primary focus of all enquiry.

Each journey, moreover, is unique in itself. Political economy arrives *a postiori* when social reality has already revealed its hand. Grand theory, however elegant, has no right to propound undying assertions. All that the economist has a right to do is to investigate each journey on its own terms.

Even the language of economics is an *ex post* construct. Words, so they will not 'be strange to the generality of readers', must correspond to the ordinary usage 'in the common conversation of ordinary persons' (DEF 6, 7). In particular, they should follow the linguistic signals already employed by 'educated persons' (DEF 4, 6, 7). A 'new and more perfect nomenclature' introduced by a scientific in-group would only be permissible if words in their 'natural and ordinary meaning'

(DEF 6, 116) were failing to describe a distinctive phenomenon like unproductive labour. Otherwise, language must be treated like any other social fact. Definitions and empiricisms 'act and react upon one another….not so much as the causes as the consequences of our advances in knowledge' (letter from Malthus to Whewell, 1833, in de Marchi and Sturges, 1973: 392, 393). Like theoretical explanations, linguistic codes arrive after the event when the facts have already settled in.

Ricardo had left school at 14 for a hands-on career in the City, Parliament and the lairdship of Gatcombe Park. Malthus had studied mathematics at Cambridge before he renounced a life of practice for the Church and higher education. As with so much in their relationship, one would have expected the intellectual positions to be reversed. In fact, it was nature and not nurture that played the sorting hat.

Robert Torrens was neither the first nor the last to say that, 'if Mr. Ricardo generalizes too much, Mr. Malthus generalizes too little' (Torrens 1821: iv). Both Ricardo and Malthus had already seen that it was so. Writing to Malthus, Ricardo put the difference as follows: 'If I am too theoretical which I really believe is the case, - you I think are too practical' (letter from Ricardo to Malthus, 1815, in Ricardo VI: 295). Answering Ricardo, Malthus said that he was doing no more than conforming to the nature of the beast: 'The science of political economy is essentially practical' (PR 12). The science of political economy could not afford to settle for *ex ante* gymnastics which contributed little to human well-being: 'There are few branches of human knowledge where false views may do more harm, or just views more good' (PR 12).

Always pragmatic, Malthus did concede that 'mathematical calculations may in some cases be introduced with advantage into the science of Political Economy' (letter from Malthus to Whewell, 1829, in de Marchi and Sturges, 1973: 387). He himself only once employed formal notation, in a footnote on logarithms (SE I 271n). Writing to William Whewell in 1829, he saw (four decades before the esoteric marginalism of W. S. Jevons and F. Y. Edgeworth) that the symbolic representation of differential calculus might be of some value in describing small changes and continuous 'degrees' (letter from Malthus to Whewell, 1829, in de Marchi and Sturges, 1973: 387): 'Many of the questions both in morals and politics seem to be of the nature of the problems *de maximis* and *minimis* in fluxions; in which there is always a point where a certain effect is the greatest; while on either side of this point it gradually diminishes' (1814 [1986]: 102).

Small gradations and optimal proportions are central to Malthus's account not just of utility but of saving, property and the composition of the labour force. In the last analysis, however, the 'algebraic notation' is of little 'practical utility' where it is not supported by facts: 'The grand difficulty….is the getting data to work upon' (letter from Malthus to Whewell, 1829, in de Marchi and Sturges, 1973: 387).

Especially difficult is to gain entry into the hidden mind. Unlike a hard science like physics or dentistry, a social science like economics is founded on passions and propensities that, internal and subjective, are not easy to read. A science that is closer to morals and politics than it is to figures and numbers will always be as inscrutable and imprecise as the workings of the human psyche itself.

Adam Smith had seen that there was no accurate measure of non-observable sensations like 'sympathy' (Smith 1759 [1966]: 124–127). Later, making sociology the science of 'interpretive understanding' (Weber 1964: 88), Max Weber was to acknowledge that a psychometric scale would always be distorted by imperfect communication. Malthus, like Smith and Weber, recognised that interpersonal utility is recalcitrant to decimal-point precision. The human mind keeps its secrets to itself. Like Smith and Weber, however, Malthus also believed that scaling upward from the one-off to the aggregate could proceed as a first approximation on the basis of revealed preference. It is imperfect but it is sound.

Different people hold different world views. They have different interests. They experience different levels of want-satisfaction. Each person is a 'compound being', motivated not by reason alone but by 'corporal propensities' and 'bodily cravings' such as 'hunger, the love of liquor, the desire of possessing a beautiful woman' (FE 163, 164). Economics must by its very nature appeal to psychology and introspection to build up a database on the strength and direction of not just of action but of consciousness: 'By inquiring into the immediate causes of the progress of wealth I clearly mean to inquire mainly into motives' (letter from Malthus to Ricardo, 1821, in Ricardo IX: 10).

Fact-gathering is imperfect and mathematics looks good. Whewell complained to Richard Jones that the public was more attracted to facile generalisations than careful documentation: 'People will not mind me when I write Political Economy, except indeed I join to it mathematics and make nonsense of it' (letter from Whewell to Jones, 1849, in de Marchi and Sturges, 1973: 382). Whewell, Master of Trinity, mineralogist, intellectual, published two papers in the *Transactions of the Cambridge Philosophical Society* (Whewell 1830, 1831) in which he attempted to translate into mathematics the essence of Ricardo's economics. He concluded that Ricardo's assumptions were unrealistic and Ricardo's inferences false. Ricardian economics did not meet the need. Instead, Whewell suggested, political economy should rely on the historical record. Interpretations founded on *what is* would not make 'nonsense' of an important branch of study.

Empiricists like Whewell saw Malthus as 'a pioneer practitioner of the inductive method' (de Marchi and Sturges 1973: 384). Malthus introduced Statistics into the British Association. He was in the London Statistics Society. He was a Professor of History. Malthus was in the spirit of practical Sir William Petty's '*Number, Weight, or Measure*' which drew upon 'only such Causes, as have visible Foundations in Nature' (Petty 1690 [1997]: I 244, emphasis in original). Great British names like Francis Bacon, David Hume and Adam Smith had shown the way when they ranked the 'grand and consistent theory of Newton' above the 'wild and eccentric hypotheses of Descartes' (FE 126). Malthus, 'establishing systems upon facts' rather than making the 'facts bend to systems', was explicitly situating himself in an ongoing tradition that went directly to 'the book of nature' for 'well authenticated proofs' that could be established by means of 'patient observation' (FE 126, 131). The Owl of Minerva flies not at dawn but at dusk. The statistician sets up his clinic when the battle is over and the strategists have all gone home.

Information being scarce, there is no substitute for experiment and experience. Thomas Tooke's *High and Low Prices* demonstrated to Malthus what best practice could achieve. Tooke had brought together an 'extensive collection of facts', all of them 'within the reach of intelligent merchants' who had a practitioner's need to know (1823: 145).

Their need, similar to that of Alfred Marshall's target readership of businessmen (Marshall 1905: 5), was not currently being met by the economic mainstream: 'Some of our ablest writers in this science have been deficient in that constant reference to facts and experience, on which alone it can be safely founded, or further improved' (1823: 145).

Tooke's statistics, Malthus said, had disproved the Ricardians' labour-embodied theory. The numbers had shown that 'all exchangeable value, and consequently the prices of all commodities, depend entirely on the supply compared with the demand' and not at all on 'the labour required to produce them' (1823: 146). It is not clear what technique Tooke had used to separate the supply curve from the labour cost that is an intrinsic component of the reservation price. What is clear is the lesson that Malthus said he personally had learned. Tooke's numbers, meticulously crunched, 'leave the truth of the proposition beyond the reach of any reasonable doubt' (1823: 147). The labour theory shrivels and dies in the pure light of the five senses. The same pure light also undermines and all but refutes the 'spirit and bent' (1823: 163) of Say's Law. Deductive reasoning has nothing to fear so much as the pure light of the truth itself.

Malthus, like Tooke, is an empiricist in search of the facts. Yet he is also, like Ricardo, a theorist who wishes to generalise and predict. Hollander goes so far as to say that Malthus, despite his 'continual lip-service to experience', was in the end 'as deductive as Ricardo' (Hollander 1997: 998). It would be a serious error to see Malthus as a pure inductivist who never sullies his economics with filters and expectations. Malthus leaves no doubt that he is mixing his model. While 'bad theories are very bad things' and bad theorists are 'pernicious' and 'mischievous' (SE II 185), still a conjectural vacuum can itself be bad.

Malthus was not a radical agnostic or a forerunner of the non-theoretical historical school. The facts, he contended, do not speak for themselves. Without general principles, any search will be hit-and-miss. While no schema can ever be universal or eternal, still a working hypothesis can be constructed out of recorded associations that have stood the test of time.

It must, however, be constructed with caution. Theoretical statements based on 'partial experience' are less likely to protect the observer against the random and the irrelevant than are track-record heuristics gleaned from 'general experience' (SE II 185) that screen out the selection bias. Since a single individual, a single industry, a single market is not the national pool, the observer should take care not to draw 'general principles from insufficient evidence' (SE II 188). If, however, the sample is representative and the associations repeated, then the observer should not shy away from *ex ante* conjectures merely because a reasonable expectation is not a documented skein.

The truth is a mix: 'I would never wish to push general principles too far, though I think that they ought to be kept in view' (SE I 365). The truth is a dialogue: 'The tendency to premature generalization occasions also, in some of the principal writers on political economy, an unwillingness to bring their theories to the test of experience..... The first business of philosophy is to account for things as they are.... An accurate yet comprehensive attention to facts is necessary, both to prevent the multiplication of erroneous theories, and to confirm and sanction those that are just' (PR 10–11, 12). The truth is a circular flow. Theoretical schemata have to be inferred from real-world experience. Relevant observations have to be selected employing theoretical spotlights. It is a two-way street.

Malthus is open in stating that he, like Ricardo, is looking for laws: 'There are indeed in political economy great general principles, to which exceptions are of the most rare occurrence, and prominent land-marks which may almost always be depended upon as safe guides' (PR 1). It is all too easy to confuse 'certain appearances, which are merely co-existent and incidental' (PR 21) with the invisible iceberg that is the true cause of the effects that are observed. Theory is essential to plot the path through the wilderness of scenarios and possibilities.

Among the 'safe guides' which serve as 'prominent land-marks' there are the 'general principles' of diminishing returns, the quantity theory of money, the gains from trade and the market-clearing price. Malthus uses 'safe guides' to estimate the respective contribution to the national wealth of private property, inequality, self-reliance and state intervention. He uses 'general principles' to model the causes of fluctuation, stagnation and secular over-saving. He relies on 'fixed laws of our nature' (FE 70) to show that population tends to increase more rapidly than the supply of subsistence. He appeals to 'a law as invariable as the action of the principle of gravity' (PR 155) to justify his evolutionary account of rent. As much as Malthus was a votary of 'number, weight and measure', he was also committed to the theoretical prism of 'strong cases' that would empower him to screen, focus and select: 'My object was to elucidate principles....To do this I imagined strong cases that I might shew the operation of those principles' (letter from Malthus to Ricardo, 1820, in Ricardo VIII: 184).

It can even happen that the *a priori* schema is more reliable than the raw data that untreated reality has thrown up. He says as much in the *Essay*: 'It will be but little consequence, if any of the facts or calculations which have been assumed in the course of this chapter, should turn out to be false. The reader will see that the reasonings are of a general nature, and may be true, though the facts taken to illustrate them may prove to be inexplicable' (SE I 238). Where the facts do not support the conjectures and the investigators are 'not fully satisfied' with the 'reference to experience' (PR 115), it will sometimes be wise to throw the naked evidence back and to trawl again.

An 'advantageous mean' (PR 10) must be found. It is a difficult task. The optimum is not marked: 'We may not know how to place it' (PR 10). The 'resources of political economy' (PR 464) may not be equal to the task. Difficult as it will be, the 'just mean' (PR 22) between conjecture and observation is the sine qua non. It is implicit in the mission statement of the science itself. Malthus, introducing his *Principles*, says that he has made it his task 'to prepare the general rules of political economy for practical application' (PR 21). Practical application necessitates the right tool for the right task. Malthus wanted to do good: 'The sole use of political economy is its application to practice' (1823: 162). He knew that in order to do good he had to get his mixed methodology right.

2.2 Population Malthus

First, there are the axioms. Then there are the deductions. At the end, there is the summing up: 'The superior power of population cannot be checked without producing misery or vice' (FE 79). Subsistence lags behind. The geometrical ratio in mouths to feed, the arithmetical expansion in natural resources, make the life of all plants, animals and human beings into a game against nature that nature must always win.

The rule is that 'population must always be kept down to the level of the means of subsistence' (FE 61). Pure logic proves it. Scarcity is inevitable. Overpopulation is 'an obvious truth' (FE 61). The conjecture is 'confirmed by experiment' (FE 69) and supported by evidence: 'The best proof that can be obtained of the capacity of mankind to increase at a certain rate is their having really increased at that rate' (SV 233). The best proof is 'Number, Weight, or Measure'.

The law of population is not an abstract proposition derived exclusively from an assumed *a priori*. Rather, it is a tentative generalisation based upon the 'past history of mankind, from which alone we can judge of the future' (SE II 229). The patterns described have been 'confirmed, in the most remarkable manner, by the state of society *as it actually exists* in every country with which we are acquainted' (PR 11, emphasis added). Grand theory can be added later to provide a structured explanation of the results. It is no more than the junior partner. The real world *as it actually exists* has revealed everything that the epistemologist needs to know.

Malthus claimed that his theory had been drawn out from 'the past history of mankind'. He must have known that it had not. The evidence did not exist. Defending 'a position not to be controverted' (FE 87), he had no choice but to rely on toy soldiers such as 'there can remain no doubt in the mind of any thinking man' (FE 86), 'I should infer with certainty' (FE 87), 'is it not probable?' (FE 110), it 'would probably have a very unfavourable effect' (FE 110), 'it is obvious' (PR 369) and 'few will be disposed to believe' (FE 187).

Toy soldiers such as these made him appear a false prophet who never dirtied his *ex cathedra* with mundane reality. As a Christian and a clergyman, he could have said that his professional cassock had accustomed him to make statements that had to be taken on trust. Instead, he appealed to the recorded *what is*. Malthus boasted in the *Principles* that he had a 'steady and unshaken confidence in the theory of population' (PR 11). His reason was that the theory had been confirmed by 'no inconsiderable evidence' (FE 61).

It was wishful thinking. The database in 1798 was fragmentary and embryonic. Different countries, all of them coloured by 'the powers of production', 'the natural resources of the soil', 'the acquired tastes and habits of the people' (PR 489, 490), were adapting the law of population to their own unique circumstances. Economic growth was moving the cross-country comparisons on. No one had the data that was needed to support or disprove the alleged laws and ratios.

Speaking of China, Malthus infers 'with certainty' that the population is 'immense' (FE 87) and that the lower classes are trapped in 'the most abject state of poverty' (SE I 125). He infers it but he does not prove it. A 'minute history....would be of the greatest use' (FE 87). Absent the time series and the cross section, all he had was general knowledge and the unsubstantiated authority of Adam Smith (1776 [1961]: I 80–81). China is 'the most fertile country in the world'. 'Almost all the land is in tillage'. The people 'live very frugally' (FE 87). Malthus cannot be faulted for theorising from vague impressions such as these when the second best was the only best he could get. But it neither confirms nor refutes his supposition.

England too was second best. Writing before the first-ever English census in 1801, Malthus in 1798 had no way of knowing whether the population of his own country was rising, falling or remaining constant. Price said it was going down. Howlett said it was going up.

Richard Price in *Observations on Reversionary Payments* had calculated in 1771 that the population of England and Wales had fallen by a quarter since 1688 (Price 1771: II 311). He had based his estimate on the number of taxable housing-units multiplied by a notional number of residents per house. Alarmed by the decline, he called on the State to get involved: 'The encouragement of population, therefore, ought to be one of the first objectives of policy in every state' (Price 1771: I 280).

John Howlett in *An Examination of Dr. Price's Essay* had responded in 1781 that Price had got it badly wrong: 'Our population, so far from rapidly declining, has long been greatly advancing' (Howlett 1781: xii, 152). The population of England and Wales had increased by a third since 1688. It had increased by a fifth in the previous twenty years alone. Britain was expanding. It was not withering away.

Choosing between depopulation and escalation, Malthus settled the issue with inference. It was an error for nations to assume that 'population was the cause of prosperity, instead of their prosperity being the cause of their population' (SE I 437). Britain had enjoyed rapid economic growth. It had been that improvement in living standards that had pulled up the headcount. At the time of the first *Essay* Malthus believed that the population was rising but not rising rapidly. The census in 1801 proved that he had underestimated the magnitude of the problem. The geometrical ratio was back in business.

Price and Howlett were writing in an English tradition of conjectural demography that made use of proxies like houses and windows to estimate the number of souls. The literature included William Petty's *Political Arithmetic* in 1690, Gregory King's *Natural and Political Observations* in 1696 and George Chalmers's *Estimate of the Comparative Strength of Great Britain* in 1782. Malthus was particularly influenced by Sir Frederick Morton Eden's *The State of the Poor*, published in 1797, and by his *Estimate of the Number of Inhabitants in Great Britain and Ireland* in 1800. Malthus described Eden's work as a 'mine of information, for everything relating to prices and labour' (1814 [1986]: 89).

Malthus in developing his theory of population was inserting himself into an ongoing debate. It had culminated in the canonical *Wealth of Nations* where Smith wrote that 'the demand for men necessarily regulates the production of men': 'Every species of animals necessarily multiplies in proportion to the means of their subsistence, and no species can ever multiply beyond it' (Smith 1776 [1961]: I 89). The *Wealth of Nations* said it all. Not, however, for the first time. Even Adam Smith was inserting himself into an ongoing debate.

Benjamin Franklin in his *Observations* explained the fact that the America had twice the weighted birth rate as Europe and that its population was doubling itself every 20 years with reference to high wages and good conditions: 'People increase in Proportion to the Number of the Marriages, and that is greater in Proportion to the Ease and Convenience of supporting a Family' (Franklin 1755: 42). David Hume in *Political Discourses* had argued that the moderns were definitely more populous than the ancients: 'Almost every man who thinks he can maintain a family will have one; and the human species, at this rate of propagation, would more than double every generation' (Hume 1752 [1955]: 111, 146). Richard Cantillon in his *Essai sur la Nature du Commerce en Général* had announced that 'the multiplication of Animals has no other bounds than the greater or less means allotted for their subsistence' (Cantillon 1755 [1959]: 67). If the food is there, the people will breed: 'Men multiply like Mice in a barn if they have unlimited Means of Subsistence' (Cantillon 1755 [1959]: 83).

There will not be enough room in the barn. There will not be enough food. It was as Robert Wallace said in his *Dissertation on the Numbers of Mankind* (1752), *Characteristics of the Present State of Great Britain* (1758) and *Various Prospects of Mankind, Nature, and Providence* (1761). Wallace, a Scottish clergyman and contemporary of Hume, had looked at population from the perspective both of a single country and of the world as a whole. He predicted a time when 'the earth would be overstocked at last, and become unable to support its numerous inhabitants.... There would not even be sufficient room for containing their bodies upon the surface of the earth' (Wallace 1761: 115, 116).

The world, Wallace, said, was doomed to sickness and plague. Men are 'laid under the cruel necessity of killing one another' (Wallace 1761: 121). Abortion and infanticide, 'unnatural and inhuman', are rife as 'the natural consequences of our depravity' (Wallace 1761: 118, 120). In politics, 'force and fraud must prevail' (Wallace 1761: 120). The real impediment to utopia was the population mechanism and the certainty of overcrowding. Smith, Godwin and Paley had read Wallace. So had Malthus (FE 120; SE I 306). Wallace's message was chilling. The population of the world will grow until it grows hungry. After that it will starve, just like the mice in the barn.

Sir James Steuart in *Principles of Political Economy* had compared the 'generative faculty' to a spring restrained by a weight. When the growth in population exceeds the growth in subsistence, 'the spring is overloaded' and 'inhabitants will diminish....in proportion to the overcharge' (Steuart 1767 [1966]: I 32). The numbers, always assuming 'that there be a demand for men', must 'ever be, in proportion to the food produced' (Steuart 1767 [1966]: I 20, 49). It all depends on the ratios: 'Whatever gives food gives numbers' (Steuart 1767 [1966]: I 94, emphasis deleted). It is true in reverse. If there is not enough food to go round, nature will bid the superfluous diners to be gone. There were positive checks even before 1798. Even in the Age of Reason, there was more to the debate than Godwin and Condorcet.

Malthus read widely. Many books, British and foreign, contributed insights that were to feed through into the *Essay*. A number of them were comparative accounts of journeys at home and abroad. Malthus had read Jean Chardin's *Journal du Voyage* (1686), Antonio de Ulloa's *Voyage to South America* (1758), James Cook's *Voyages* (1773), Arthur Young's *Tour of Ireland* (1780) and *Travels in France* (1792), Joseph Townsend's *Dissertation on the Poor Laws* (1786) and *Journey through Spain* (1791), Mungo Park's *Travels in the Interior of Africa* (1797). There was also the section on 'Population and Provision' in Paley's *Principles of Moral and Political Philosophy* in 1785 about which Anthony Waterman says: 'Virtually the whole of Malthus's *population* theory, narrowly considered, is to be found in Paley's brief exposition.... including strong hints of Malthus's own phraseology' (Waterman 1996: 681, emphasis in original).

Paley had anticipated the checks and the mathematical increase. He had criticised the 'irregular gratifications' and 'licentious indulgences' so frequently pursued by 'the male part of the species' (Paley 1785: II 372). He had looked forward to a 'fivefold' improvement in 'the fecundity of soil' (Paley 1785: II 372). He had foreseen the effect of luxuries, 'habitual superfluities' and the 'accustomed mode of life' in discouraging early marriage, even among 'the common people', lest marginal offspring 'reduce their mode of living' (Paley 1785: II 375). He had said that a country which wants adequate subsistence should budget for a surplus: 'It is impossible to have enough, without a superfluity' (Paley 1785: II 420). He had said that the mechanisation of industry was no threat to jobs, incomes or childbearing: 'The number of persons employed in the manufactory of stockings has not, I apprehend, decreased, since the invention of stocking mills' (Paley 1785: II 424). It is all in Malthus because it is all in Paley.

On one point, however, there was a fundamental disagreement. Paley, Malthus believed, had greatly underestimated the imminence of excess. As a utilitarian Paley had asserted that 'the quantity of happiness....

depends upon the number of inhabitants' (Paley 1785: II 368). Paley in 1785 had contended that, one counted as one, it would be in an 'exact proportion': to double the nation's population would be to double its stock of happiness. In 1802, after reading the *Essay*, he changed his mind. Convinced by Malthus's geometrical and arithmetical progressions, Paley accepted in his *Natural Theology* that numbers could mean not collective happiness but real poverty.

Malthus in 1798 had influenced Paley. Paley in 1785 had influenced Malthus. It is even possible that it had been Paley's *Principles* that had awakened Malthus's interest in Smith. 'There is very little evidence', Waterman writes, 'that *Wealth of Nations* was much read in Cambridge before 1800' (Waterman 1996: 675), when the *Essay* in 1798 and the establishment of the *Edinburgh Review* in 1802 raised the profile of the new field of inquiry. Paley, a clergyman, had nonetheless been interested enough in economics to read the whole of Smith's long treatise. Paley had borrowed the butcher, the brewer and the baker. He had also adopted Smith's account of the doubling of the population in 25 years. Paley in that way may have been the broker who introduced Malthus to Smith.

Paley was an influence. There were others. There were Plato and Aristotle. From them Malthus learned that colonisation in ancient Greece had confirmed 'the strong tendency of population to increase beyond the means of subsistence' (SE I 135). There were Tacitus, Caesar, Machiavelli, Montesquieu, Crome, Graunt and Gibbon. There were the reports of the Jesuits. There was Dionysius of Halicarnassus. There was Johann Peter Süssmilch's *Göttliche Ordnung*, also cited by Richard Price despite the fact that neither he nor Malthus (whose only modern foreign language was French) could actually read German. Malthus wrote to his father in 1799 that he hoped for a translation: 'If it should be in German, it will be of no use to me' (quoted in Bonar 1885 [1924]: 414).

Primary data was not easy to obtain. Secondary material, not always substantiated, was easier to access. It fleshed out the deductions. In the New England colonies the population, benefiting from ample subsistence, was doubling itself every 25 years (FE 74). It was conforming to the expectation of the geometrical ratio. Sooner or later, nature would put paid to that: 'Even civil liberty, all powerful as it is, will not create fresh land' (FE 197). Among the Amerindians, Cape Hottentots (FE 81), South Sea Islanders and Australian aborigines (SE I 25–26), the 'want of room and nourishment' was pushing into the history books Rousseau's deceptive fiction of the Noble Savage. Noble or ignoble, the population is 'always greater than the means to support it' (FE 81).

The secondary literature, inevitably selective, confirmed his conjectures. What he really wanted, however, was the raw library of experience. Normally relying on the published research of other scholars, Malthus made what use he could of parish registers to document the births, marriages and deaths. From the records, he was able to draw 'many useful inferences' (SE II 7). Using the statistics, he made cross-national comparisons of 'the varying effect of soil and climate' (SV 253). He compared mountainous versus flat terrain, corn countries with cattle countries, and showed a sociologist's sensitivity to the variance in habits and customs. Norway had a lower mortality rate and a higher ratio of births to deaths than did Sweden. He explained this by the relative lack of urban conglomerations and 'unwholesome manufactories' that in Sweden were unleashing the positive checks (SE I 153, 158). He took advantage of his study-trips to Scandinavia and later to France and Ireland to inspect at first hand both the living conditions and the economic basis.

Original data was hard to obtain. Much of it was inconsistent or 'deficient' (SE I 254). The tables could not be trusted: 'Few just inferences can be drawn from them' (SE I 281). Marriage and death in the upper classes were better documented than the equivalent patterns among the poor. Statistics collected in wartime could not be extrapolated into peace: because the males will have returned, it is 'difficult to conceive that they approach nearer the truth' (SE I 282). Even the 1801 Census was only a first approximation (SE II 1). Unregistered births, unbaptised dissenters and unrecorded deaths were omitted. There was no distinction between first, second and further marriages. There was no allowance for the rural–urban divide. There was no disaggregation into income groups and cultural classes.

The published data left much to be desired. Yet it did open a door. Malthus made use of Census data to estimate the significance of the inter-temporal increase (SE I 273). He relied on tabulated frequencies for the statistic that the average marriage in Europe was producing four children (SE II 2). He discovered in 1817 that the British population was doubling itself every 55 years (SE I 445). He made, 'with tolerable exactness' (SE II 14), cross-country comparisons of preventive checks correlated with differential birth rates. He knew that he was being held back by the data. At least he recognised that he had to go further than mathematics and revelation alone.

Malthus had formal training in mathematics and revelation. He had no formal training in statistics. He was being held back not just by the paucity of the records but by his own inability to net out the 'limitations', the 'exceptions', the 'unforeseen' and the 'various and complicated causes' (PR 8, 11). They left even the data that he could obtain behind a thick veil of ambiguity. Malthus could not be confident that he had drawn the correct inferences. Empirical evidence, inadequately processed, could be the cause of 'crude and premature theories' that are always 'the principal cause of error' (PR 5, 6). Malthus must have known that he lacked the computational skills to winnow out the wheat from the chaff.

The problem is especially acute since Malthus, as Pullen says, was 'constantly looking for causative plurality' (Pullen 2016: 350). Although he accepted Occam's rule not to admit more causes that are necessary for a specific problem Malthus also believed that too few variables were as unsatisfactory as too many. If a cause is really necessary, Malthus said, there is no choice. It 'must be admitted' (PR 7).

Where there are many causes, incidental, repeated, primary, secondary, it is easier to assume *ceteris paribus* than it is to measure the impact of a single variable factored out from the rest. The value of land is determined jointly by fertility, population, trade, partial demand, total demand. The size of the population is a function of subsistence, *embourgeoisement*, habit, emigration, poor relief. All variables are in flux. None is held constant. Assertions are simplifications. The testing of hypotheses is difficult.

Time complicates the calculations. Malthus knew that there was a feedback loop, a 'circle of causes and effects in political economy which are acting and re-acting on each other' (PR 16). The kaleidoscope of combinations can 'alone adequately account for the variable and complicated phenomena observable' (PR 7). It is, clearly, 'a task of very great difficulty' (PR 16) not merely to think out a general rule but also to find credible confirmation in the 'actual situation and circumstances' (PR II 14) of a single country at a single moment in its history. Treading the middle course between induction and deduction, Malthus is wise enough to recognise that it brings 'permanent discredit' (PR II 14) on economic science to claim a degree of knowledge that it does not possess.

References

By T. R. Malthus

(1798 [1970]). *Essay on the Principle of Population, as It Affects the Future Improvement of Society, with Remarks on the Speculations of Mr. Godwin, M. Condorcet, and Other Writers* (abbreviated as FE), ed. by A. Flew. Harmondsworth: Penguin.

(1803 et seq. [1989]). *An Essay on the Principle of Population: Or a View of Its Past and Present Effects on Human Happiness, with an Inquiry into Our Prospects Respecting the Removal of the Evils Which It occasions* (2nd edition, 1803; further editions in 1806, 1807, 1817, 1826) (abbreviated as SE I and SE II), 2 vols., ed. by P. James. Cambridge: Cambridge University Press.

(1814 [1986]). *Observations on the Effects of the Corn Laws, and of a Rise or Fall in the Price of Corn on the Agriculture and General Wealth of the Country*, reprinted in *The Works of Thomas Robert Malthus*, ed. by E. A. Wrigley and D. Souden. London: Pickering and Chatto, 7, 87–109.

(1820 [1989]). *The Principles of Political Economy* (abbreviated as PR), ed. by J. Pullen. Cambridge: Cambridge University Press.

(1823 [1963]). 'Tooke—On High and Low Prices', review of Thomas Tooke's *Thoughts and Details on the High and Low Prices of the Last Thirty Years*', *Quarterly Review*, 1823, reprinted in *Occasional Papers of T.R. Malthus*, ed. by B. Semmel. New York: Bert Franklin, 145–170.

(1827 [1986]). *Definitions in Political Economy, Preceded by an Inquiry into the Rules Which Ought to Guide Political Economists in the Definition and Use of Their Terms, with Remarks on the Deviation from These Rules in Their Writings*

(abbreviated as DEF), reprinted in *The Works of Thomas Robert Malthus*, ed. by E. A. Wrigley and D. Souden. London: Pickering and Chatto, 8.
(1830). *A Summary View of the Principle of Population* (abbreviated as SV), in FE, supra, 219–272.
(1836 [1989]). *The Principles of Political Economy: The Alterations to the First Edition* (abbreviated as PR II), ed. by J. Pullen. Cambridge: Cambridge University Press.

Secondary Literarture

Bonar, J. (1885 [1924]). *Malthus and his Work* (2nd. ed.). London: Macmillan.
Cantillon, R. (1755 [1959]). *Essai sur la Nature du Commerce en Général* (H. Higgs, Ed. & Trans.). London: Frank Cass.
de Marchi, N. B., & Sturges, R. P. (1973). Malthus and Ricardo's Inductivist Critics: Four Letters to William Whewell. *Economica, 40,* 379–393.
Franklin, B. (1755). *Observations Concerning the Increase of Mankind, Peopling of Countries, etc.* Boston: John Clarke.
Hollander, S. (1997). *The Economics of Thomas Robert Malthus.* Toronto: University of Toronto Press.
Howlett, J. (1781). *An Examination of Dr. Price's Essay on the Population of England and Wales, and the Doctrine of an Increased Population in This Country Established by the Facts.* Maidstone: J. Black.
Hume, D. (1752 [1955]). Of the Populousness of Ancient Nations. In E. Rotwein (Ed.), *David Hume: Writings on Economics* (pp. 108–184). London: Nelson.
Keynes, J. M. (1933 [1972]). Thomas Robert Malthus. In *Essays in Biography* (Reprinted in *The Collected Writings of John Maynard Keynes,* Vol. 10, pp. 71–108, London: Macmillan).
Keynes, J. M. (1936 [1973]). *The General Theory of Employment, Interest and Money.* In *The Collected Writings of John Maynard Keynes.* London: Macmillan.
Marshall, A. (1905, December 29). Letter to *The Times.*
Paley, W. (1785). *Principles of Moral and Political Philosophy* (2 vols.). Dublin: Exshaw, White and others.
Petty, W. (1690 [1997]). *Political Arithmetic.* In C. H. Hull (Ed.), *The Economic Writings of Sir William Petty* (2 vols.). London: Routledge and Thommes Press.

Price, R. (1771). *Observations on Reversionary Payments, on Schemes for Providing Annuities for Widows, and for Persons in Old Age* (2 vols.). London: Cadell.

Pullen, J. R. (2016). Malthus on Causality. *European Journal of History of Economic Thought, 23,* 349–377.

Ricardo, D. (1951–1955). *The Works and Correspondence of David Ricardo* (abbreviated as Ricardo) (P. Sraffa with M. Dobb, Ed., 11 vols.). Cambridge: Cambridge University Press.

Smith, A. (1759 [1966]). *The Theory of Moral Sentiments.* New York: Augustus M. Kelley.

Smith, A. (1776 [1961]). *The Wealth of Nations* (E. Cannan, Ed., 2 vols.). London: Methuen.

Steuart, J. (1767 [1966]). *An Inquiry into the Principles of Political Oeconomy* (A. S. Skinner, Ed.). Edinburgh: Oliver & Boyd.

Torrens, R. (1821). *An Essay on the Production of Wealth; with an Appendix in Which the Principles of Political Economy Are Applied to the Actual Circumstances of the Country.* London: Longman, Hurst, Rees, Orme and Brown.

Wallace, R. (1761). *Various Prospects of Mankind, Nature, and Providence.* London: A. Millar.

Waterman, A. M. C. (1996). Why William Paley Was "the First of the Cambridge Economists". *Cambridge Journal of Economics, 20,* 673–686.

Weber, M. (1964). *The Theory of Social and Economic Organization* (T. Parsons, Ed.). New York: The Free Press.

Whewell, W. (1830). Mathematical Exposition of Some Doctrines of Political Economy. *Transactions of the Cambridge Philosophical Society, 3,* 191–230.

Whewell, W. (1831). Mathematical Exposition of Some of the Leading Doctrines in Mr. Ricardo's "Principles of Political Economy and Taxation". *Transactions of the Cambridge Philosophical Society, 4,* 155–198.

3
The Law of Population

Malthus wanted to do good. He wanted to see the greatest happiness of the greatest number. Empson says that 'Mr. Malthus owed the discovery, which will immortalize his name, mainly to his benevolence' (Empson 1837 [1963]: 244), Utopian perfectionists like Godwin and Condorcet had put their faith in the rational redesign of human institutions. They had failed to understand the unbending law of nature. Malthus was a social scientist who predicted that biological instinct in association with the exhaustion of the soil must inevitably turn all the demons loose.

3.1 The Optimum Population

Population in itself is good: 'The power of a country to increase its resources or defend its possessions must depend principally upon its efficient population' (SE II 207). As producers, people are workers who add value to the national wealth. As consumers, people are 'a powerful and necessary element of increasing demand' (PR 347). William Petty had said that 'fewness of people, is real poverty' (Petty 1662 [1997]: I 34),

D. Reisman, *Thomas Robert Malthus*, Great Thinkers in Economics,
https://doi.org/10.1007/978-3-030-01956-3_3

Josiah Child that the true wealth of a nation is 'multitudes of People' and 'an encrease of People' (Child 1693: xii), William Paley that 'the decay of population is the greatest evil that a state can suffer' (Paley 1785: II 369). It is a considerable body of expert opinion. There is more. Even before 'the writers of old' had made themselves 'the warmest advocates of increase' (SE II 206), there had been a still more distinguished authority: 'It is the intention of the Creator that the earth should be replenished' (SE II 206). The Creator had declared that population in itself is good. He was unlikely to have made a mistake.

A growing population grows the national wealth. The hidden assumption is, however, that the basic needs can be met: 'An increase of population is in itself a very decided advantage, if it not be accompanied by an increased proportion of vice and misery' (letter from Malthus to Senior, 1829, in Senior, 1831: 85). Fruitfulness and multiplication are unequivocally in the national interest. Vice and misery are not: 'I see no objection to the greatest possible increase of population, which does not produce, or threaten after a moderate time to produce low wages, misery and vice' (letter from Malthus to Wilmot-Horton, 1830, in Ghosh, 1963: 54). The optimum population is neither *too few* nor *too many* but rather the number in the middle that maximises the felt well-being of the whole. It is important to get the balance right.

Malthus in the 1798 *Essay* had been the Cassandra who knew with certainty that the shipwreck was imminent: 'I see no way by which man can escape from the weight of this law which pervades all animated nature. No fancied equality, no agrarian regulations in their utmost extent, could remove the pressure of it *even for a single century*' (FE 72, emphasis added). By the 1803 *Essay*, he was conceding that perhaps he had over-egged his pudding. As things now stand, he said, 'not more than half of the prolific power of nature is called into action' (SE I 253). The end of days had not been cancelled. Apparently, however, it had been deferred.

In the 1806 *Essay*, the date of the apocalypse slipped again. In the 'course of some centuries', Malthus announced, the British population will be two times or even three times as large and yet each individual citizen will 'be both better fed and better clothed' (SE II 210). Living standards will have risen as the cause and effect of a rise in population.

It was not yet the time to call for a stationary population or, still less, for the population to decline.

In the 1817 *Essay*, the invocation to build an ark was diluted still further. The time span was not infinite but it was strictly speaking indefinite: 'The power of the earth to produce subsistence is certainly not unlimited, but is strictly speaking indefinite....The time *will probably never arrive* when we shall be able to say, that no farther labour or ingenuity of man could make further additions to it' (SE II 211, emphasis added). It *will probably never arrive.* Petty, Child and Paley were right. Subsistence is not unlimited but it is indefinite. There is no demographic time bomb primed to explode.

This is not to deny the existence even now of 'low wages, misery and vice'. The short run can be a veil of tears. The human passions demand immediate gratification. The increase in the supply of food is lagged, gradual and diminishing. Already 'there are more children born than the country can properly support' (SE I 253). In the long run, it might not be the march to the abyss. In the here-and-now, it is neither a confirmation nor a refutation of the law of population to say that life at the Hobbesian margin will be nasty, brutish and short.

It is no reason to disparage the passion between the sexes. Good times or bad times, marriage and family are a considerable source of satisfaction. 'So delightful a passion as virtuous love' could 'more than counterbalance' the 'attendant evils' of more dependents to feed (FE 90). Parental affection is 'one of the most delightful passions in human nature' (SE II 141). Virtuous love for the family man is 'the sunny spot in his whole life, where his imagination loves most to bask' (SE II 91).

Having 'some object of affection', sharing in 'the endearing engagement of parent and child', the family man develops a 'gentleness, kindness, and suavity of manners' (SE II 91, 92) which distinguishes him from the bachelor. Malthus was unmarried at the time of the first *Essay* and a family man from the third. It did not affect his views. Malthus never eulogised puritanism or advocated monastic abstinence. Godwin said the passion between the sexes would be extinguished. Malthus welcomed married love. Without the conjugal unit, the pleasures of 'the evening meal, the warm house, and the comfortable fireside' (SE II 91) would be greatly diminished.

Yet it is Steuart's spring loaded by a weight. A nation ought to pursue the two great *desiderata* of a large population and minimal deprivation. There are limits beyond which it cannot go. W. S. Jevons said that coal was running out (Jevons 1865), Fred Hirsch that the moral legacy was being depleted (Hirsch 1977), the Club of Rome that irreplaceable resources were being exhausted (Meadows and others 1972). Ecology, recycling, congestion, solar energy, good neighbours, Neo-Malthusian is open-ended. Malthus himself said that the limit was food. 1798 or 1817, Malthus never denied that the crocodile of famine was lurking unseen. Sooner or later it would have the last laugh.

3.2 The Ratios

Subsistence increases in an arithmetical ratio: 1, 2, 3, 4. Population increases in a geometrical ratio: 1, 2, 4, 8. Left unchecked, the human species would increase 512-fold in 225 years but subsistence only by a factor of 10. In a single century, the population would increase 16-fold but subsistence only 5. It is not good news. The increase in population is 'indefinitely greater' (FE 71) than the power of the earth to provide.

It is a race against time. It is a race that the non-ego environment must win and 'all animated nature' lose. There is a 'strong and constantly operating check from the difficulty of subsistence' (FE 71). Sooner or later it must end in 'low wages, vice and misery'. There is no other way: 'By the laws of nature man cannot live without food' (SV 242).

Trained in the logical deductions of mathematics, Malthus anchors his theory in two postulates, two 'fixed laws of our nature'. The first is that 'food is necessary to the existence of man'. The second is that 'the passion between the sexes is necessary and will remain nearly in its present state' (FE 70). The iron law of population is rooted in two irrevocable truths, universal and eternal. The dismal prediction is derived through a chain of reasoning that is entirely dependent on the strength of the two initial constants.

The mathematical logic does not lie. Deduction is 'incontrovertible' (SE II 197). Besides that, it is 'uniformly confirmed by experience'

(SE I 336). Observation bears 'too convincing a testimony' (FE 79), not just in Britain, witnessed by 'almost every register of a country parish' (SE I 338), but further afield, 'in every age and in every part of the world' (SE I 336). Evidence from every age and every part of the world confirms the core contention, that population 'does invariably increase' (FE 79) to the limits of subsistence. Extrapolating from an estimated 7 million in 1798, the British population would swell to 14 million in 1823 and 28 million in 1848 (FE 75). Soon it will be standing room only, red in tooth and claw. Scarcity means crowding and in the end crowding out. That is how it is: 'I can see no way by which man can escape from the weight of this law which pervades all animated nature' (FE 72).

3.3 The Checks

Population 'when unchecked' (FE 71) will more than equal the whole of nature's mighty feast. Where there is meat there are mouths. Without any checks, the population will ultimately go beyond the supply of food: 'The perpetual tendency in the race of man to increase beyond the means of subsistence is one of the general laws of animated nature' (FE 199).

Without any checks, the natural increase 'would evidently be much greater than any increase that has been hitherto been known' (FE 74). That counterfactual is the key: 'In no state that we have yet known has the power of population been left to exert itself with perfect freedom' (FE 73). History confirms it. Countervailing forces must have been at work. They must have been pushing against the geometrical series. They must have arrested its further advance before it reached the danger zone.

Malthus insists that 'no theories are entitled to confidence in reference to the future, which will not give a satisfactory solution of past phenomena' (1823 [1963]: 152). Nature abhors a frictionless vacuum and economics must respect the *ceteris paribus*. In order to draw out the lessons of history, Malthus knew that he had to rely on 'that enlarged and comprehensive experience' (PR 6) which goes beyond a one-dimensional, two-variable model of procreation and nutrition.

'In the actual state of every society' (SE II 87), Malthus said, there are countervailing forces which, functioning as an inevitable law of nature, are stepping in to ensure the balance. There are two such checks, mutually exclusive: 'The sum of all the positive and preventive checks, taken together, forms undoubtedly the most immediate cause which represses population' (SE I 146). The history of demography is the record of the checks.

A positive check is one which 'represses an increase which is already begun' (FE 93). Mortality rates rise and life expectancy falls. In London, one-half of all newborns are dead before the age of 3 (SE I 257). Hard times thin out the competitors. The fall is not permanent. New births and internal migration replenish the supply. When a third of the population of Prussia and Lithuania was wiped out by the plague in 1710, one year later, in 1711, the number of marriages was twice its earlier average (SE I 203). In 1710 and even 1711, however, the pressure on scarce resources was undoubtedly relieved.

Pestilence, famine, miscarriage, abortion and infanticide are all positive checks that sweep away the excess. Malignant fevers and epidemic disease cull the sickly and the old. Farmworkers are packed into urban black spots, so much 'less healthy than country situations and country employments' (SE II 197). Foul air in the inner-city slums is 'unfavourable to the tender lungs of children' (SE I 257). Child labour decimates the vulnerable. The lower orders, on poverty wages and exposed to cyclical unemployment, 'are disabled from giving the proper food and attention to their children' (FE 89). Their children in turn pass on to their own children the intergenerational handicap of malnutrition and debility. Their resistance is less. It makes them more susceptible to delayed euthanasia through plague, cholera or smallpox.

In 1796, two years before Malthus's *Essay*, Edward Jenner had discovered his game-changing, life-saving vaccine. Logically speaking, Malthus should have been opposed to anything that would snooker nature's investment in the positive checks. He must initially have been torn between compassion and economics since he does not refer to Jenner in the 1798 *Essay*. By the 1806 *Essay*, he had decided that human life had to be put first. Declaring himself 'one of the warmest friends to the introduction of the cow-pox' (SE II 210), he left unexplained what the life-course was to be of the children, vaccinated, that the earth could not feed.

There is also war. Historically speaking, it has been, among all the positive checks, 'the most prominent and striking' (SE I 147). Population pressures are 'partly the effect and partly the cause of incessant war' (SE II 101). Decimating battles are fought for arable land, valuable herds, essential wells and *Lebensraum* for the superfluous headcount. Continuing conflict diverts scarce resources from production to predation: 'The evils seem mutually to produce each other' (SE I 79). Labour and capital are destroyed in war even if new land is successfully annexed. Wages rise because of the deaths. Couples marry earlier and have more children. Rising population then makes the next war inevitable.

Positive checks from pestilence to conquest attack the overhang that diminishing returns to labour on the land can no longer support. Malthus describes what it is like to arrive too late in an evocative passage from the second *Essay* of 1803: 'A man who is born into a world already possessed, if he cannot get subsistence from his parents on whom he has a just demand, and if the society do not want his labour, has no claim of *right* to the smallest portion of food, and, in fact, has no business to be where he is. At nature's mighty feast there is no vacant cover for him. She tells him to be gone' (SE II 127, emphasis in original). More diners demand more provisions until in the end 'the plenty that before reigned is changed into scarcity' (SE II 127). A compassionate host 'fills the hall with numerous claimants' (SE II 127) until in the end there is nothing but disappointment and distress left to share. One diner destroys another diner's happiness. It is the law of nature.

Positive checks wash away the surplus. Preventive checks are more merciful. They ensure that an unwanted excess never sees the light of day.

Unlike bad harvests or a hard winter, preventive checks are under human control: 'Reason, that faculty which enables us to calculate consequences, is the proper corrective and guide....Improved reason will always tend to prevent the abuse of sensual pleasures' (FE 148). Plants and animals do not have the telescopic vision to foresee the consequences of a fleeting diversion. Human beings do. Their voluntary restraint has the beneficial consequence that children sentenced to die are never conceived and never born.

Voluntary restraint is a wise and thinking choice: 'No man would bring beings into the world, for whom he could not find the means of support' (FE 141). Afraid both of distress and of 'disgrace' (FE 141), constantly aware of 'the difficulties attending the rearing of a family' (FE 89), such a man will defer marriage or remain permanently celibate. Subsistence is scarce. Self-control is the sensible choice until the breadwinner is able to cover the costs.

The middle and the upper classes are more likely to have the foresight. The lower classes are more likely to live for the day. While voluntary restraint is found 'in some degree' (FE 89) in all strata of society, Malthus points to 'the improbability that the lower classes of people in any country should ever be sufficiently free from want and labour to obtain any high degree of intellectual improvement' (FE 149). The lower deciles make up the largest proportion of the nation's population. They are also the most susceptible to short-horizoned temptation and myopic indulgence: 'There are few countries in which the common people have so much foresight as to defer marriage till they have a fair prospect of being able to support properly all their children' (SE I 193). In most countries, the common people rush unthinkingly into marriage and procreation. Only later do they become aware that they cannot provide. The excess is thinned out by positive checks.

Some preventive checks are 'natural'. Deferred marriage is natural. Others are 'unnatural'. They are vice. They are checks to the growth in population that a morally minded society will properly eschew.

The list of preventive roadblocks that Malthus classifies as vice extends to abortion, prostitution, 'concubinage', 'promiscuous intercourse', 'unnatural passions' 'irregular connexions' and 'violations of the marriage bed' (SE I 18). Homosexuality (prohibited in *Leviticus*: 18) is out. Adultery (prohibited by the Seventh Commandment) is out. Fornication (prohibited in *Matthew*: 15) is out. There is also a blanket condemnation of anything that renders women 'unprolific' (SV 250).

Contraception, even for a married couple, falls into this last category: 'I should always particularly reprobate any artificial and unnatural modes of checking population, both on account of their immorality and their tendency to remove a necessary stimulus to industry' (SE II 235). The separation of 'the sex' (SE I 18) from its consequences was a flagrant invitation not to do God's will on earth: 'The indolence of the human race would be very greatly increased' (SE II 235). Family planning would leave the poorer countries even poorer than before.

Contraception could cause the rate of change in population to swing from excessive to inadequate. Keynes in particular had seen that depopulation where it resulted could deprive the nation of essential labour, of capital and, most of all, of effective demand: 'When the devil P of Population is chained up we are free of one menace; but we are more exposed to the other devil U of unemployed Resources' (Keynes 1937 [1973]: 132). There would also be guilt by association. Sheaths and sponges were widely taken to be the playthings of rakes and libertines. Malthus regarded them as a bad citizen's abdication of responsibility. A far better check would be 'looking forward to marriage' (SE II 235) while in the interim living frugally in order to pre-pay a family home. It is how the middle-class subculture is already checking its increase. The lower classes ought to mimic the cultural *mores* of the role models who went before.

Malthus is propounding a scientific theory but he is also expressing his own moral values and those of his Church. Depravity is in the eye of the beholder. Francis Place, tailor, Benthamite, reformer, father of 15 children, took a different view. In 1820, in *Illustrations and Proofs of the Principle of Population*, he defended contraception, the propagation of which was still illegal in England, with the argument that it would reduce the supply of labour and raise the average wage: 'The proposals of Mr. Malthus, to persuade the poor that they have no right to eat....commence at the wrong end. The remedy can alone be found in preventives' (Place 1820: 150). The 'Malthusian League' was later to make a totally inappropriate use of Malthus's assumed authority in support of a cause for which Charles Bradlaugh and Annie Besant went to trial in 1877. Place saw contraception as the solution to a problem which no one but the 'driveller' Malthus (Place 1820: 174) would regard as a natural law. Positive checks and poor relief would then die a natural death. The individual and the collective interest would be the same.

There are positive checks and there are preventive checks. All are unpleasant: 'All these checks may be fairly resolved into misery and vice' (FE 103). In China, the poor eat dogs (Smith 1776 [1961]: I 81). In Kamschatka, even the dogs eat dogs (SE I 99). That is misery. In industrial Britain, some unmarried men contract disease in brothels and some married couples commit birth control. That is vice. Misery and vice involve 'both sexes in inextricable unhappiness' (FE 92). Unhappiness is bad.

There is nothing that can be done. Misery and vice are the product of 'the immediate agency of divine power' (FE 114). They conform to 'fixed laws', in operation 'since the world began' (FE 114). Population tends to increase more rapidly than the means of subsistence (FE 79). The geometrical and the arithmetical ratios do not march in step. Misery and vice are the correctives that make peace between demand and supply.

3.4 Moral Restraint

In 1798, it was misery and vice. In 1803, it was misery and vice *and* moral restraint (SE I 292). Malthus in the second edition of the *Essay* declared that the preventive check was becoming 'the most powerful of the checks which in modern Europe keep down the population to the level of the means of subsistence' (SE I 305). Societies were evolving from the positive checks of the savages to the preventive checks of the capitalists.

Persuaders like Malthus are an afterthought. They are preaching to the masses that 'the *only* source of an essential and permanent improvement of their condition, is the improvement and right direction of their moral and religious habits' (letter from Malthus to Senior, 1829, in Senior, 1831: 86, emphasis in original). As valuable as their advice will be, it is the material environment that will ultimately provide the greater stimulus to moral restraint. Economics matters. Ideas matter less. Prophets matter hardly at all.

Moral restraint is 'abstinence from marriage, either for a time or permanently, from prudential considerations, with a strictly moral conduct towards the sex in the interval' (SV 250). Marriage must be delayed. A woman who marries at age 28–30 (SE II 99; SV 263) is unlikely to experience more than five pregnancies. The postponement reduces the misery caused by child and adult mortality later on.

In advance of marriage, both sexes ought to remain celibate. It is a duty as well as a diagnosis: they have an 'obligation to practise this virtue' (SE II 87). While unmarried they should abstain from 'irregular gratifications' and 'illicit intercourse' (SE I 18, 19n) even if a relapse into vice will not culminate in an uneconomic new birth. Unmarried people are deferring their private gratification in the expectation of greater private gratification later on. It is the same good judgement backed up by self-control that causes them to save and invest in the capitalist market economy.

Passion is repressed by a rational choice. Moral restraint is validated by the utilitarian consequences. Irresponsible indulgence diminishes both personal utility and, aggregating, 'the general happiness and virtue of the society' (SE I 18). Postponement followed by monogamy is the better way. There are no free riders. No one wants to see his offspring in rags, 'clamouring for bread that he cannot give them' (FE 76). Only a man who wants his children to starve will default on his obligation to keep his country's population at a manageable level.

Malthus in the 1803 edition said that he had 'endeavoured to soften some of the harshest conclusions of the first essay' (SE I 3). He was saying that he had modulated the melancholy prediction that the lower classes might have little to look forward to but promiscuity, malnutrition and an early grave. He was being unfair to himself. Even in 1798, there had been a mighty feast of moral restraint.

In the first *Essay*, Malthus said that the well-to-do suffer from a 'fear of lowering their condition in life' (FE 73). It is the fear of relative deprivation even more than the fear of material want that leads them to repress their libido. It is not just their bodily needs but their societal insecurities that make the anxious postpone family life until they are confident that the expense will not demote them from their status group: 'A man of liberal education, but with an income only just sufficient to enable him to associate in the rank of gentlemen, must feel absolutely certain that if he marries and has a family he shall be obliged, if he mixes at all in society, to rank himself with moderate farmers and the lower class of tradesmen. The woman that a man of education would naturally make the object of his choice would be one brought up in the same tastes and sentiments with himself and used to the familiar intercourse of a society totally different from that to which she must be reduced by marriage. Can a man consent to place the object of his affection in a situation so discordant, probably, to her tastes and inclinations' (FE 90). Fearing to descend, driven by the endowment effect, determined to shield the 'object of his affection' from downward social mobility, he delays marriage until he is confident that he can retain his existing rank, symbols, pleasures and privileges.

Malthus in the first *Essay* focuses first and foremost on the moral restraint of the well-to-do. Even in 1798, however, he was saying that the same precautionary abstention was already to be found in the lower orders of society: 'The preventive check to population in this country operates, though with varied force, through all the classes of the community' (FE 91-2). The sons of a tradesman or a farmer put off marriage until they are able to afford a shop or a cottage. The manual labourer who can live 'with some degree of comfort as a single man' will 'hesitate a little' before opting for the 'harder fare and harder labour' (FE 91) that are the price of a family. Children focus the mind. Moral restraint is already preventing 'a very large number' (FE 76) from breeding themselves into relative or absolute deprivation.

Deprivation is relative as well as absolute. In fact, 'almost all poverty is relative' (SE I 351). It is all in Adam Smith: 'It is the vanity, not the ease, or the pleasure, which interests us' (Smith 1759 [1966]: 71). Malthus in the first *Essay* maintained that even the lower orders live in fear of losing what little they have. Social conventions and learned habits of living—'moral causes' (PR 250)—make the peer group and the handed on into arguments in the subsistence threshold: 'The labourers of the South of England are so accustomed to eat fine wheaten bread that they will suffer themselves to be half starved before they will submit to live like the Scotch peasants' (FE 116). The labourers of the South of England are already thinking like the 'man of liberal education'. They are reluctant to economise on their customary standard of life.

In the short run, it will be the social and not the physical minimum that functions as the bedrock check. Only in the long run will the ratchet slip as reckless childbearing depresses the English labourers into the lifestyle of the boorish Scots. After that, 'the sex' continuing to multiply the supply, it will be the 'hard law of necessity' (FE 116). Sensitive parents are repelled by 'the idea of the expenses they must retrench, and the fancied pleasures they must deprive themselves of' (FE 89). It need not happen. Moral restraint can protect the *done thing* from an avoidable loss of face. Later marriage and fewer children can defend the accustomed niche.

To Malthus, consumption is the supreme contraceptive. Even if the family does not descend into absolute poverty and charity gruel, sensitive social actors will experience 'degradation in the community' (SE I 17) analogous to Hindu Brahmins 'sinking from their caste' (SE I 118). A man will suffer a severe loss of self-respect when it is seen that he can no longer afford the necessaries and conveniences that are the customary signifiers of his social role. He will feel ashamed by his inability to 'transmit to his children the same advantages of education and improvement that he had himself possessed' (SE II 17). Calculating the 'distant consequences', resisting the 'bent of his inclinations' (SE I 16), he will keep the size of his family under control. Middle-class respectability has him by the throat.

As in the first *Essay*, so in the subsequent revisions: the preventive check 'operates with considerable force throughout *all the classes of the community*' (SE I 252, emphasis added). There is room for improvement. Compared with the positive checks, cautious prudence still operates 'very feebly indeed' (SE I 147). Even so, the standard of expectations is on a rising curve. It is likely to make 'still further advances' (SE II 198). 'Improved habits of cleanliness' have 'more than counterbalanced' the risk factors in the towns (SE I 201). In Scotland, the common people enjoy better accommodation and a healthier diet precisely because they have developed 'a habit of later marriages' (SE I 283). In France, the common people have secured 'a greater share of the produce of the country' in consequence of their 'greatly diminished proportion of births' (SE I 378). Towards the end of his life, Malthus said: 'The principal check which *at present* keeps the population down to the level of the actual means of subsistence is the prudential restraint on marriage' (SV 254, emphasis added). It is happening *at present.* Moral restraint is replacing misery and vice because the lower classes are limiting their births.

In England, Scotland and France the residuum is escaping from the positive checks. In Ireland, they are not. Degraded and impoverished, the Irish 'propagate their species like brutes, totally regardless of consequences' (SE II 147). Already at the bottom, the paupers feel that they cannot fall much further regardless of when they start their family.

Malthus had visited Ireland in 1817. He had formed the impression that cheap potatoes and small family farms had left the people indolent, ignorant and feckless. The Irish were following their inclinations and marrying young. They were living out the tragedy of bare subsistence that was destroying 'all vigorous exertion' (SE I 439) and extinguishing all ambition. There was also the political climate. Civil unrest and martial law were reinforcing the positive checks of hunger and disease.

Trapped between poverty and oppression, the Irish were badly lacking in foresight and prudence: 'They are inclined to be satisfied with the very least degree of comfort, and to marry with little other prospect than that of being able to get potatoes for themselves and their children' (1827: 319). They had lost all hope and could see no opportunity. Ireland was in a dead-end rut that led straight to overpopulated China and even to Kamschatka. Moral restraint was the only way. The experience of England, Scotland and France showed that it could be done.

3.5 The Road to Moral Restraint

Economic development begins in the mind. Deficient in the 'prime cheerer' (SE II 200) of moving up, the indigent remains trapped in hard times and dependent poverty. They lack the imagination and the will to escape from the mould: 'It is the hope of bettering our condition, and the fear of want, rather than want itself, that is the best stimulus to industry' (SE I 439).

Aspiration is the prime cheerer. At present, 'its most constant and best efforts will almost invariably be found among a class of people above the class of the wretchedly poor' (SE I 439). At present, it operates only 'in a very trifling degree' in 'the great mass of the human condition' (1829 [1831]: 64). Things must change. The will to succeed is the 'masterspring of industry' (SE II 187). It is 'the true mode of improving the state of the lower classes' (SE II 187). It must become the tide that raises up even the smallest craft.

The desire to move up is at once a consequence of past economic improvement and a cause of future economic growth. Men are social creatures. They 'hope to rise or fear to fall in society' as a consequence of their own 'diligence and exertion' and not primarily by virtue of their ascribed station at birth (SE II 194). Translated into economics, their pursuit of higher status results in 'a most laudable spirit of industry and foresight' (SE II 145). Economics is education. 'Industrious habits' are produced by 'regular employment' (SE II 174). The habits are passed on to the children. Affected 'in their moral and civil constitution' (SE II 143), children emulate their role models and strive to achieve.

There is hope for the Irish yet: 'Decent pride….will make the lower classes of society look forward to something besides mere support' (1808: 49). Potatoes will not satisfy their upgraded wants for wheaten bread and discretionary luxuries. They will experience 'an increasing taste for comforts and conveniences' (1809: 66). Higher wages might not after all lead to earlier marriage. There is a ratchet effect. The Irish, once they become accustomed to 'other comforts beside the mere support of their families upon potatoes' (1808: 50), will have no desire to return to absolute necessities and nothing more.

Subsistence wages, Malthus said, 'will be unfavourable to the generation of those habits of prudential restraint' (SE II 27). The 'wretchedly poor' live for today and not for a big step up. If we are equally poor, there is no incentive to excel. That is why moral restraint is more common in a high-wage economy while positive checks are the thermostat in a low-income reference group. Good pay and upward mobility are correlated with moral restraint. The same mental baggage that produces smaller families also produces faster growth: 'Industry cannot exist without foresight and security' (SE I 438). It cannot exist without the saver's propensity to plan ahead.

It is a complex of causality. The rich can afford large families but they put saving and status first. The poor cannot afford large families but they live for today. Excessive population is both the cause and the effect of low self-esteem. It has a sociopolitical component. The lower classes in Ireland 'are not treated with proper respect by their superiors; they are treated as if they were a degraded people' (1827: 326). Adam Smith had seen it all before. A ruling class in Ireland holds power because of 'the most odious of all distinctions, those of religious and political prejudices' Smith (1776 [1961]: II 483). Ireland, Smith had said, was divided internally into 'the insolence of the oppressors' at the top, 'the hatred and indignation of the oppressed' at the bottom (Smith 1776 [1961]: II 483). Malthus built on Smith. The Irish population was doubling itself every 40 years (1827: 327). The 'insolence', the 'hatred' and the 'indignation' were turning inward.

The Irish are being treated as if they were a 'degraded people' (1827: 326). Debased as well as deprived, they are so lacking in self-respect and 'a spirit of independence' (SE II 170) that they grow up socialised into 'vicious habits' (SE II 114) and immoral conduct. Only extraordinary people 'can continue to respect themselves when no other person whatever respects them' (SE II 114). 'Squalid poverty' is 'unfavourable to chastity' (SE II 114).

It is self-image as well as living standards that will draw the Irish to moral restraint. In his evidence in 1827 to the Select Committee on Emigration, Malthus, asked what would shake the Irish out of their low-income population trap, stated without hesitation that it would have to be 'civil, religious and political liberty', 'education', and, crucially, 'better habits of respecting themselves' (1827: 319, 320, 326). Self-respect breeds self-respect. It is not the accumulation of capital alone that will end the logjam. It is also self-worth.

Catholics feel oppressed by Protestants. Irish labourers feel degraded by English landowners. Psychologically and not just economically lower class, the victims of institutional discrimination have taken refuge in alcohol and 'the sex'. If the increase in population is to be kept down, then there is no alternative but to integrate the alienated into the mainstream of national activity: 'By raising their responsibility you can inspire them with a taste for comforts' (1827: 326).

Inclusion in the common culture is the trigger. Mainland bigots should display 'kindliness and conciliation' (1808 [1963]: 47) towards their fellow countrymen. They should treat Irish Catholics as 'fellow Christians worshipping the same God, and fellow subjects entitled to the same privileges' (1808 [1963]: 33). The common culture is more than a topic in economics alone. Integration is a cause of moral restraint.

3.6 Employment

Higher earnings are correlated with moral restraint. It is an economic bar. Creature comforts and conspicuous consumption are nothing if the out-of-work lack the wherewithal to travel upwards into the affluent society: 'Though the ample subsistence of a man for a day might be purchased for a penny, yet nobody will give these people a farthing for their labour' (SE I 102). Even one-quarter of one penny was not to be had. Lacking decent jobs that will pay them a decent income, the unemployed economise on moral restraint. A passport to the suburbs is increasingly believed to be beyond their reach.

Adam Smith had seen the link between employment and procreation. Growth generates saving and investment swells the wages fund. Marriages and births are more common, Smith said, when the demand for labour 'is continually increasing' (Smith 1776 [1961]: I 89). It was a positive development and not a cause for alarm. Population is the cause and effect of the nation's wealth. So long as the demand for labour continues to outstrip the growth in population, there is no danger of a labour surplus that festers into vice and misery.

Arthur Young, two years before Smith, had said that it was all a matter of common sense: 'Population is proportioned to employment' (Young 1774: 66). It was self-evident to him that the '*ease of acquiring income*' (Young 1774: 66, emphasis in original) is the ultimate thermostat that regulates the supply of hands. Subsistence is not: 'Increase your people as much as you please, food will increase with them' (Young 1774: 69). Improvements in agriculture ensure that a growing people will be fed. An arithmetical ratio is not a constraint.

The bottleneck will always be the jobs. Without them, the population will shrink: 'A *want of employment*...is the only cause of depopulation' (Young 1774: 68, emphasis in original). Richard Price had said that the population was going down. John Howlett had said that it was going up. Arthur Young knew instinctively which one was right. England is 'more populous than ever' (Young 1774: 84). The proof is that there had been a steady growth in the demand for labour. Demand had created its own supply. Decent jobs were empowering the poor to consume a 'greater quantity of superfluities' (Young 1774: 76). The employment opportunities were there. An increase in population would augment still further the wealth that was funding the work.

Economic growth to Smith and Young was creating the jobs and the incomes that would contribute so much to the moral restraint that Malthus associated with a rising standard of living. Marx and Engels invoked the reserve army of unemployment and the organic composition of capital to overturn any inference that Malthus might have drawn. Malthus, they said, had confused 'means of subsistence with means of employment' (quoted in Meek 1953: 60). It is the jobs and not the food that will always lag behind.

Malthus had failed to anticipate 'the inexhaustible reservoir of disposable labour' that is forever assured by the substitution of fixed for variable capital (quoted in Meek 1953: 100). Instead, he had pyramided his expectation of falling birth rates on his prediction that working-class living standards would evolve upward from grain and potatoes to tea, sugar, spices and rum. Marx and Engels said that it could not happen. They accused Malthus of neglecting the iron law of capitalism, that 'a surplus labouring population is a necessary product of accumulation' (quoted in Meek 1953: 88). Torn between celibacy and starvation, they said, the human beast of burden will have little time for moral restraint.

Malthus knew that employment in the sense of Arthur Young was the sine qua non for survival: 'Man, though he may often be produced without a sufficient demand for him, cannot really multiply and prosper unless his labour be wanted' (SE I 101). He knew that incomes might never advance to the stage where moral restraint becomes an option if saving, accumulation and growth were not properly balanced and aligned. He had also learned from thinkers like John Barton that labour displacement in the sense of Marx and Engels could conceivably leave the human beast of burden in no fit state to think himself into the comfortable middle class.

Things could go wrong. In spite of that, Malthus was optimistic about steady *embourgeoisement*. As economic growth spreads outward from the centre to the periphery, the middle classes will expand and the manual classes contract. A 'more favourable distribution of the abundant produce' (PR 482) gives the climbing estate a growing presence in the national wealth. General and vocational education together with the capitalist premium on achievement allows the manual to tap in to the open road of meritocracy. The proletariat becomes more like the bourgeoisie 'as the lower classes of people continue to improve in knowledge and prudence' (SE I 338). Learning to 'look before and after', the socially mobile become aware that family planning through a later start is the only way to be 'respectable, virtuous, and happy' (SV 252).

It is moral restraint in a growing economy but there is a crucial step. There must also be a growing supply of middle-class jobs if an expanding cohort of ambitious aspirants is to succeed in bettering their condition. Malthus is confident that the jobs will be created. New technology is on the side of enriched employment. 'Processes for abridging human labour' are reducing the proportion of the labour force engaged in 'severe toil' (SE II 194). Simultaneously, the economy is creating new openings as clerks, overseers and retailers for 'the more intelligent of the working classes' who have received 'a tolerable education' (PR 482-3). Economic restructuring is producing a society 'with fewer blanks and more prizes' (SE II 195). There is room in the middle. There is room for the new middle class that is driven into moral restraint because no one wants to go home.

3.7 Emigration

Emigration is a safety valve but not a lasting solution. In the 1817 *Essay*, Malthus said that it would provide a stopgap breathing space in the post-war recession but that the quick fix 'could not be of long duration' (SE II 237). In 1803, he said that he regarded it mainly as a temporary release that only in the short run would be 'favourable to the population of the mother country' (SE I 296). In 1798, he said that the overspill could conceivably be expatriated but that worldwide beggar-thy-neighbour would not make sense. What one country can dump the earth as a whole cannot (FE 75).

It all adds up to this. Exportation of the surplus is never an 'adequate remedy' (SE II 237). It is today's haircut that postpones but does not obviate the need for tomorrow's trim. In the long run, the engineered deficit will be made up through higher wages, earlier marriages and new births: there is a 'strong tendency of population to recover lost numbers' (letter from Malthus to Wilmot-Horton, 1830, in Ghosh, 1963: 53). As a transitory expedient, however, the policy is popularly known as 'shovelling out the paupers' undeniably reduces the misery and the burden on relief.

Malthus gave evidence in 1827 to the Select Committee on Emigration. He said that subsistence in England 'probably has not been furnished as amply as before' and that the poor were increasing in numbers: 'If they are not removed by emigration, it cannot be done without producing most extreme distress' (1827: 311, 312). Extrapolating from the decade between the census of 1811 and the census of 1821, he calculated that 'the rate of increase was such as would double the population in forty-eight years' (1827: 327). England could not absorb them. Schemes such as those of Edward Gibbon Wakefield to make Australia the extensive margin would have to be considered seriously.

Whereas Wakefield wanted the passages to be financed from the sale of colonial land, Malthus had a preference for self-funding by the individual beneficiaries. In the 1806 *Essay*, he said that 'it is both the duty and interest of government to facilitate emigration' (SE II 220n) but was silent on the source of the money. In 1823, writing to Wilmot-Horton, he was equally vague: 'I have always thought it very unjust on the part of Governments, to prohibit, or impede emigration; but I have doubted whether they could reasonably be expected so to promote it' (letter from Malthus to Wilmot-Horton, 1823, in Ghosh, 1963: 48).

Public funding would have the effect of 'weakening the exertions of the settlers themselves' (letter from Malthus to Wilmot-Horton, 1823, in Ghosh, 1963: 48). Unable to make good at home, their industry and efficiency were already weak. A change of surroundings will not necessarily make an indolent man less indolent. There is a selection bias where the emigrants are uneducated paupers without a track record of initiative. If the colonists are educated, there would be a loss of manpower and skills. On the plus side, assisted passages would arguably cost the public less than the Poor Laws at home. Also, physical removal is quick. Moral improvement takes time.

R. J. Wilmot-Horton was the Under-Secretary of State for War and the Colonies. He was a strong supporter of State-aided resettlement to Canada. In the course of their correspondence between 1823 and 1830, Malthus seems to have become more willing to compromise. By 1830, he was writing: 'I am a decided friend to emigration myself in the present state of the country, and would willingly pay my share of any tax necessary to accomplish it' (letter from Malthus to Wilmot-Horton, 1830, in Ghosh, 1963: 52).

In spite of the obstacles, the New England settlers are proof that it can be done. On their side was an abundant supply of cheap land, little manufacturing, little urban congestion. Pay was good because labour was scarce. The colonists were free from the old-country incubus of primogeniture, tithes and poor rates. They had brought with them the English values of liberty, property and equality before the law. The 'knowledge and habits of the people' (FE 113) were in their favour.

The New England colonies had been a success. Even in North America, however, the countdown had begun. Once the initial hardships had been overcome, the population doubled itself in 25 years precisely as the geometrical ratio would predict (FE 105). What the colonists did not foresee is that the arithmetical ratio too was inexorably progressing towards a frontier of its own. Good pay was only 'a weak palliative', 'a partial degree of improvement' (SE I 340). It would postpone the evil of vice and misery to a 'distant period' (SE I 340) but it would not cancel forever the nature-driven margin of cultivation. Sooner or later, the colony will be full. So, in time, will the home country that made the mistake of thinking that its excess had permanently disappeared into a virgin wilderness.

At the same time that the English were going out, the Irish were coming in. The vacuum in the mother country was being filled by new immigrants who were keeping wages down despite the contraction in the home-grown workforce. English people would be 'very much worse off in every respect….moral and physical' (1827: 313). The Irish would 'defeat all the benefits of the plan proposed' (letter from Malthus to Wilmot-Horton, 1827, in Ghosh, 1963: 49).

Cheap labour might make British exports more competitive. Clearly, if immigrant manpower exceeds the growth in the wages fund, then pay is likely to be bid down: 'Nothing will increase the rate of wages but an alteration in the capital and revenue of the country, as compared with the number of the people' (1827: 318). As attractive as low pay will be for foreign trade, it by definition contributes less than high pay to total demand. In that way, it will 'have a tendency to diminish the home trade, and I think the home trade much more important than the foreign' (1827: 317).

Arguably, the Irish immigrants will be having a dynamic effect on the national income and, crucially, the national expenditure. Malthus is not optimistic that the new saving and new investment that are being created will necessarily match the increase in the workforce: 'There is no immediate prospect of it; I do not mean to say it may not take place' (1827: 318). If it does not take place, then an influx of new immigrants would 'be at the expense of great misery' (1827: 314). There is nothing analogous to the Corn Laws that can obstruct the free movement of labour from Ireland. The emigration of the home-grown population is the only choice.

3.8 Statement, Prediction and Tendency

Economics is rhetoric. Words are weapons. Language is a code that is made to conceal. Malthus's law of population is the proof that contentions and assertions are not always what they seem. On the surface, it is a maze of contradictions, exaggerations and thundering Jeremiads that make the reader wish for a fortified bunker on a distant planet. At the core, it is all of a piece.

The law of population is a statement of *what is*: 'The period when the number of men surpass their means of subsistence has long since arrived' (FE 124). It is a prediction of *what is to come*: 'There are few states in which there is not a constant effort in the population to increase beyond the means of subsistence' (SE I 20). It is a tendency towards *what might be* that might be blocked, frustrated, reversed or diverted by the never-sleeping *ceteris paribus*: 'Population *invariably* increases when the means of subsistence increase, *unless* prevented by powerful and obvious checks' (SE I 304, emphasis added). Population *invariably* increases *unless* it does not. Logician or statistician, few readers will take issue with that.

It is a statement: 'Wherever, therefore, there is liberty, the power of increase is exerted; and the superabundant effects are repressed afterwards by want of room and nourishment' (SE I 10). It is a prediction: 'This constantly subsisting cause of periodical misery, has existed ever since we have had any histories of mankind, does exist at present, and will for ever continue to exist' (FE 124). It is a 'general tendency': there is a '*natural tendency* of population to increase beyond the powers of the earth to produce food for it' (SE II 244, emphasis in original). It cannot be all three. All three are present, side by side, in all six editions of the influential *Essay*.

Whether in 1798 or 1826, Malthus seems to have been reluctant to make up his mind. Schumpeter felt that the obsessive diffidence ultimately robbed the theory of its action-clause: 'The only valuable things about Malthus's law of population are its qualifications' (Schumpeter 1942 [1976]: 115n). Boulding expressed the same frustration with the ceaseless mix and match. Is it the 'Utterly Dismal Theorem' or is it the 'Cheerful Theorem' (Boulding 1955: 195)? Is it optimism or pessimism? Is it the lower depths or an English summer's day?

Malthus may not have been clear. Yet there is another possibility. Malthus was not a political activist but a scientist with a sincere interest to get at the truth. A scientist speaks in a multitude of tongues. Some propositions are one-dimensional, two-variable simplifications. Other propositions are multi-plane, multi-causal cornucopia. Malthus never intended that his statements and his predictions should be taken at face value. They are no more than the inferences that could be drawn if association were causation and there were no further causes to associate. The Malthusian law of population is a tendency law. That is all.

Malthus assumed that his readers could tell a ceteris paribus from a perfect vacuum. In fact, he had to spell it out even to Ricardo. He explained to Ricardo that he was not making categorical pronouncements but simply trying to show what the effect would be if 'undisturbed by any other operating cause' (letter from Malthus to Ricardo, 1820, in Ricardo VIII: 184). It may be that he was expecting too much from a general public that had already made up its mind. Malthus is frequently cited in support of factions and policies which he did not and could not have supported. Language conceals. In 1830, he had to write his *Summary View* to make clear to the wider public what he had meant all along. It made little difference to the street.

Writing to Whewell in 1831, he expressed his regret that he had so often been misunderstood: 'The general and practical conclusions which I have myself drawn from my principles both on population and rent, have by no means the gloomy aspect given to them by many of my readers' (letter from Malthus to Whewell, 1831, in de Marchi and Sturges, 1973: 390). Malthus told Whewell that his theory was based on a *tendency* and predicated on an *if.* He told Nassau Senior that many of his readers had simply missed the point: 'I was certainly not aware that, in saying that population had a *tendency* to increase faster than food, I should be considered as denying that it might practically at times increase slower' (letter from Malthus to Senior, 1829, in Senior, 1831: 60, emphasis in original).

Malthus himself is partly to blame for the conflicting messages. He seems to be crying doom when in fact he is only using doom as a worst-case benchmark. Yet doom is there and it focuses the mind.

Malthus states that all countries even now 'are peopled up to their actual produce' (SE I 46). In America and Ireland, 'the increase of population….has been nearly in proportion to the relative quantity of the customary food awarded to the labourers' (SE II 26). The pressure of population on scanty subsistence is not a distant possibility but rather a social fact which 'actually exists at present over the greatest part of the globe' (SV 247). 'With few exceptions', he said in the *Summary View*, it has 'been almost constantly acting upon all countries of which we have any account' (SV 247). The *Summary View* was written to make his position clear. Instead, he makes his prognosis sound like the nuclear winter.

Malthus warns that the demographic time bomb is primed to explode at any time: 'In the actual circumstances of every country, the principle of population seems to be always ready to exert nearly its full force' (SE I 362). Then he lets his cat out of the bag. The statements and the predictions, he suggests, are only the *obiter dicta*. They are deliberate hyperbole intended to ensure that the reader pays proper attention to the core message. The core message is the *tendency*: 'Population was always ready, and inclined, to increase faster than food, *if* the checks which repressed it were removed' (letter from Malthus to Senior, 1829, in Senior, 1831: 61, emphasis added). It would happen *if*. It would not happen *if not*. The keyword is the *if*.

The geometrical and arithmetical ratios, Malthus is saying, are only a 'supposition' (SV 264), not yet fully documented. What is constant is not the misery and the vice but simply the 'constant *tendency* in the human race to increase beyond the means of subsistence' (SE I 60, emphasis added). It is a tendency that might have prevented the sensible Swiss from enjoying 'an extraordinary degree of healthiness…*if* it had not been accompanied by a proportionate action of the prudential restraint on marriage' (SV 261, emphasis added).

The Swiss lived well. The Irish did not. The divergence in the historical trajectory confirms the existence both of the trajectory and of the *if*: 'Scarcity and extreme poverty….may or may not accompany an increasing population, according to circumstances' (SE I 46). It may or may not be standing room only. Sometimes it is the Swiss scenario and sometimes it is China: 'The proportion of births, deaths, and marriages are extremely different in different countries….They are very different in the same country at different periods, and under different circumstances' (SE I 245). It is good to have an open mind. It all depends.

Population might expand in a less than geometrical ratio if moral restraint arrested the rise. Subsistence might expand in a more than arithmetical ratio if technical progress offset the diminishing returns. Countervailing forces 'for some time' (SV 239) might be able to avert the fatal intersection, Perhaps they will be able to do so for all time.

Perhaps the problem of overpopulation is already shrinking into an also-ran *memento mori*: 'The evils resulting from the principle of population have rather diminished than increased' (SE II 202). We cannot know: 'We can certainly draw no safe conclusion' (SE I 146).

What is safe is minimax. So long as the tendency is there, the disease might recur. History is a graveyard of the misguided and the complacent: 'So far as we can judge from history, there has never been a period of any considerable length, when the premature mortality and vice, specifically arising from the pressure of population against food, has not prevailed to a considerable extent' (letter from Malthus to Senior, 1829, in Senior, 1831: 64–65). Even America is not an exception. Once the abundant land has become 'well-peopled' and the frontier has been closed, an 'actual increase in population faster than food is not only probable, but absolutely certain' (letter from Malthus to Senior, 1829, in 1831: 67). *Absolutely certain*. Malthus's message to the Americans was that life could only get worse.

It is a tendency law, but it is packaged as the end of time. Moral restraint is no match for diminishing returns: 'The most intense desire of bettering our condition, can do nothing towards making food permanently increase at the rate at which population is always to increase' (letter from Malthus to Senior, 1829, in Senior, 1831: 63). The future is already upon us: 'From 1720 to 1750 the labourer earned about a full peck of wheat a day. Since that period, I believe, he has never for five years together earned so much as a peck hardly, indeed, so much as five-sixths of a peck' (letter from Malthus to Senior, 1829, in Senior, 1831: 69).

The *tendency* in population may be stronger than the tendency in subsistence. Armageddon may be stronger than *if*. Nassau Senior said that the nightmare scenario would not occur: 'There is a natural tendency in subsistence to increase in a greater ratio than population' (Senior 1831: 49). Malthus said that the future was in the pecks. He pointed to the facts. The pecks from 1720 to 1750 suggested that Senior was wrong. Chinese or British, Swiss or Americans, all of them had a tendency to end up one day in filth and rags. That much at least was absolutely certain.

References

By T. R. Malthus

(1798 [1970]). *Essay on the Principle of Population, as It Affects the Future Improvement of Society, with Remarks on the Speculations of Mr. Godwin, M. Condorcet, and Other Writers* (abbreviated as FE), ed. by A. Flew. Harmondsworth: Penguin.

(1803 et seq. [1989]). *An Essay on the Principle of Population: Or a View of Its Past and Present Effects on Human Happiness, with an Inquiry into Our Prospects Respecting the Removal of the Evils Which It Occasions* (2nd edition, 1803; further editions in 1806, 1807, 1817, 1826) (abbreviated as SE I and SE II), 2 vols., ed. by P. James. Cambridge: Cambridge University Press.

(1808 [1963]). Review of Thomas Newenham's *A Statistical and Historical Inquiry into the Progress and Magnitude of the Population of Ireland, Edinburgh Review*, 24, reprinted in *Occasional Papers of T.R. Malthus*, ed. by B. Semmel. New York: Bert Franklin, 33–52.

(1809 [1963]). Review of Thomas Newenham's *A View of the Natural, Political and Commercial Circumstances of Ireland, Edinburgh Review*, 27, 1809, reprinted in *Occasional Papers of T.R. Malthus*, ed. by B. Semmel. New York: Bert Franklin, 52–71.

(1820 [1989]). *The Principles of Political Economy* (abbreviated as PR), ed. by J. Pullen. Cambridge: Cambridge University Press.

(1823 [1963]). 'Tooke—On High and Low Prices', Review of Thomas Tooke's *Thoughts and Details on the High and Low Prices of the Last Thirty Years*', *Quarterly Review*, 1823, reprinted in *Occasional Papers of T.R. Malthus*, ed. by B. Semmel. New York: Bert Franklin, 145–170.

(1827). Evidence to the Select Committee on Emigration (Third Report), in *Parliamentary Papers*. London: House of Commons, 5, 311–327.

(1830). *A Summary View of the Principle of Population* (abbreviated as SV), in FE, supra.

Ghosh, R. N. (1963). Malthus on Emigration and Colonization: Letters to Wilmot-Horton. *Economica*, 30, 45–62.

Secondary Literature

Boulding, K. E. (1955). The Malthusian Model as a General System. *Social and Economic Studies, 4,* 195–205.

Child, J. (1693). *A New Discourse of Trade*. London: John Everingham.

de Marchi, N. B., & Sturges, R. P. (1973). Malthus and Ricardo's Inductivist Critics: Four Letters to William Whewell. *Economica, 40,* 379–393.

Empson, W. (1837 [1963]). Life, Writings and Character of Mr. Malthus. *Edinburgh Review,* 64 (Reprinted in *Occasional Papers of T.R. Malthus,* pp. 231–268, by B. Semmel, Ed., New York: Bert Franklin).

Hirsch, F. (1977). *Social Limits to Growth*. London: Routledge.

Jevons, W. S. (1865). *The Coal Question*. London: Macmillan.

Keynes, J. M. (1937 [1973]). Some Economic Consequences of a Declining Population. *Eugenics Review, 29* (in *The Collected Writings of John Maynard Keynes,* Vol. 14, pp. 124–133, by D. Moggridge, Ed., London: Macmillan).

Meadows, D. H., Meadows, D. L., Randers, J., & Behrens III, W. W. (1972). *The Limits to Growth: A Report for the Club of Rome's Project on the Predicament of Mankind*. New York: New American Library.

Meek, R. L. (Ed.). (1953). *Marx and Engels on Malthus*. London: Lawrence and Wishart.

Paley, W. (1785). *Principles of Moral and Political Philosophy* (2 vols.). Dublin: Exshaw, White and others.

Petty, W. (1662 [1997]). *A Treatise of Taxes and Contributions*. In *The Economic Writings of Sir William Petty* (C. H. Hull, Ed., 2 vols.). London: Routledge and Thommes Press.

Place, F. (1820). *Illustrations and Proofs of the Principle of Population*. London: George Allen & Unwin.

Ricardo, D. (1951–1955). *The Works and Correspondence of David Ricardo* (abbreviated as Ricardo) (P. Sraffa with M. Dobb, Eds., 11 vols.). Cambridge: Cambridge University Press.

Schumpeter, J. (1942 [1976]). *Capitalism, Socialism and Democracy*. London: George Allen & Unwin.

Senior, N. W. (1829 [1831]). *Two Lectures on Population with a Correspondence Between the Author and T.R. Malthus*. London: John Murray.

Smith, A. (1759 [1966]). *The Theory of Moral Sentiments*. New York: Augustus M. Kelley.

Smith, A. (1776 [1961]). *The Wealth of Nations* (E. Cannan, Ed., 2 vols.). London: Methuen.

Young, A. (1774). *Political Arithmetic*. London: W. Nicoll.

4
Public Policy

There is much automaticity in a nation. The Great Designer wound up the eternal spring. Supply and demand gravitate to the market-clearing price. The ratios and the checks grind out the equilibrium population. Nature is the only drug a healthy person will ever need: 'The ablest physicians are the most sparing in the use of medicine, and the most inclined to trust to the healing power of nature' (PR 20).

It is all a question of nature. Matter in motion is taking its course. There is not much the visible hand can do to improve on that: 'Almost all medicine is in itself bad; and one of the great evils of illness is the necessity of taking it. No person can well be more averse to medicine in the animal kingdom, or a system of expedients in political economy, than myself' (SE I 408).

Healthy people do not need pills and powders to make them well. Nature has a will of its own which statesmen, like doctors, would be well-advised to respect: 'It is….one of the most general rules in political economy, that governments should not interfere in the direction of capital and industry, but leave every person, so long as he obeys the laws of justice, to pursue his own interest in his own way' (PR 13).

D. Reisman, *Thomas Robert Malthus*, Great Thinkers in Economics,
https://doi.org/10.1007/978-3-030-01956-3_4

It is Adam Smith's 'obvious and simple system of natural liberty' (Smith 1776 [1961]: II 208). It is the classical liberals' laissez-faire.

Malthus was drawn to the minimal State. The market is efficient. Governments make mistakes. First principles dictate a cautious response. Governments should act with an eye to 'the *least possible* prejudice to the prosperity of the state, and the happiness of individuals' (PR 19, emphasis added). It was not doctrinaire ideology but problem-solving pragmatism that drew him to minimax. When in doubt, the bias must always be in favour of supply and demand in order that the *least possible* damage should be done to the felt well-being of the whole: 'The sole object of our consideration ought to be the permanent interest of the consumer, in the character of which is comprehended the whole nation' (SE I 410).

The greatest happiness of the greatest number will best be promoted through factoring down. Nature comes first. The government should only intervene if it is convinced that the self-stabilising balance wheel is unable to regulate or provide. Where it is 'obviously.... impossible for a government strictly to let things take their natural course' (PR 20), there politics must step in to bend back the bent rod.

4.1 Law and Order

Safety and security are the precondition for 'higgling and bargaining'. Without the protective State, it is a natural law that human beings would seek not to add value but to seize an existing endowment. Leviathan is preferable to anarchy if the players cannot know in advance which of them will hold the ace: 'Security with moderate wealth is a wiser choice, and better calculated for peace and happiness than insecurity with greater wealth' (PR 485).

Pastoral tribes act out the Hobbesian *bellum*. Always on the move, they migrate in search of fresh pastures which they make their own through conquest and theft: 'Scythian shepherds have been uniformly actuated by a most savage and destructive spirit' (SE I 74). Because they are always on the move, the warriors only plunder what is already in store. Had they remained behind to grow their endowment, the land, 'if it were properly cultivated....would be sufficient for the support of four times the number of its present inhabitants' (SE I 75). Not all of vice and misery can be blamed on the niggardly soil. Some of the shortfall is due to the compulsory transfers demanded by violent neighbours who reap where they never sowed.

The Tartars too are bad neighbours. At home, they are experiencing the vicissitudes of the ratios: 'Their population presses so hard against the limits of their food' (SE I 79). They could have alleviated their hunger through economic activity. Instead, they made a choice to snatch and grab: 'They choose rather to expose themselves to the thousand fatigues and dangers necessarily attendant on such a life, than apply themselves seriously to agriculture' (SE I 77). It was the best they could do. Property was insecure. Marauders laid waste to dams and long-term improvements. There is little incentive to invest if the harvest can at any time be seized by a jealous neighbour.

It is a self-aggravating feedback loop and a school for aggression. Desperate people become accustomed to taking what they need: 'A scarcity of subsistence might at first perhaps give occasion to the habits of war' (SE I 79). Because the military power of the tribe depends on the breeding of sons, the survival of the fittest prescribes a rising population to make up for the battlefield losses. Polygamy is practised because males are in short supply. As population rises, the scarcity of food becomes more intense. The habits of war 'powerfully contribute to narrow the means of subsistence' (SE I 79). Neglecting plus-sum productivity because it is susceptible to early transfer, they had no alternative but to go to war again: 'He who determines to be rich, or die, and does not scruple the means, cannot long live poor' (SE I 82).

The law of nature did not feed the tribe. Captain Cook in the South Seas found that depredation was constant and 'provisions....in consequence insecure' (SE I 47). Cannibalism was practised because the islanders were hungry. Because of the ratios and the checks, moral values like benevolence were thin on the ground. As Adam Smith says, 'before we can feel much for others we must in some measure be at ease ourselves' (Smith 1759 [1966]: 205). The struggle to produce and to retain tends to 'harden the heart, and narrow all the sources of sympathy' (SE I 58). There is simply no surplus to share. Virtues, like other commodities, 'will be produced in the greatest quantity for which there is the greatest demand' (SE I 59). There is not much demand for altruism where the resources are not there.

Ethics is marginalised by overpopulation. The protective State fills the moral and the material void. Production for profitable sale is the antidote to the culture of conflict and theft. Today's Scythians enjoy a standard of living that yesterday's savages could never expect: 'Activity in bettering our condition….now forms the master-spring of public prosperity' (SE II 194). Economics has been the way forward, but the precondition has been the protective State: 'A certain degree of security is perhaps still more necessary than richness of soil' (SE I 79).

Top-down authority is essential. The rights of person and property must be protected. Institutions count. They are 'necessary….to promote the general good' and 'the increase of human happiness' (SV 269). Exposure to plunder 'must necessarily have a baneful effect on industry' (SE I 87). An economic actor, savage or modern, will rationally be 'improvident' if he 'feels little security of reaping what he has sown' (SE I 438): 'No people can be much accustomed to form plans for the future, who do not feel assured that their industrious exertions, while fair and honourable, will be allowed to have free scope' (PR 251). It is the right to title, 'from which everything that is valuable to man has hitherto arisen' (SE I 362), that lies behind moral restraint to limit the numbers and purposive endeavour to augment the subsistence. Government in that sense is a cause of the wealth of nations. Positive law in tune with natural law is a part of the nation's production function.

4.2 Good Government

Government is essential but it must be good government. Some governments are bad governments, 'tyrannical and oppressive', who 'think only of enriching themselves' (SE I 96). Egypt ruled by the Ottoman Turks is a case in point.

The Ottomans are experts in 'seizing wealth wherever it may be found', in 'wresting it by violence from the possessor', in 'imposing continually new and arbitrary contributions' (SE I 96). Fearing to attract unwelcome attention to himself, 'no individual proprietor dares to undertake any improvement which might indicate the possession of capital' (SE I 96). Oppression in this way destroys 'the springs of industry' (SE I 439). The risk of confiscation is too great.

Public investment is just as deficient as private. The Turkish administrator is what Olson calls a 'roving bandit' (Olson 2000: 60). Uncertain how long he will be in post before he is rotated, he does not have a personal stake in 'enriching the country, the better to prepare it for their plunder' (SE I 96). There is no point in fattening up the goose if it will be his successor who brings the goose to market: 'Uncertain of to-morrow, he treats his province as a mere transient possession, and endeavours to reap, if possible, in one day, the fruit of many years' (SE I 110). His personal and private incentive structure is strictly short term. It is at variance with the needs of the people that he rules. An administered territory such as Egypt is no more than a fowl to be plucked.

The soil is fertile, irrigated by the Nile and its floods. In spite of that, the population is well below its maximum. The scarcity of food limits the supply of labour. Inadequate labour means inadequate output. It is a vicious circle, and an important cause is 'the nature of the government' (SE I 108). Bad laws, corrupt bureaucrats, and extortionate taxation, make it difficult for farmers to increase the supply of food in line with the rising population.

It is the ratios at work but it is also the State. The infrastructure has been neglected because Egypt is afflicted with bad government: 'The causes of this neglect, and consequently of the diminished means of subsistence, are obviously to be traced to the extreme ignorance and brutality of the government' (SE I 96). Government has been the immediate cause but at bottom it is rational choice. Malthus treats the State in Egypt as if it were an economic market. People, self-interested and calculative, respond to incentives. The incentives in Egypt were perverse. The game being flawed, the Turkish expatriates had no reason to improve the wealth of a nation that they were planning first to loot and then to quit.

The State is people. People are a problem. Even in Britain, there cannot be an assumption that, the feudal aristocracy once relegated to a watching brief, the post-1688 settlement will automatically meet Locke's requirement that public policy should be accountable to its constituents. Political liberty presupposes a viable constitution. Where the lawmakers exempt themselves from the law, 'the vices of government' (SE II 28) may significantly discourage long-term investment, job creation and economic progress. Egypt or Britain, the meta-goal of maximum happiness is not being attained.

The ideal is due process and impartial arbitration. The 'duty of government' is 'not to be actively assisting – first one party, and then another' (1809 [1963]: 67): 'In the turns of the wheel of fortune all parties should have fair play; no class of persons can be justified in endeavouring to lift themselves up by using unfair and dishonourable means to pull others down' (1823: 220). It is not always so. Even the 'best-established governments' are 'continually assailed by partial and individual interests' (1809 [1963]: 52, 53). Some governments are 'dastardly, servile and useless': 'There is nothing that the great interests of society more imperiously call for, than the appointment of governors, who have the knowledge to detect, and vigour to resist, those mercantile clamours, the uniform object of which is to sacrifice the whole to a part' (1809 [1963]: 61, 60).

Malthus believed that 'mercantile clamours' were doing great harm to the well-being of the whole. Adam Smith had said that in the setting of wages the government had inequitably relied on advice from the narrow-minded employers' cartel (Smith 1776 [1961]: I 158–159). In trade policy, it had fallen into the hands of a self-appointed clique of shop-soiled dealers: 'The interest of the home-consumer has been sacrificed to that of the producer' (Smith 1776 [1961]: II 80). Mancur Olson in a very different economic climate has demonstrated that the public good of rapid growth was incompatible with the special pleading of small but determined coalitions that had sought to redistribute the wealth of the nation rather than to increase it (Olson 1982: 74). Malthus was clearly in distinguished company when he expressed his reservations about the venal 'jobbing' (1809 [1963]: 55) and the 'officious meddling' (PR 14) that were rolling the logs and sectionalising the outcomes. Taxes have a bias and services are discriminatory. Philosopher-rulers do not have the ability to screen out the lobby.

The result, he said, is government failure: 'Good roads may be purchased too dear' (1809 [1963]: 55).

The proof is the state of the Irish economy. It was not the masses but the merchants that had dictated to Parliament the 'disgusting detail of the various commercial regulations', truly 'among the worst that ever came from such suspicious advisers' (1809 [1963]: 59). It was not the people of Ireland but 'the monopolizers of England' (1809 [1963]: 59) who had passed the law prohibiting the exportation of Irish woollens to the mainland. They had persuaded the politicians that competition was not the British way: 'The interest of the British and Irish consumers.... was sacrificed to a few English traders....The poor resource of a poor country in the neighbourhood of a rich one, was denied to it' (1809 [1963]: 60).

The Irish woollen industry was crushed. Enterprise was stifled. Overpopulation and emigration were the downstream spillovers. Irish agriculture stagnated. Irrespective of the national interest, the special-interest minorities had managed to corner the cream for themselves.

4.3 The Politics of Fear

In the age of the dictators and after that the managed mix there was James Buchanan. Fearing the worst more than he hoped for the best, Buchanan said that 'it is rational to *have a constitution*' (Buchanan and Tullock 1962: 81, emphasis in original). The leaders and not just the followers must be bound by multi-period rules that they may not violate to suit their personal convenience or intellectual outlook. It was the politics of minimax. Malthus was unmistakeably on side: 'The great advantage of a free country does not consist in its requiring higher qualities in its governors, but in its being better secured against their bad qualities – in being better fenced against the folly or wickedness of a sovereign' (1809 [1963]: 53).

Folly and wickedness are all around. So, and even worse, is ignorance. In common with the masses and the ideologues, the politicians themselves simply do not know: 'If once we admit the principle that the government must know better with regard to the quantity of power which it wants....we must just as well, at the same time, surrender up the whole of our constitution' (SE II 126). Bounded rationality makes the choices into guesstimates and sometimes into guesses. There is a great deal of ruin in a nation if someone presses the wrong button by mistake.

It is what Friedrich von Hayek calls the 'fatal conceit' (Hayek 1988: 66) to assume that bumbling old Sir is better placed to alleviate our woes than are we, the people, ourselves. Trusting to the White House, the Pink House or the Blue House to keep us well fed and warm, we, the people, would become 'inattentive to our great interests' (SE II 126). We would blind trust the administration of our estate to self-styled *virtuosi* who lack the skill to manage our lives: 'It is the height of folly and unreasonableness, to expect that government will attend to them for us' (SE II 126). We would enjoy greater happiness if we could escape from the yoke of dependence: 'Any great interference with the affairs of other people is a species of tyranny' (SE I 360).

It is man versus the State, the sovereign individual versus the 'wretched system of governing too much' (SE II 140). Were top-down authority to win out, it would be the 'end of British freedom' (SE II 126). We do not want that. The alternative is the minimal State: 'Government is a quarter in which liberty is not, nor cannot be, very faithfully preserved' (SE II 126). No in-group with a monopoly of force should ever be entrusted with more than the essential functions of the protective State.

Social democrats will say that Malthus is being too cautious. In his haste to block the great evils of despotism, tyranny, false starts and 'extreme mismanagement' (1809 [1963]: 71), it may be that he was also tying the hands of far-sighted leaders to introduce welfare-enhancing reforms. Not every decent statesman, as Richard Henry Tawney observed, will necessarily be a 'Totalitarian monster' who treats political power as a self-serving privilege: 'Fools will use it, when they can, for foolish ends, criminals for criminal ends. Sensible and decent men will use it for ends which are sensible and decent' (Tawney 1966: 172).

It was not a gamble into which Malthus had any urgent desire to enter. Baby or bathwater, the fundamental truth is that the law of nature cannot be repealed: 'The principal cause of want and unhappiness is unconnected with government, and totally beyond its power to remove' (SE II 132). To argue otherwise, to make ordinary people believe that good lawmakers can 'alter by a *fiat* the whole circumstances of the country', is to work 'an unpardonable deceit upon the poor' (SE I 356, 364).

4.4 The State as Leader

Malthus was drawn to the minimal State: 'More evil is likely to arise from governing too much, than from a tendency to the opposite extreme' (PR 14). The balance of advantage must be presumed to lie with 'the freedom of trade, and the leaving every person, while he adheres to the rules of justice, to pursue his own interest his own way' (PR 3). Mercantilism belongs to the past. What is needed today is the protective State and not much more. The consensus increasingly takes the view that philosopher-rulers should limit themselves to the law-courts and the constables. They 'should not interfere in the direction of capital and industry' (PR 13).

The State should remain on the sidelines. It should ensure the 'strict and equal administration of justice' (1827: 326). It should backstop 'the perfect security of property' (1827: 326). Contracts should be enforced and personal integrity assured. Beyond that, the State should resist the temptation to nanny, shepherd or micro-manage. The presumption must always be that the individual has a natural right to do as he likes with his own.

Yet there is a problem. One individual's natural right may be at variance with another individual's natural right. One person's freedom may restrict the freedom of another person to enjoy *as much* and *as good*. Every action has externalities. Every person is another person's neighbour. Malthus knew that the nation as a whole is a stakeholder in every decision that is made. The three Ps of population, pay and property demonstrate his recognition that not a sparrow falls but Big Ben must toll.

4.4.1 Population

The increase in population generates positive spillovers such as a rise in labour supply and in effective demand. It also imposes new burdens on third-party bystanders. Food prices go up. Charity overstrains the parish rates. Malthus was aware of the uncontracted diswelfares. He knew that the cat had to be belled. He also knew that it was easier said than done.

Malthus could have called for legislation to limit family size, prescribe a minimum age or prohibit marriage altogether in the lower income groups. Command and control would keep the numbers down. In spite of that, it was unacceptable. Even paupers without the resources to support their children should have 'the most perfect liberty so to do': 'Any positive law to limit the age of marriage would be both unjust and immoral' (SE I 374).

The lower classes do not foresee the vice and misery that will be the delayed consequence of their unthinking gratification. Regrettable as it is, the State has no right to protect the sovereign citizen from himself. There is nothing that can be done by law 'without a great violation of natural liberty, and a great risk of producing more evil than good' (SV 251). Tolerance is a key liberal value. Overpopulation is a negative spillover. A violation of natural liberty would, however, be even worse.

Altering the parameters of the game is a different matter. The State can and should act indirectly to foster habits of prudence in the lower classes. Persuasion is superior to force even where the masses, suffering from 'scanty knowledge', are all too liable to be 'deceived by first appearances, and by the arts of designing men': 'It must always be the wish of those who are better informed, that they should be brought to a sense of the truth, rather by patience and the gradual diffusion of education and knowledge, than by any harsher methods' (SE I 334, 335). Education, economic growth and social mobility are all favourable to moral restraint. The government should trust to the free market to turn loose the sleeping giants of rationality and upgrading that in time will limit the marriages and the births.

There is also the possibility of Pigou-like taxes and subsidies. Pronatalists like Montesquieu and Johann Peter Süssmilch had advocated financial premiums to encourage larger families. Malthus could have recommended the use of economic incentives to keep the number of children down. He did not see the need. If the subsistence is abundant, the tax will only marginally discourage the births. If the food supply is thin, the tax will be an irrelevance. So, for the same reason, will a subsidy for agricultural improvement. Grain prices rise when the population rises. The invisible hand will pay the premium that increases the supply. State intervention is not needed to bring about the targeted result.

Rising grain prices do, of course, cut the real wage of the poor-in-work. An alternative strategy would be price ceilings to cap the burden of essential cereals. Malthus opposes such limits with the economist's argument that they would have perverse and unintended consequences. Cheaper grain would trigger earlier marriages. At the same time, the price caps would drive discouraged farmers to reduce their supply: 'There is no check more fatal to improving cultivation, than any difficulty in the vent of its produce which prevents the farmer from being able to obtain, in good years, a price for his corn, not much below the national average' (SE I 65). Lower prices lead to lower output even as they lead to more children and more mouths to feed. They exacerbate the shortage that they are intended to relieve.

4.4.2 Pay

Grain prices should not be regulated. Nor should wage rates: 'The price of labour, when left to find its natural level, is a most important political barometer.... It further expresses clearly the wants of society respecting population' (SE I 355). The free market is socially in touch and allocatively efficient. It calibrates the revealed preferences on both sides of the bargain. That is enough.

The free market should set the wage. Yet bargaining power, always opposite, is seldom equal. Employers, often in tacit cartels, are in a stronger position than isolated workmen, powerless and desperate. Unions of price-takers would facilitate a more level playing field. Trades unions were, however, prohibited under the Combination Acts of 1799 and 1800. They were only permitted after 1825.

Malthus knew about employers' compacts formed expressly to keep the workers' wages down. Since it would be unrealistic to expect the employers' side to renounce its competitive imperfections, the only alternative would be to allow the labour side to acquire countervailing power of its own. The Combination Acts were 'pernicious': 'They evidently appear not to be just, and ought to be avoided' (1824: 601). Prohibition was inconsistent with equality before the law. The State should intervene to repeal existing intervention that had always been biased and unsound.

Repeal of the Combination Acts would, however, only correct market asymmetry at the cost of market freedom. A struggle between concentrated blocs need not end in convergence on the economists' natural wage. There is worse to come. Unions, 'irrational and ineffectual', cause unemployment and misery in the working class: 'If they could raise their wages above what the state of demand and the prices of goods will warrant, it is absolutely impossible that all, or nearly all, should be employed' (SE I 375n).

Higher wages for the insiders mean lower pay and fewer jobs for the out-of-work. It is 'an *absolute impossibility* that all the different classes of society should be both well paid and fully employed, if the supply of labour on the whole exceed the demand' (SE I 375, emphasis in original). To maximise 'the happiness of the great mass of the community' (SE I 375), the ideal is for powerless supply to be equal to powerless demand. Since, however, original power cannot be broken up, the balance of terror is better than no balance at all.

4.4.3 Property

The leaderly State should not legislate to shape the size of the population or the market price of labour. Nor should the State become directly involved in the economic administration of land. Inefficiencies and inequities exist. It is not the function of the State to correct them.

The protective State should enforce existing titles. Only, however, in exceptional circumstances should it reallocate them. Producing 'more evil than good', compulsory redistribution would be an undemocratic encroachment into private property 'on which all progress in civilization, improvement, and wealth, must ever depend' (PR 507).

Compulsion is unacceptable. Yet excessive dispersion is unacceptable too. The fact that Malthus had little sympathy with the dead-level holdings of the utopian anarchists 'by no means infers that the present great inequality of property is either necessary or useful to society. On the contrary, it must certainly be considered as an evil' (FE 177). It is not 'necessary or useful'. It is 'an evil'. It is an aberration that either nature or government is obliged to address.

At one extreme, there is *too small.* Minuscule holdings are wasteful and undercapitalised. In France, the peasants are poor because of 'the extreme subdivision of property' (SE II 169). In the Shetlands, 'few have a plough' (SE I 284). Low productivity on the farms has meant 'naked and starving crowds of people' (SE I 285). The plots could not cover the smallholders' own requirements, let alone produce a surplus for the towns.

At the other extreme, there is *too large.* Vast estates mean that the number of landowners is restricted and the number of labourers excessive. A better distribution of landed property would be beneficial to felt well-being and productivity per acre alike: 'A greater part of society would be in the happy state of possessing property; and a smaller part in the unhappy state of possessing no other property than their labour' (FE 198).

Owner-occupiers would be more likely to practise moral restraint. Middle-class and proud of their independence, they would have more self-respect than they would under the tutelage of 'feudal servitude': 'If society be held desirable, it must surely be free, equal, and reciprocal society, where benefits are conferred as well as received, and not such as the dependent finds with his patron' (FE 90). Unequal estates lead to unequal relationships. In a society that is 'free, equal, and reciprocal', the servant thinks himself more nearly the equal of his master. He can change his master or himself buy land on the market. Capitalism is free, equal and reciprocal. It is not the birth and privilege of the 'feudal servitude' that it was inexorably replacing.

In the capitalist industrial sector, the person-to-person nexus is the dignified bargain and the 'amicable exchange': 'The man who does a day's work for me confers full as great an obligation upon me as I do upon him. I possess what he wants, he possesses what I want' (FE 179). When manufacturing and trade developed in the towns, 'liberty came in their train' (FE 179). In agriculture, the rule of right relationships ought to be the same: 'The poor man walks erect in conscious independence;

and the mind of his employer is not vitiated by a sense of power' (FE 179). It would be equality of citizenship at its best. It is, however, not possible without the more equal distribution of land.

Malthus is not in sympathy either with *too small* or *too large*. A believer in proportion, his ideal is the equilibrium compromise that will give 'the best stimulus to production' (PR 10). Economic output but also right relationships circumscribe the ideal. The means to the end is more of a problem. As with the size of the population and the fabric of the wage-bargain, Malthus is not really convinced that it is the function of the leaderly State to reallocate the land: 'Whether a government could with advantage to society actively interfere to repress inequality of fortunes may be matter of doubt' (FE 177). Smith's perfect liberty should not be exchanged for restraint.

The cat should be belled: 'The numbers in the extreme regions would be lessened, and the numbers in the middle regions increased' (FE 207). It is not, however, the function of the leaderly State to do the belling. Critics will say that Malthus is being too conservative, too accepting and possibly even too timid. His reply to the impetuous would be that all change takes time. It is the conviction of the liberal that, ultimately, economic underperformance will be squeezed out by market competition. Given time, it will be free enterprise that will bell the cat.

Malthus was cautious but not doctrinaire. His vision of the political economy is not just free enterprise supported by the constables and the judges. Malthus was opposed to the Poor Laws. He was, however, in favour of the Corn Laws, subsidised schooling, assisted emigration, bounties for grain exports and parish relief for the genuinely destitute. He also made common cause with Robert Owen to restrict child labour: 'Every friend of humanity must heartily wish him success in his endeavours' (SE I 334). Parliament in 1802 voted to limit the hours and impose a minimum age. Malthus felt it was the right thing to do: 'It is hoped that much good will result' (SE I 383n).

Malthus did not always reject regulation. In a minority of cases, he deviated from freedom *from* to espouse the cause of freedom *to*. In Bonar's view, he had no hard-and-fast rule but utility: 'His only axiom in political philosophy was that the end of politics is the greatest happiness of the great body of the people; and his only rule for securing that end was the observation of what, as a matter of experience, actually did secure it' (Bonar 1885 [1924]).

Happiness to Malthus normally pointed to individual choice. Pragmatism is, however, a foot in the door. The criterion that the State should intervene where collective choice puts up the sum total of happiness is a rubber rule. National Health, nationalised rail, the Arts Council, there is little that Malthus could not support if his rubber rule told him that felt well-being would be shifted up to a higher plane.

4.5 Education for Citizenship

Adam Smith said that the common people had to be taught. They had to learn to 'read, write, and account' even if the training would have a low economic pay-off once the alienating sub-division of labour had made them 'as stupid and ignorant as it is possible for a human creature to become' (Smith 1776 [1961]: II 303, 305). More important than the vocational skills, they had also to be inoculated with a focused understanding of how their society actually functions. Without this true and unimpeachable lens, they would be easy prey for false preachers and rabble-rousers who would entice them into faction, superstition and rebellion. They would be more likely to 'be misled into any wanton or unnecessary opposition to the measures of government' (Smith 1776 [1961]: II 309). The very stability of the social order would be at risk. It is all in Smith, and Burke, and 1789.

Malthus saw precisely what Smith was trying to say. As with Smith, he realised that education involved not just the inculcation of economically relevant *how tos* but the transmission of mainstream values and valuations without which social interaction would become a powder keg. Education for citizenship socialises the impressionable into the common value system. It conditions their behaviour patterns. It makes them fit for the society in which they live. There is even a hint, never subsequently developed, that comprehensive schooling might one day serve as an engine of social integration: 'To give respectability to the schools, it would be very desirable that those who are a little above the class of labourers, should send their children to them, which they would never do' (LW 17).

Education gives children the training they need to advance beyond the manual grades. Whereas Smith had feared that the working classes would become mentally stunted through dead-end employment, Malthus was more optimistic about economic evolution. Modern industry is creating new jobs. Education is teaching the skills. The schools are giving children the technical knowledge and the social values that will enable them to succeed at work.

The lower classes acquire the will and the way to better their condition. Improved self-esteem integrates the masses into a going concern. The role models show that it can be done. The prudence of the first to ascend tends to 'improve the condition of his fellow labourers' (SE II 190). They follow him up the ladder of success. Both the school places and the occupational slots are in their nature plus-sum: 'All may share without interfering with each other' (SE II 189). It is the antithesis of misery and vice.

The superiors and the inferiors in One Nation enjoy 'a more equal and liberal mode of treatment' (SE II 131). Respect and self-respect have an effect on the population multiplier. Once a man acquires 'that decent kind of pride' (SE II 190) that accrues to achievement, he will postpone the founding of a family in order to preserve his new-found status. Education in that way contributes to moral restraint: 'The degree of proper pride and spirit of independence, almost invariably connected with education and a certain rank in life, will secure the operation of the preventive check' (SE II 150).

Governments cannot supersede the geometrical and the arithmetical ratios. To promise more only arouses false hopes. What governments can do is to indulge in background social engineering. People's attitudes should be redirected 'in such a way as to be the least prejudicial to the virtue and happiness of society' (SV 249). It may be propaganda but it does ensure convergence. Education for citizenship reinforces the 'general rectitude of character' (PR 346). In collaboration with the spill-over of faster growth, it raises the total utility of the nation.

The untutored do not understand the link between population and hunger, indolence and distress, achievement and accomplishment. Resentful of low wages, Spartan relief, 'unjust institutions' and 'the avarice of the rich, who suffer him to want what they can so well spare'

(SE II 160), the common man reifies the enemy into a privileged '*they*' (SE II 140, emphasis in original). Blinkered by 'erroneous views', suffering from 'total misapprehension', the uneducated have a 'habit of expecting too much' (SE II 131, 133).

A lack of knowledge is 'of all monsters the most fatal to freedom' (SE II 123). *Vox populi* is not *vox dei*. Instead, it is 'the voice of error and absurdity' (SE II 124), 'false expectations and extravagant demands' (SE II 136), 'ignorance and delusion....among the common people' (SE II 125). There is 'insubordination and turbulence' on the part of the lower classes when they ought to be 'peaceful and orderly' (SE II 201). They challenge what they do not understand. They riot and protest against abuses that are all in the mind.

A lack of knowledge is a dangerous thing. Education for citizenship is the antidote. Religion teaches selective precepts. Urgently required, however, is something more. The lower classes must be given a good grounding in 'the common principles by which markets are regulated': 'Political economy is perhaps the only science of which it may be said that the ignorance of it is not merely a deprivation of good, but produces great evil' (SE II 152n).

Political economy makes the civics clear. The deprived should seek out well-paid employment, limit the number of their dependents and practise self-denial through frugality. They should learn that they alone are the captains of their fate: 'Nothing perhaps would tend so strongly to excite a spirit of industry and economy among the poor, as a thorough knowledge that their happiness must always depend principally upon themselves' (SE II 111).

Charity begins at home. It is the lesson of 'nature and reason' that ordinary people, not the capitalists, the landowners or the politicians, are 'themselves the cause of their poverty' (SE II 106). While Malthus is not blaming the poor for their poverty, he is directly blaming their ignorance. They need education. They need to be told why they are poor. There will be 'a very decided improvement in the habits and temper of the lower classes, when their real situation has been clearly explained to them' (SE II 227).

The masses need to understand that the State is not the answer to their prayers: 'It is of the very highest importance....to know distinctly what government *cannot* do, as well as what it *can*' (SE II 131, emphasis added). Their first reaction is to blame a social failing on their leaders. Untutored, they have not understood 'how small a part of their present distress was attributable to government' (SE II 128). It makes 'the mob' an easy target for orators, revolutionaries, ideologues and demagogues. 'Turbulent and discontented men in the middle classes' (SE II 128), cranks and misfits like these take advantage of the poor whom they pretend to represent.

Political opportunists compete for popularity without any attempt to cost their manifesto. They manipulate and misinform because it is not in their interest to focus on the truth. Malthus cites the example of Tom Paine, whose *Rights of Man* of 1792 'has done great mischief': 'He falls into the common error of attributing all want of happiness to government' (SE II 126, 127). Tom Paine had failed to grasp the basic truths of economics. False promises and distortions like his 'cannot but be disheartening to every friend of freedom' (SE II 153). It is doubly disheartening since without education for citizenship it would be all too easy for forked-tongue fanatics to trick the fickle crowd.

That is why the lower classes should not have the vote. Like Adam Smith, Malthus believed in multi-party democracy but not in manhood or universal suffrage. Like Hobbes, Burke and Smith, Malthus warned of the lawlessness that lies just beneath the veneer: 'Every free government tends constantly to destruction' (SE II 122). The *Essay* was written at a time when the French were thought poised to invade. The Defence of the Realm Act in 1798 had suspended Habeas Corpus because English Jacobins were believed to be the Trojan Horse. Malthus knew that it was not the moment to make politics more inclusive. Populism, radicalism and sedition within had, for now, 'paralyzed the exertions of the best friends of liberty' (SE II 136).

At the same time, Malthus did believe that even the disenfranchised should have 'some share in the government', 'some influence' in the framing of the laws (SE II 131). It is the advantage of 'the representative system' that it accords 'to the lower classes of society a more equal and liberal mode of treatment' (SE II 131). Presumably, the representatives voted in by a small and propertied élite could be trusted to legislate for the general interest. Distributive coalitions and marginal constituencies are not all there is to representative democracy.

Malthus said in the year of Peterloo ('this terrible Manchester business…cruel and unjust') that he was 'a decided friend to a moderate reform in Parliament' (letter from Malthus to Ricardo, 1819, in Ricardo VIII: 66, 107). A Whig, he favoured an extension of the franchise to the commercial middle classes who met the property qualification. Malthus supported the 1832 Reform Act. He would probably have welcomed subsequent extensions. First, however, there would have to be education.

The Education Act of 1870 followed on the heels of the 1867 Reform Act because the leaders knew that they had urgently to educate their masters. It was what Malthus had envisaged all along. There is only one test, and that is education for citizenship. No good would come of an election where scheming entrepreneurs were tempting the gullible into their shop with fanciful utopias on which they would not be able to deliver. They would turn public policy into a battlefield in which every contender is doomed to disappointment. Education is high-powered. Literacy is the only way to prevent the left-behind from being poisoned by the work of Tom Paine. A literate workman would prefer to read Adam Smith instead.

References

By T. R. Malthus

(1798 [1970]). *Essay on the Principle of Population, as It affects the Future Improvement of Society, with Remarks on the Speculations of Mr. Godwin, M. Condorcet, and Other Writers* (abbreviated as FE), ed. by A. Flew. Harmondsworth: Penguin.

(1803 et seq. [1989]). *An Essay on the Principle of Population: Or a View of Its Past and Present Effects on Human Happiness, with an Inquiry into Our Prospects Respecting the Removal of the Evils Which It Occasions* (2nd edition, 1803; further editions in 1806, 1807, 1817, 1826) (abbreviated as SE I and SE II), 2 vols., ed. by P. James. Cambridge: Cambridge University Press.

(1807). *A Letter to Samuel Whitbread, Esq, M.P., on His Proposed Bill for the Amendment of the Poor Laws* (abbreviated as LW), reprinted in *The Works of Thomas Robert Malthus*, ed. by E. A. Wrigley and D. Souden. London: Pickering and Chatto, 4, 3–19.

(1809 [1963]). Review of Thomas Newenham's *A View of the Natural, Political and Commercial Circumstances of Ireland, Edinburgh Review*, 27, 1809, reprinted in *Occasional Papers of T.R. Malthus*, ed. by B. Semmel. New York: Bert Franklin, 52–71.
(1820 [1989]). *The Principles of Political Economy* (abbreviated as PR), ed. by J. Pullen. Cambridge: Cambridge University Press.
(1823 [1986]). *The Measure of Value Stated and Illustrated, with an Application of It to the Alterations in the Value of the English Currency Since 1790*, reprinted in *The Works of Thomas Robert Malthus*, ed. by E. A. Wrigley and D. Souden. London: Pickering and Chatto, 7, 179–221.
(1824). Evidence to the Select Committee on Artizans and Machinery (Sixth Report), in *Parliamentary Papers*. London: House of Commons, 5, 598–601.
(1827). Evidence to the Select Committee on Emigration (Third Report), in *Parliamentary Papers*. London: House of Commons, 5, 311–327.
(1830). *A Summary View of the Principle of Population* (abbreviated as SV), in FE, supra.

Secondary Literature

Bonar, J. (1885 [1924]). *Malthus and His Work* (2nd ed.). London: Macmillan.
Buchanan, J. M., & Tullock, G. (1962). *The Calculus of Consent*. Ann Arbor: University of Michigan Press.
Hayek, F. (1988). *The Fatal Conceit*. London: Routledge.
Olson, M. (1982). *The Rise and Decline of Nations*. New Haven: Yale University Press.
Olson, M. (2000). *Power and Prosperity: Outgrowing Communist and Capitalist Dictatorships*. New York: Basic Books.
Ricardo, D. (1951–1955). *The Works and Correspondence of David Ricardo* (abbreviated as Ricardo) (P. Sraffa with M. Dobb, Eds., 11 vols.). Cambridge: Cambridge University Press.
Smith, A. (1759 [1966]). *The Theory of Moral Sentiments*. London: Augustus M. Kelley.
Smith, A. (1776 [1961]). *The Wealth of Nations* (E. Cannan, Ed., 2 vols.). London: Methuen.
Tawney, R. H. (1966). *The Radical Tradition* (R. Hinden, Ed.). London: Penguin Books.

5
The Poor Laws

The Poor Laws were enacted in 1601 when the Tudor enclosures were forcing farmers with traditional tenures to give up their land. They were joined in 1662 by the Law of Settlement which confined relief to the pauper's own parish lest desperate incomers such as pregnant women make themselves a burden on an alien community. In the Napoleonic Wars, when the economy was disrupted there was the Speenhamland system. It topped up the wages of the able-bodied in work so as to give them index-linked access to bread.

The intention had been to relieve and assist. The outcome had been even greater distress. Malthus was a persuader. His *Essay* was a determined attempt to rescue public policy from false consciousness. The laws cannot eradicate the misery of the poor. All they can do is to 'throw a veil of obscurity over this subject' (SE II 106). It is not the practice that is flawed so much as the expectation that wise leaders can make water into wine: 'I attribute still more evil to the original ill conception than to the subsequent ill execution' (SE II 112n).

It is all a question of inadequate education for imperfect citizenship. The poor are led to believe that the government can do the impossible. It cannot: 'A revolution would not alter in their favour the proportion

D. Reisman, *Thomas Robert Malthus*, Great Thinkers in Economics,
https://doi.org/10.1007/978-3-030-01956-3_5

of the supply of labour to the demand, or the quantity of food to the number of the consumers' (SE II 154). A responsible leadership must acknowledge the double constraint of human instinct and exhaustible subsistence. Both the masses and their leaders have a strong desire to repeal the natural law and elect another. There no way that they can do this. Public poverty to relieve the poor is counterproductive: 'If the poor laws had never existed…the aggregate mass of happiness among the common people would have been much greater' (SE I 361). The Poor Laws had to go.

5.1 Income Maintenance: The First *Essay*

Churchgoers will have been familiar with *Matthew* 26.11. It informed the worshippers that 'the poor you will always have with you'. The Bible had revealed that poverty is 'the lot of humanity' (LW 6). At the same time, it had preached the duty to share. In the Old Testament, the farmer is enjoined not to glean his whole crop in order that the scavenger may feed himself from the margin. In the New Testament, there is the parable of the Good Samaritan and the tithe paid for Christian charity.

Adam Smith had made benevolence, together with self-interest and justice, one of the three pillars of the moral sentiments (Smith 1759 [1966]: 112, 119). Malthus, steeped in the philosophy of Adam Smith even as he was a Christian clergyman, was quick to agree that there is more to social obligation than economic exchange. Benevolence, Malthus says, 'is one of the noblest and most godlike qualities of the human heart' (FE 179). Benevolence can 'correct the asperities' and 'smooth the wrinkles' of self-love (FE 179). That, however, is all: 'It can never be substituted in its place' (FE 179). Malthus knew that even moral absolutes had to fit in with the real world.

Poor relief redistributes purchasing power to the least advantaged. The neglected have 'a command of food so much greater than their degree of skill and industry entitled them to' (SE I 351). The prosperous take home less than they 'would naturally possess' (SE I 351). It verges on a violation of natural justice. What men naturally possess must normally be regarded as their own.

The redistribution is horizontal as well as vertical. Men who irresponsibly father children in the expectation of the safety net 'injure all in the same class with themselves' (SE I 359). Poor rates cut into wage capital. The transfers are a threat to employment. The price of grain is competed up. Increasing the pressure on a finite stock, well-intentioned handouts 'spread the general evil over a much larger surface' (FE 94).

The well-to-do can pay the higher prices. The very poor are obliged 'to live upon the hardest fare and in the smallest quantity' (FE 95). The moderately deprived situated just above the welfare cut-off are the most vulnerable. Intra-class exploitation becomes a fact. Workers on wages suffer because workers on welfare bid up the grain. Adding it all up, the partial amelioration secured by the destitute is 'much more than counterbalanced by the general deterioration in the condition of the great mass of the society' (SV 270). Money cannot raise some to a higher plane 'without proportionately depressing others' (FE 96). It is a fact of life.

The first *Essay* was written in a time of war, disruption and need. In spite of that, the First *Essay* and all the succeeding *Essays* were not about compassion but about the ratios. The population is going up. The supply of food is not. There is no way that musical chairs can correct the imbalance: 'The transfer of three shillings and sixpence a day to every labourer would not increase the quantity of meat in the country' (FE 94).

The food does not exist. The promise of income maintenance is nonetheless attracting the poor into earlier marriage and larger families. An induced expansion in population can only exacerbate the pressure on subsistence. Open-handed assistance, because it gives a free pass to spineless improvidence, 'will always defeat its own purpose' (FE 98). The Poor Laws 'create the poor which they maintain' (FE 97). It is all the fault of the geometrical ratio: 'It is better that it should be checked from a foresight of the difficulties attending a family and the fear of dependent poverty, than that it should be encouraged, only to be repressed afterwards by want and sickness' (FE 99).

The Poor Laws cut into the real wage. They also have a detrimental effect on the propensity to save. The poorer classes 'live from hand to mouth': 'Their present wants employ their whole attention, and they seldom think of the future' (FE 98). It is not just the wherewithal that they lack but the cultural valuation of deferred gratification: 'Even when they have an opportunity of saving they seldom exercise it.... All that is beyond their present necessities goes, generally speaking, to the ale-house' (FE 98). Destitution holds no terror for them. The welfare parish will provide.

Low incomes and a live-for-today mentality cannot be attributed exclusively to permissive and non-judgmental welfare. It is not the free-money mentality alone that is tempting otherwise decent men into drunkenness and dissipation. Even so, Malthus has no doubt that the insurance principle which educates men in the escape clause of moral hazard is in itself an important cause of preventable poverty. The Poor Laws 'diminish both the power and the will to save among the common people, and thus....weaken one of the strongest incentives to sobriety and industry, and consequently to happiness' (FE 98). Low pay or high pay, there is no need to budget for a rainy day.

It is a dependency culture in which the negative spillovers are absorbed by the caring community. The spirit of independence is weakened and in the end eradicated by the citizenship guarantee (FE 91). This is especially so if the transfers are delivered without stigma. If irresponsible procreation is relieved without discredit, the lack of sanctions will be an invitation to abuse.

There must be probing questions, shaming hurdles and stern gatekeepers primed to keep the chancers out. The deterrents are a necessary evil but they are an evil nonetheless. Malthus expresses his regret that the poor must 'sacrifice the valuable blessing of liberty' (FE 103) when they are required to beg. The means tests and the debasing disclosures are 'grating, inconvenient, and tyrannical', 'utterly contradictory to all ideas of freedom' (FE 100). The fault lies not with the individual officers but with the very essence of the relationship. Sensitively managed or not, 'any great interference with the affairs of other people is a species of tyranny' (FE 101). Tyranny is a part of the system. Shame is needed to ensure that only the truly deserving will venture their way through the minefield.

Stigma is the sine qua non. Welfare must be cruel to be kind: 'Hard as it may appear in individual cases, dependent poverty ought to be held disgraceful. Such a stimulus seems to be absolutely necessary to promote the happiness of the great mass of mankind, and every general attempt to weaken this stimulus, however benevolent its apparent intention, will always defeat its own purpose' (FE 98). The alternative to the culture of shame is to do away altogether with the handout-trap. Malthus is a friend of the poor. He contends that any friend of the poor must also be an enemy of welfare.

In an ideal world, the Poor Laws would have to go (FE 101). In the short run, they can at least be reformed.

One step would be to phase out the Law of Settlement: 'The market for labour would then be free' (FE 101). Freedom is an end. The sovereign labourer would take pride in his liberty and individual autonomy (FE 103). Freedom is also a means. Geographical mobility is allocatively efficient where workers are attracted into scarcity areas by supernormal pay. Impeded circulation seals in sub-markets that are incompatible with the competitive law of one price.

Another reform would be the privatisation of relief. Voluntary bodies and self-appointed charities could take over the financial overhead. Sickness funds and mutual aid could share between their members the contingency of dependence. Bountiful donors and sealed-off risk pools do not eliminate the burden of moral hazard but they do shield the outside community from an involuntary imposition.

At the end of the day, the parish will still have to provide outdoor relief for the fault-free 'deserving poor'. It will also have to operate workhouses for the able-bodied who have fallen into destitution. Conditions in the workhouses will be 'less eligible' than in the world outside but the inmates will be paid the going market wage for their work (FE 102). The institution will in this way, relying on education through quasi-capitalism, be resocialising the dependent into acceptable standards of conduct. It will be doing more than supplying life's essentials to lean against the positive checks.

It can all be summed up in a phrase: 'To prevent the recurrence of misery, is, alas! beyond the power of man. In the vain endeavour to attain what in the nature of things is impossible, we now sacrifice not only possible but certain benefits' (FE 102). The Poor Laws should be tightened up. Sooner or later they will have to go.

5.2 Poor People: The Later *Essays*

From the second *Essay* of 1803 to the sixth edition in 1826, Malthus never departed from his bedrock text. Doing right can never be wrong: 'Both humanity and true policy imperiously require that we should give every assistance to the poor' (SE I 357). Assistance to the needy fulfils 'the great moral duty of assisting our fellow-creatures in distress' (SE I 368). The gift relationship is 'the bond which unites the rich with the poor' (SE II 216). The kindly Malthus may have been seriously misrepresented by the nay-sayers and the point-scorers. Or perhaps not. Ultimately, he did recommend that the Poor Laws should be scrapped.

The later editions repeat the warning of 1798. Poor relief undams the flood of irresponsible procreation. Whatever happens, the children will not starve. There is no need for self-restraint. The preventive check is an archaic deterrent 'which the distribution of this assistance tends obviously to destroy' (SE II 188).

It 'tends' and it 'tends obviously'. The tendency by itself is not enough. For a causal relationship to go beyond an unfounded assertion, there must also be the facts. Malthus had the facts. They did not confirm his hypothesis but at least they were the facts.

In 1806, he cited evidence which, to him, 'clearly proves that the Poor Laws…. do not encourage marriage so much as might be expected from theory' (SE II 170n). In 1817, he showed that the Poor Laws had indeed increased the population but had not done so 'greatly' (SE II 226n). Comparative data suggested that marriages and births were not radically different in England from foreign countries which did not have a social floor. Even the Irish who did have a welfare net had managed to promote themselves from a 'wretched and degraded state' in the 1803 *Essay* to nothing worse than a 'depressed state' (SE II: 145, 145n) in 1817. The Poor Laws had evidently not stranded them in 'barbarism' and 'filth'. A tendency law is not an ineluctable sequence.

The facts were there but Malthus was not convinced. More persuasive than the selective and the anecdotal were the national correlations. The population of England was, he calculated in 1817, doubling every 48 years. The growth in numbers had not been 'regulated by the demand for labour' (SE II 169). England did, however, have a Poor Law. That says it all. Unstinting assistance had clearly been the cause of the explosion. *Post hoc* and *propter hoc* were lending strong support to the law of population: 'The number of the dependent poor continually bears a greater proportion to the whole population' (LW 11). The facts speak for themselves.

Malthus had seen the hovels and the hunger on his study tours. The Poor Laws, he reported, had 'done great good, or at least prevented great evil' (SE I 368). They had alleviated the distress of the rural and urban residuum. Yet there is an adding up problem. Succor granted to the part may cause unexpected misery for the whole: 'The partial and immediate effects of a particular mode of giving assistance are so often directly opposite to the general and permanent effects' (SE II 186).

The 'general' and the 'permanent' are the benchmark. The 'particular' and the 'immediate' are not. The greatest happiness of the greatest number cannot be estimated by the unique happiness of one individual, one allowance once. Using the criterion of the 'general' and the 'permanent', it is obvious that the Poor Laws will be defeated by 'the absolute impossibility' (SE I 368) of delivering on their promise. Anti-poor, 'an inhuman deceit' (SE I 127), they lower wages (SE I 374) and 'depress the general condition of the poor' (SE I 358). They lead to 'carelessness and want of frugality' (SE I 359), 'ignorance', 'imprudence' (SE II 212), 'indolence' 'want of foresight', early marriage and 'too rapid multiplication' (SE II 219). Relief introduces a further circle of inferno to their wretchedness. The Poor Laws are a license for arrogant churchwardens and supercilious overseers to conduct themselves in a 'capricious and insulting manner', 'inconsistent with the genuine spirit of the constitution' (SE I 363, 360).

Big-hearted welfare passes on to the lower classes the message that there is no need to 'put any sort of restraint upon their inclinations', 'exercise any degree of prudence in the affair of marriage' or 'cultivate habits of economy' (SE I 376). The assistance guaranteed, they will have no reason to 'make use of the means afforded them by saving-banks' or to 'lay by their earnings when they are single' as an investment in 'decency and comfort' when the children arrive (SE I 376). The window that never shuts has a 'pernicious tendency' to weaken the incentive to 'sobriety and industry, and consequently to happiness' (SE I 359). The Poor Laws are a school for scoundrels. They inculcate attitudes and values that are incompatible with a mighty leap out of the vicious circle.

Alcohol and indolence come in. Foresight and prudence go out. The Poor Laws have been the cause of 'much evil, both with regard to the habits and the temper of the poor' (SE II 215). It is all in vain. The grain and the meat are simply not there: 'The commodity would not be divided among many more than it is at present' (SE I 349). As in the first *Essay*, it is the rich and not the poor who will corner the supply: 'He that offers the most money, becomes the possessor' (SE I 349). The deprived will be priced out. They will live on scanty commons. Some will die.

The ratios have not gone away. The umbrella of paternalism has promised more than it can deliver: 'Poverty and misery have always increased in proportion to the quantity of indiscriminate charity' (SE II 161). Malthus was not in favour of poverty and misery. He believed that the welfare system had imposed an inequitable burden on the deprived who most need its support.

5.3 Institutional Reform

Seeking to raise up the poor, Malthus in the succeeding editions of the *Essay* repeated that it was in no one's interest for poor relief to be an easy touch: 'No man should look to charity as a fund on which he can confidently depend. He should be taught that his own exertions, his own industry and foresight, are his only just ground of dependence' (SE II 160). By 'taught' Malthus is not thinking only of formal lessons, augmented by Sunday sermons and party-political oratory. He is also looking to the material conditions of existence to breed and form the behaviour patterns that will prevent men from ever sinking to the lower depths.

The relief of poverty is a footnote. What Malthus most wants is a social order built around self-reliance and achievement in which a cry for help is seldom heard. It all hinges on institutional reform. People should be placed in situations where the incentive structure will strengthen the core values of hard work and personal responsibility. Conditions should be created that are conducive to moral restraint and prudential frugality. Market capitalism will be the university that turns out the new, post-Poor Law man.

Allocative efficiency aside, the competitive market has the great attraction that it instils a 'spirit of independence' (SE I 359). It can be seen in the countryside where the farmer operator has a 'natural and becoming pride' (SE I 363) in his capacity to earn life for himself and his family. In France after the Revolution, the reallocation of land and the destruction of the feudal networks had the same effect on the national character. It tended to 'make every person depend more upon himself, and less upon others. The labouring classes are therefore become more industrious, more saving and more prudent in marriage' (SE I 378). They are better able to look after themselves.

The ownership of property is an upgrading influence. It encourages self-respect and discourages premature marriage: 'Those cottagers who keep cows are more industrious and more regular in their conduct than those who do not' (SE II 191). It is reciprocal causality. The 'better sort of labourers' will purchase their cows 'with the fruits of their own industry': 'It is therefore more just to say that their industry has given them a cow, than that a cow has given them their industry' (SE II 191). Once a farmer has some land, he will save for a cow. Children will be put off until his finances are secure.

That is a reason for the parish not to supply residential accommodation. The aspiration to have a home of one's own is 'one of the most salutary and least pernicious checks' (SE II 190). The housing shortage in the case of the lower classes will 'always operate as a powerful check to their increase' (SE II 191n). Samuel Whitbread, speaking in Parliament in 1807, had outlined a plan for the local authorities to provide affordable cottages. Malthus replied to Whitbread that the proposal would 'produce more harm than good' (LW 16). Low-cost units would encourage early childbearing and with it 'the greater part of our labouring classes dependent on parish relief': 'Whatever accommodations you may make for them at present, the difficulty would shortly recur' (LW 13). Dependent poverty would increase. The policy would be counterproductive. Rather than moving into a new cottage, it would be better for a young couple to wait patiently for an old cottage to fall vacant: 'The number of annual marriages is regulated principally by the number of annual deaths. They reciprocally influence each other' (SE I 193).

Self-reliance is the most reliable way to eradicate the smothering influence of over-permissive welfare. It is also a move towards a more inclusive society. Rather than the needy soliciting a subsidy from the successful, the lower classes would be adopting the plus-sum strategy of pulling themselves up: 'Prudence in marriage, which is the only moral means of preventing an excess of workmen above the demand, can be the only mode of giving to the poor permanently a large share of all that is produced in the country' (SE I 377). All classes travel upward with growth. The poor left behind travel upwards the fastest of all. *Enrichissez-vous*. Entitlements must and will be earned.

The primary source of help is self-help. It is a virtuous circle that encompasses saving as well as earning. Abstinence being 'the touchstone' of betterment, the habit of saving goes to 'the very root of the evil' (SE II 181). It tends to 'strengthen the lessons of Nature and Providence' (SE II 182). Most of all will this be so if the funds can be left to accrue interest in a financial institution. In that way, the capitalist bankers can assist the poor to better their condition.

Savings banks are 'the best, and the most likely' (SE II 182) way to universalise the practice of thrift. Ideally, a young man will begin to put money aside at 14 or 15. His nest egg would then build up over a notional ten years before the usual age of marriage. The banks must play their part in taking small deposits from the poorer classes. Even a bank can be a school: 'We wish to teach the labouring classes to rely more upon their own exertions and resources' (SE II 183). The Poor Laws teach a very different lesson.

5.4 The Right to Welfare

The first line of defence, in the later editions as in 1798, should be self-defence. Only after all else has failed should the out-of-luck be able to approach their fellow citizens for help. Even then, it will never be a citizenship entitlement. Tom Paine just after the French Revolution declared that mutual aid from 'the common stock' had become an incontrovertible expectation: 'Every man is a proprietor in society, and draws on the capital as a matter of right' (Paine 1792 [2000]: 90).

T. H. Marshall at the inception of Britain's post-1945 Welfare State proclaimed that each citizen had a social right 'to live the life of a civilised being according to the standards prevailing in the society' (Marshall 1950 [1992]: 8). Malthus poured cold water on the humanitarian idealism of the warm-hearted collectivists. He said that the transfer-in-need was not an entitlement but merely a hope and a dream: 'The poor have no claim of *right* to support' (SE II 218, emphasis in original). Welfare is not backed up by social justice. Even if it were, the earth is simply not able to provide. Philosophy and economics are in agreement. There is no right to welfare: 'No person has any claim of right on society for subsistence' (SE II 128). The only right is society's right to bid him to be gone.

Children have a claim of right on their parents. Parents have a duty of care to their children. The nexus becomes attenuated as the concentric circles move out. No one has a natural claim on distant strangers. Anonymous others have no quasi-parental duty to assist. They may, of course, choose to do so out of pity and compassion. Whatever they do, the gift is optional and voluntary. It is not a social obligation. The Poor Laws are on shaky ground when they are funded through a tax. Property cannot be secure if it is taken compulsorily to acquit a discretionary commitment.

The gift is not a right. Even so, a nation sometimes provides a gift because of a loose consensus that something has to be done. Intervening because it feels involved, a society will nonetheless have reservations about equal treatment for equal distress. Widows and orphans may be deemed 'worthy objects of relief' (SE II 160). Inveterate scroungers, just as hungry, may legitimately be turned away.

Generally speaking, the public are more likely to say that 'unmerited calamities' are 'the genuine objects of charity' (SE II 161). There being no element of moral hazard or self-inflicted dysfunction, such claimants should be relieved 'liberally and adequately': 'Good conduct, and not mere distress, should have the most valid claim to preference' (SE II 162, 190). Relief to 'the worthless', the 'idle and improvident' should, on the other hand, be 'very scanty': 'They should on no account be enabled to command so much of the necessaries of life as can be obtained by the worst-paid common labour' (SE II 162). In the 1817 edition, the recommendation that it should be 'very scanty' was downgraded to 'not be abundant' (SE II 162n). The metric does not make a difference to the principle. The test remains 'good conduct', free from 'indolence or improvidence' (SE II 161). It remains 'not having brought myself into distress by my own idleness or extravagance' (SE II 216).

The moral cut-off extends to premature marriage. Although it is an 'immoral act' (SE II 140), a person who has no expectation of supporting his children should not be prevented by law from starting a family. Natural law will impose its own sanctions of hunger and death. What is important for social policy is that 'all parish assistance should be most rigidly denied him'; while private charity, always uncertain, 'should be administered very sparingly' (SE II 140). The sins of the fathers should be visited on the children. Harsh as this may be, it is a necessary deterrent to irresponsible parenting.

The children born, there should never be an expectation that public institutions will take in the unwanted excess. Malthus does not say that infants should be allowed to starve on the streets. What he does say is more oblique. Foundling homes, 'miscalled philanthropic', are 'in every view hurtful to the State' (SE I 165, 175–176).

In financial terms, such institutions are a drain: 'The period of failure cannot be very distant' (SE I 174). A more fundamental problem is the value system that they embody. Foundling hospitals foster 'habits of licentiousness, discourage marriage, and thus weaken the main spring of population' (SE I 176). They convey the message that parents can reasonably discard an unloved newborn because the bystander community will provide. Foundling windows strike at 'some of the best and most useful feelings of the human heart' (SE II 177). They come between conception and its consequences. If they were to be scaled down, moral restraint would be that much more attractive.

Help should be thin and, as in the first *Essay*, it should be accompanied by stigma. For 'humane reasons', 'dependent poverty' ought to be sanctioned by 'disgrace': 'Such a stimulus seems to be absolutely necessary to promote the happiness of the great mass of mankind' (SE I 359, 360). Compassion is counterproductive. Deterrence is 'utility' (SE II 156). The 'great mass of mankind' must be protected against the ratios which have not gone away.

5.5 The Social Contract

The pauper is indolent and improvident. The pauper is drunken and dissipated. The pauper breeds children that he cannot afford. The pauper travels free on the Poor Laws because the benevolent are an inexhaustible pool that will never cease from among us. It is the individual wherever you look. Society is never the cause of the diswelfares. Society only arrives at closing time to pick up the pieces.

James Bonar was concerned that there seemed to be no social contract in the remorseless factoring down: 'Malthus looks at social problems too much from the individual's point of view.....He speaks little of the duty of the citizen to the community....The citizen is lost in the householder' (Bonar 1885 [1924]: 353). There may be sympathy but there is no debt. The individual has no duty to the community. The community has no duty to the individual.

That is one interpretation. There is an alternative. The earlier editions of the *Essay* were written at a time when wartime disruptions and harvest failures were triggering successive 'seasons of distress' (SE I 4). No one could blame the destitute for drunkenness and destitution when everyone knew that a crop failure had made poverty not specific but general. The 1817 edition of the *Essay* and the *Principles* in 1820 were written in the post-war recession when demobilisation, readjustment and deficient demand were depriving even the most assiduous and prudent of the chance to work. In 1817, Malthus estimated that one-fourth of the population of England and Wales was dependent on poor relief. It was a national problem that had spread, like an epidemic disease, throughout the whole of the integrated matrix. It was not the alehouses and the ratios that had caused the misery but an interruption in the national flow.

Even in good times, the economy might not provide. Taste is fickle. Innovation costs jobs. Market capitalism is a kaleidoscope of profit *and loss*. It is bad luck but not an individual shortcoming when the sovereign consumer moves on to something new: 'The weavers of Spitalfields were plunged into the most severe distress by the fashion of muslins instead of silks; and great numbers of workmen in Sheffield and

Birmingham were for a time thrown out of employment owing to the adoption of shoe strings and covered buttons, instead of buckles and metal buttons' (SE II 83).

The weavers and the button-moulders had become what Richard Titmuss calls 'the social pathologies of other people's progress' (Titmuss 1968: 157). In the long run, they will make a new start in a sunrise sector. Broken legs heal. In the short run—'for a time'—they may not be able to support even the children they had cost-consciously conceived when their incomes were good. Moral restraint does not come with an all-seasons guarantee. The economic system had cost them their livelihood. It is social causality and not an individual shortcoming that had stranded them on the sidelines.

Malthus knew about the weavers and the button-moulders. He knew about involuntary unemployment when there was not enough spending to go round: 'The country has been wholly unable to find adequate employment for the numerous labourers and artificers who were able as well as willing to work' (SE I 128). Able and willing, honest workmen cannot reasonably be stigmatised for a shortcoming that is not their own. The failure of 'the country' sheds a new light on the Poor Laws. It also suggests that income maintenance might after all be money well spent: 'As a temporary measure, it is not only charitable but just to spread the evil over a larger surface' (SE I 370).

It must be 'temporary' but it is also 'just'. The recipient has not brought his misfortune upon himself. The social order and not the blameless monad is the cause of the diswelfare. Malthus, so often an implacable critic of the Poor Laws, is prepared to concede that in certain circumstances the Poor Laws do meet the strict test of equity. Even the Poor Laws can be regarded as citizenship compensation that puts right a previous wrong: 'Violence on particular parts may be so mitigated as to be made bearable by all' (SE I 370).

Outdoor relief in a downswing is just. It is an acknowledgement of 'both humanity and true policy' to provide 'temporary aid' in 'seasons of distress' (SE I 357). It is a social duty to assist the involuntarily unemployed who are being denied the freedom to earn. The poor were blaming the government for their misery. Malthus was still saying that the secular solution is moral restraint. In the short run, however, he was saying that it is the state.

In the downswing, there can legitimately be public assistance. There should also be direct employment. Malthus proposes that in bad times the government should take up the slack through contra-cyclical public works like roads, bridges, railways and canals (SE I 369–370). They were unlikely to cut into private capital or compete with private production. They would inculcate attitudes at the same time that they created employment, Workfare would in this way combat the 'bad moral effects of idleness' and the 'evil habits' of welfare dependency (SE I 369). When good times return, the habits the workers have acquired in government employment would hopefully be carried forward into new private sector openings.

Job creation, like Poor Law relief, can only be temporary: 'The permanent remedy which we are seeking cannot possibly come from this quarter' (SE II 181). Since the remuneration is not alms but the market wage it could have an undesirable impact on marriage and childbearing. Direct employment does not 'apply to the source of the specific evil' (SE II 182). The specific evil is the ratios. Poor Laws or public works, it all leads to vice and misery.

5.6 The End of the Poor Laws

Left untreated, the 'evils attendant on the poor laws seem to be irremediable' (SE I 360). Poor relief in producing poverty was 'producing effects totally opposite to those which were intended' (SE II 139). The deadweight cost was putting a damper on jobs and output: 'The farmer pays to the poor's rates, for the encouragement of a bad and unprofitable manufacture, what he would have employed on his land with infinitely more advantage to his country' (SE I 365). Poor rates had doubled in the quarter-century between the *Wealth of Nations* and the second *Essay*. It was current affairs and not just moral philosophy.

A solution had to be found. There was only one possible solution. It was 'the total abolition of all the present poor-laws' (FE 101): 'We come to the conclusion not to interfere in any respect, but to leave every man to his own free choice, and responsible only to God for the evil which he does' (SE II 119).

In the end, it would be a return to individual responsibility: 'The knowledge and prudence of the poor themselves, are absolutely the *only* means by which any general improvement in their condition can be effected. They are really the arbiters of their own destiny; and what others can do for them, is like the dust of the balance compared with what they can do for themselves' (PR 306, emphasis in original). Social causes and social duties ended the day as the dust of the balance. There was no way but the positive and the preventive checks. Blameless children would go hungry. Panhandlers would importune the affluent on the streets. Workhouses would impose a penal discipline. Only the victims of 'misfortunes which no common prudence could have avoided' (LW 14) would qualify for cash. Private charity would be the last resort. Peterloo would say what it thought of his justice. Malthus must have known that public opinion was not on his side. It did not deter him from calling for abolition because there was no other choice.

Abolition was contentious. A stricter administration of benefits might have been sufficient. Malthus nonetheless persevered in his call for repeal. In the 1806 *Essay*, he proposed that families already on support should continue to receive relief but not couples who married after the cancellation. In 1817, he was saying that it should be done but not done all at once: 'What I have really proposed….is the *gradual* and very *gradual abolition* of the poor-laws' (SE I 37, emphasis in original). In a footnote, he added that it should be 'so gradual as not to affect any individuals at present alive, or who will be born within the next two years' (SE I 374n). After that, the poor would have to live out their destiny with the 'fortitude of men and the resignation of Christians' (SE II 140). At least they would be emancipated from 'the wretched system of governing too much' (SE II 140).

References

By T. R. Malthus

(1798 [1970]). *Essay on the Principle of Population, as It Affects the Future Improvement of Society, with Remarks on the Speculations of Mr. Godwin, M. Condorcet, and Other Writers* (abbreviated as FE), ed. by A. Flew. Harmondsworth: Penguin.

(1803 et seq. [1989]). *An Essay on the Principle of Population: Or a View of Its Past and Present Effects on Human Happiness, with an Inquiry into Our Prospects Respecting the Removal of the Evils Which It Occasions* (2nd edition, 1803; further editions in 1806, 1807, 1817, 1826) (abbreviated as SE I and SE II), 2 vols., ed. by P. James. Cambridge: Cambridge University Press.

(1807). *A Letter to Samuel Whitbread, Esq, M.P., on His Proposed Bill for the Amendment of the Poor Laws* (abbreviated as LW), reprinted in *The Works of Thomas Robert Malthus*, ed. by E. A. Wrigley and D. Souden. London: Pickering and Chatto, 4, 3–19.

(1830). *A Summary View of the Principle of Population* (abbreviated as SV), in FE, supra.

Secondary Literature

Bonar, J. (1885 [1924]). *Malthus and His Work* (2nd ed.). London: Macmillan.

Marshall, T. H. (1950 [1992]). *Citizenship and Social Class*. London: Pluto Press.

Paine, T. (1792 [2000]). *The Rights of Man*. In T. Benn (Ed.), *Common Sense and the Rights of Man*. London: Phoenix Press.

Smith, A. (1759 [1966]). *The Theory of Moral Sentiments*. New York: Augustus M. Kelley.

Titmuss, R. M. (1968). *Commitment to Welfare*. London: Allen & Unwin.

6

Balanced Growth

An economy is an organism. The parts are separate but they are also symbiotic. Population is linked to land. Agriculture is linked to industry. It is a circular flow of institutions and activities. Critical to the effective functioning of the whole is a viable balance between the evolving parts.

Malthus lived at a time when the balance of the economy was in the melting pot. Technology and capital were raising productivity in both industry and agriculture. The towns were emerging as a second economic powerhouse. Self-made capitalists were challenging the landed aristocracy for political and commercial influence. A new mix was evolving out of the old. New was good. Old was good too. Malthus had a foot in each camp. His divided loyalties underlie his discussion of the balance between the primary and secondary sectors.

6.1 The Surplus

The debate was framed by Adam Smith. He saw exploitation in every hedgerow that partitioned the commonwealth: 'As soon as the land of any country has all become private property, the landlords, like all

D. Reisman, *Thomas Robert Malthus*, Great Thinkers in Economics,
https://doi.org/10.1007/978-3-030-01956-3_6

other men, love to reap where they never sowed, and demand a rent even for its natural produce' (Smith 1776 [1961]: I 56). David Ricardo continued the practice of treating rent as a monopoly surplus. It is 'advantageous only to the landlord' but 'proportionately injurious to the consumer' (Ricardo 1821 [1951–1955]: 400). Rent, Ricardo said, is a demand-driven transfer that 'adds nothing to the resources of the country' (Ricardo 1821 [1951–1955]: 400). It is an unearned acknowledgment of a fixed quantity that, high rent or zero rent, has no supply-price.

Ricardo felt that the land per se made no independent contribution to the nation's value-added. Malthus approached the factor land from a different perspective. Concentrating on Smith's 'natural produce', Malthus proclaimed that the land was unique because, alone among the economic inputs, it was 'a bountiful gift of Providence' (PR 226). Nature joins forces with capital and labour to meet the basic needs of a growing population.

The French Physiocrats were the original *économistes*. Writing mainly between 1750 and 1770, they had said that land was the sole source of new value. Malthus came under the influence of French authors like Quesnay, DuPont de Nemours and Mirabeau. In Britain, there was William Spence who described trade and manufacturing as a mere 'transmutation of wealth': 'Agriculture is the sole source of the revenue of a society' (Spence 1807: 40, emphasis deleted). Agriculture was the sole source but a dual economy was the precondition for the monetisation of the increment: 'In Britain, agriculture has thriven only in consequence of the influence of manufactures' (Spence 1807: 22). The same may be said of industry: 'All those countries which have abounded in manufactures, have been extensively cultivated' (Spence 1807: 26). Each sector creates a market for the other. Action is reaction even if in the last analysis the *produit net* comes exclusively from the land.

Spence took Malthus as early as 1808 to be a kindred spirit. He was convinced that 'nearly all the main tenets of the Economists, have been embraced and defended by Mr. Malthus' (Spence 1807: 24). Spence may have overestimated the debt. Malthus accepts that some of the Physiocrats' ideas are 'quite just' but dismisses others as 'preposterous and contradictory', lost in a mass of 'superincumbent error' (1815a

[1986]: 116–117). Bernard Semmel is nearer the mark than Spence when he says that Malthus was 'an agrarian economist' but probably not 'a doctrinaire physiocrat' (Semmel 1965: 523). Malthus was too much a creature of mix to be stubbornly doctrinaire about any proposition that could not be seen to be pulling its weight.

John Duncan Inverarity was a student at the East India College. The notes he took in Malthus's lectures reveal that as late as 1830 the professor was devoting considerable attention to the 'Economists' (Pullen 1981: 806–811). Malthus criticised the Physiocrats for contending that all value originated in agriculture when the truth was that the secondary sector too was contributing to the national wealth. Without industry, Malthus said, there would in England be 'only a few large proprietors living splendidly and profusely but all the rest miserably poor' (quoted in Pullen 1981: 807).

Industry, Malthus told the boys at the East India College, is not mere 'transmutation'. It is in truth 'value superadded': 'If agriculture alone be productive of wealth how would the Economists account for the many rapid and brilliant fortunes, the fruits of manufactures and commerce?' (quoted in Pullen 1981: 808). The Economists could not answer the question. The economists could: 'Although manufactures do not produce any new matter, yet…. they add a great value to what is already produced' (quoted in Pullen 1981: 810). Manufactures 'add a great value'. If they 'add a great value', they cannot be said to be unproductive.

Yet the shadow of the land is undeniably there and sometimes the substance as well. The soil is a productive input. High rent or zero rent, Malthus never compromised on that. Here is Malthus in 1803: 'In the history of the world, the nations, whose wealth has been derived principally from manufacturing and commerce, have been perfectly ephemeral beings, compared with those the basis of whose wealth has been agriculture' (SE I 395). Here is Malthus in 1817: rent is 'the surplus produce which particularly distinguishes the industry employed upon the land' (SE II 30). Here is Malthus in 1827: rent is 'that portion of the produce of land which remains to the owner after all the outgoings belonging to its cultivation are paid, including the ordinary profits of the capital employed' (DEF 109). The natural increment from the land supports the natural increase of the people. The earth adds value. The earth is good.

Malthus was at his most Physiocratic in the second edition of his *Essay*: 'Manufactures, strictly speaking, are no new production, no new creation, but merely a modification of an old one….A revenue is transferred, but not created' (SE I 391). Land, he declared in 1803, is 'the essential and permanent source of wealth', 'incontrovertibly the sole source of all riches': 'The great position of the Economists will always remain true, that the surplus produce of the cultivators is the great fund which ultimately pays all those who are not employed upon the land' (SE I 392, 393). By 1807, he was thinking that in saying 'ultimately' he had gone too far. In 1807, his 'ultimately' was downgraded to a limit that bounded a range: 'The surplus product of the cultivators measures and limits the growth of that portion of the society which is not employed upon the land' (SE I 393n).

Even in 1803, he was aware that industry and trade, productive or not, were essential to the realisation of the circular flow: 'No great surplus produce of agriculture could exist without them' (SE I 430n). Essential is not the same as 'productive'. Commerce and manufacturing, Malthus wrote in 1803, are not the causes but the 'consequences' of England's supremacy. They are the 'ornaments and embellishments' but not the 'foundations' (SE I 430n). It would be a mistake to say that manufactures are 'almost the sole cause of the wealth, power, and prosperity of England': 'They may be more justly considered as the consequences than the cause of this wealth….No error is more frequent than that of mistaking effects for causes' (SE I 395).

In the 1807 *Essay* Malthus shows signs of having softened his position on the surplus: 'Manufactures evidently form a considerable part of it; and the raw produce alone would not be an adequate representation either of its quantity or of its value' (SE II 394–395n). This would be in line with the statement he made in the *Inquiry* in 1815 that 'profits may, without impropriety, be called a surplus' (1815a [1986]: 142n). The secondary sector is said to be capable of producing a surplus. It is for all that the junior partner. Rent is 'a clear indication of a most inestimable quality in the soil, which God has bestowed on man – the quality of being able to maintain more persons than are necessary to work on it' (1815a [1986]: 122).

We are what we are because of the land. It enjoys the lexicographic priority. The 'bountiful gift of Providence' is 'the source of all power and enjoyment', without which 'there would be no cities, no military or naval force, no arts, no learning, none of the finer manufactures, none of the conveniences and luxuries of foreign countries, and none of that cultivated and polished society, which not only elevates and dignifies individuals, but which extends its beneficial influence through the whole mass of the people' (1815a [1986]: 123). Without the bountiful gift of nature, there would be no army, no industry, no trade, no universities, no painting, no 'cultivated and polished society'. Nature is the ultimate provider. Without nature our mills and our foundries would grind to a halt.

The land is nature. It is the gift of God. Land is the lead sector in the process of growth. Assessing the case for free trade in 1815, Malthus warns of the general contraction that would ripple out from any decay in farming: 'No loss, in proportion to its amount, affects the interest of the nation so deeply, and vitally, and is so difficult to recover, as the loss of agricultural capital and produce' (1815b [1986]: 165). Farmers who migrate to the towns should think of England and return to their farms.

Every citizen has a private stake in a high price of agricultural produce. It is what the Physiocrats called the *bon prix*. No capital employed in industry can reproduce itself so rapidly as a capital on the land. The same sum of money will not deliver the same stream of benefits to the investor: 'The one employed in manufactures will leave nothing behind it, while the one employed on the land will probably leave a rent of no inconsiderable value' (1815b [1986]: 168). A backward nation in search of 'real wealth and revenue' should make its farmers the cutting edge.

Agriculture is unique and necessary. Even the gift of God must, however, respect the law of proportions. A nation should have a presence in each sector but with 'neither preponderating greatly over the other' (SE II 40). Being different but equal, being 'nearly balanced' (SE II 43), the nation will then have 'the advantages of both systems' while remaining 'free from the peculiar evils which belong to each, taken separately' (SE II 40). Capital from one sector can alleviate a shortage in the other. Profit rates will converge on a single equilibrium level. It is sound market economics but it does not make the agricultural surplus a thing apart. Physiocracy by 1807 seems to have lost its primacy. There was more to wealth than land.

In 1820, however, there was the *Principles* and with it Farmer Malthus again. In 1820, returning to the thrust of the 1803 *Essay*, Malthus wrote of 'the natural pre-eminence of agriculture', 'in the first rank', 'the greatest natural capability of wealth that a country can possibly possess' (PR 39, 40, 375). The land comes first. Without food the breeding mechanism would hit the buffers of the positive checks.

Rent is a physical surplus. It shadows 'the fertility of the land'. It is also a value surplus. It rises or falls in line with market demand for 'the necessaries of life'. It is in this way that Malthus in the *Principles* brings together his theory of population with his theory of rent. Purchasing power, allowing for its distribution, 'tends strongly and constantly to give a value to this surplus by raising up a population to demand it' (PR 144). An increase in the supply of food generates an increase in the demand for food. The necessaries of life possess the peculiar quality 'of being able.... to create their own demand' (PR 139–140). It is a microeconomic sub-species of Say's Law. Growing wealth, growing population, growing rents—they all grow together.

6.2 The Primary Sector

The primary sector enjoys pride of place. Writing in 1803 Malthus was saying that there is something special about the land: 'Our commerce has not done much for our agriculture; but ....our agriculture has done a great deal for our commerce' (SE I 399). In the 1817 *Essay* he was continuing to argue that there is more to an economy than the white heat of steel: 'Commerce and manufactures are necessary to agriculture; but agriculture is still more necessary to commerce and manufactures' (SE II 29). Capital is 'more usefully employed' (FE 194) in agriculture. People 'cannot exist without the food to support them' (SE I 430n). Manufactures are the 'embellishments'. Foodstuffs are the foundation. It is the law of nature.

Logically and historically, the agricultural minimum comes first. The farms must first feed the farmers. Only later, when a tradeable surplus has been generated, can the farmers share their superfluous crops with the commercial and manufacturing population: 'No step can be taken in any other sort of industry until the cultivators obtain from the soil more than they themselves consume' (SE II 30). The surplus of provisions makes possible the release of labour for non-agricultural activity. In that way too the natural dividend is the precondition for an industrial revolution.

The transition is not a smooth one. Meat has a higher income elasticity than grain. As industry and trade advance, so labour-intensive arable gives way to labour-saving pasturage. Enclosures, adding push to pull, displace the shepherds and accelerate the internal migration (SE I 225). Economically, it is a retrograde tendency. A sheep, like a machine, only transforms existing value. Animal husbandry adds nothing new: 'A fatted beast may in some respects be considered, in the language of the French economists, as an unproductive labourer: he has added nothing to the value of the raw produce that he has consumed' (FE 188). Wealth creation aside, the conversion of tillage to sheep runs reduces the supply of grain that is essential to feed the growing population. Vice and misery become the uninvited guests at the feast.

It need not be so. 'Very great improvements in agriculture' (PR 165) are taking place in response to rising demand and rising prices: 'Inferior land may be cultivated at higher profits' (SE II 46). Because capitals employed 'skillfully and economically' have 'prodigiously increased the produce' (PR 176n), the land will be better able to satisfy the geometrical ratio.

Rising productivity is playing against diminishing returns. The two teams, unequally matched, 'do not by any means always keep pace with each other' (SE II 68–69). All things considered, the improvement in skills and complements may 'more than counterbalance the tendency of an extended cultivation and a great increase of capital to yield smaller proportionate returns' (SE II 46). The betterment may be 'so great that its limit is not easily calculated' (SE II 69). Vice and misery may be no more than a tendency law.

In the short-run science and investment may prove stronger than nature: 'No great surplus produce of agriculture could exist without them' (SE I 430). In the long run the trend will reassert itself. Inferior plots and the intensive margin will in the end be the vanishing point. Sooner or later, and it may take 'centuries', 'it is evident that both the population and produce must come to a stand' (SE II 44).

It must happen; but still it need not happen 'for a long period' (SE II 46). In 1817, referring to a country that has used up all its land, Malthus says: 'This is evidently the extreme practicable limit to the progress of population, *which no nation has ever yet reached, nor indeed ever will*' (SE II 44, emphasis added). No nation has ever been forced into zero-population-growth. In Britain at least, 'no near approach to this limit has yet been made' (SE II 69). Britain is 'far short of the utmost power of the earth to produce food' (SE II 45). Looking ahead, it can expect in several centuries to feed two or three times its present population (SE II 68). Europe as a whole is 'by no means so fully peopled as it might be' (SE I 14). It could be three centuries or more before the earth was fully cultivated and Britain sank into decline (SE I 430n). The end of history was 'necessarily at a great distance' and 'after the lapse of a great number of ages' (SE II 32).

The stationary state is not just round the corner. The apocalypse for all that may be biding its time. *No nation ever will* may not mean what it says. Nature may prove stronger than science in the end.

6.3 The Secondary Sector

Agriculture in the past had been the lead sector. An industrial revolution was making manufacturing a strong contender for the throne. Liberals and radicals welcomed the economic transformation because it was rooting out the dysfunctional survivals of the feudal *ancien régime*. Social conservatives, more cautious, expressed serious reservations about the dark, Satanic materialism that was calling into question the primacy of the tried-and-tested. Malthus, who believed in growth but also in balance, could see that both the new and the old had solid arguments on their side.

Malthus in the first *Essay* warned that the swing to industry might be too much, too fast (FE 198). Manchester might be Gibbon's *Decline* if not already Gibbon's *Fall.* Manufactured luxuries, contributing nothing to 'the society in general….only tend to gratify the vanity of a few rich people' (FE 194, 195). The 'ornamental luxuries of a rich country' add little to 'the mass of happiness' (FE 192–193). Fashions, conspicuous consumption, 'the capricious taste of man' (FE 185) cause unnecessary oscillations. They upset business forecasts.

Progress is not a one-way street. There is 'increased turbulence' in the modern sector (SE II 65, 81). There is displacement of labour when, through 'improved skill and machinery', 'the same number of hands' can produce a greater quantity of output (SE II 77). There is 'greater unhealthiness and immorality owing to a larger proportion of the population being employed in manufactories' (SE II 70).

The condition of the millworker and his family, 'even in their best state', is 'not by any means desirable' (1814 [1986]: 101). Factory operatives, 'crowded together in close and unwholesome rooms' (FE 186), are degraded into drink and dissolution. Work-functions are repetitive and monotonous. Urbanisation and mechanisation are exacting a toll. The health and virtue of the internal migrants would have been better protected if they had not been sucked into the smoke.

Malthus could see the costs as well as the benefits. He believed nonetheless that the take-off on balance was a change for the better. Commerce and manufactures are 'the most distinguishing characteristics of civilisation, the most obvious and striking marks of the improvement of society, and calculated to enlarge our enjoyment and add to the sum of human happiness' (SE I 430). Balanced diversification was improving living standards and creating new jobs.

Backward Poland was an under-developed country. Agriculture was not enough. Its people would remain forever poor so long as they were afraid to mimic the stages of successful England that had gone before: 'In this miserable state of things, the best remedy would unquestionably be the introduction of manufactures and commerce' (SE II 29). The shadow of Physiocracy is always there. The Poles should not neglect their grain. Yet the message is clear. There must be a dual economy for either sector fully to realise its potential.

6.4 The Dual Economy

Malthus treats the circular flow, on the model of Quesnay's *Tableau Economique*, as a dialogue between agriculture and industry. The two sectors are interdependent, the causality two-way. They 'act and re-act upon each other in turn' (SE II 42). Malthus was the forerunner of later theories of economic dualism such as that of Arthur Lewis (1954).

6.4.1 Reciprocal Demand

Rising incomes in urban manufacturing create a vent for food and raw materials. Wages in rural agriculture are bid up as farmers compete for labour: 'Both the profits of stock and the wages of labour will be high' (SE II 24). The secondary sector is absorbing the agricultural harvest. In that limited sense, the manufactures may have 'indirectly, if not directly, created it' (SE I 396).

Urban industry does not augment the supply of food. What it does is to exchange the cooked for the raw. The secondary sector pays for its primary produce with manufactures which, where the bundle includes farm implements, 'wonderfully increases' (PR II 27) the per acre productivity of the land. Farmers and landowners have an incentive to invest when demand is high, profits competitive and the rent residual on a rising curve.

There were no foreign donors and no inward multinationals in Malthus's time. British banks for their own part preferred self-liquidating collateral to long-lived assets. The shortage of risk capital meant that finance for development had to be internally generated from income saved out of growth. Funds had to be attracted into agriculture from urban industry and international trade. Profits generated on the land had also to be recycled.

Malthus was curious to find out 'if the agricultural capital which has so much increased the produce of this country….has been furnished chiefly by tenants or landlords' (letter from Malthus to A. Young, 1818, in Arthur Young Papers, 3. ff.187). The answer was that tenant farmers, no different from their fellow capitalists in the towns, were a saving estate. The profits they earned were the seedcorn that they ploughed back. The landlords were more of a mix. Some were spendthrift prodigals who spent freely on menials and fashion. Others were clear-headed businessmen who were co-investing with their leaseholders in order to grow their profits.

It is because of the harm it would do to this latter class of landlords that Malthus was opposed to the Physiocrats' single tax. A single tax on land would reduce the landlords' ability to contribute to improvements that would enhance the supply of food. It would also cut into the rural wages fund that keeps low-income farm-hands in work. Economic policy is social policy. It is not just the Poor Laws that improve the living standards of the poor.

The bi-sectoral economy alters the cultural fabric both in the countryside and in the towns. A widening range of 'conveniences and luxuries' makes the indolent more assiduous and more productive. By inspiring the cultivator with new tastes, the revolution of rising expectations has had the effect of enlarging the internal market. The villages as well as the cities have made consumer-led growth self-sustaining.

It has a negative effect on the geometrical ratio. In itself well-suited 'to enlarge our enjoyment' (SE I 430n), 'a taste for comforts' also brings about 'a favourable change' (SE I 388n) in the age of marriage and the number of offspring. 'The custom of enjoying conveniences and comforts' has the unintended consequence of generating 'those habits of prudential restraint' (SE II 27) which keep down the growth in population. Savings and investment create more jobs at higher wages. The proportion of the middle classes goes up. Moral restraint spreads. Smaller families mean higher standards of living. Affluence keeps the pressure on primary produce within limits. Shopping in the secondary sector is a preventive check.

All things considered, the farmer and the mill-hand should be friends. Industry and trade are precarious and uncertain. The cultivation and improvement of land, Adam Smith had said, is a better bet: 'The man who employs his capital in land, has it more under his view and command' (1776 [1961]: I 403). Smith had shown the way (SE II 70). Each sector has its own disadvantages and its own 'sudden reverses' (SE

II 43). Crop failures and industrial downturns will be less damaging in a bi-sectoral economy because the cyclical triggers will not be the same.

Agriculture and manufacturing are complements. The union of the two sectors together 'is calculated to produce the greatest national prosperity' (SE II 48). Each single sector in isolation is not.

6.4.2 A Balanced Economy

The two sectors must do more than coexist. They must also be in balance. Balance does not mean equality. While the precise proportions in a dynamic economy 'cannot be permanent', still the bias must be towards the land. It will be preferable, as a general rule, 'if the commercial part of the population never essentially exceeds the agricultural part' (SE II 43).

A country lives best where its industrial revolution does not crowd out its primary base: 'Its agriculture should keep pace with its manufactures, even at the expence of retarding in some degree the growth of manufactures' (1814 [1986]: 102). The industrial revolution is going too far: 'By encouraging the industry of the towns more than the industry of the country, Europe may be said, perhaps, to have brought on a premature old age' (FE 198). Industry carried to excess brings on early senility. A society should opt for the via media. It should not overload its green belt with production lines that uglify its quality of life.

There is agriculture and there is manufacturing. The two great departments must remain in balance. The invisible hand can only do so much. Where the self-stabilising mechanism fails to bring harmony to the circular flow, there is no alternative but to 'interrupt the natural course of things' (1814 [1986]: 102). Where Marx's 'anarchy in production' (Marx and Engels 1848 [2011]: 93) is unable to determine the proper proportions, the only solution is the philosopher-pilot's experienced nudge. What 'would not take place naturally, ought, under certain circumstances, to be maintained artificially' (SE II 63).

Market economics has a bias towards natural liberty. Restrictions are inefficient and wasteful in that they 'prevent the most profitable employment of the national capital and industry' (SE II 62).

Sometimes, however, there is a national need to target higher goals than private profit alone. To recognise the intervention point is, Malthus says, 'the most important practical question in the whole compass of political economy' (SE II 63). It is a question which cannot be ignored. A healthy balance between town and country has the character of a public good. It cannot be left to chance.

Food is life. The government must do what is needed. An 'adequate stimulus' to agriculture is 'absolutely necessary' if there is to be a balanced 'admixture' (SE II 70) of the sectors. There are regulations and there are incentives. Malthus is drawn to money rather than to law. A useful option, he says, would be premiums paid to farmers in order to ensure that agriculture is placed on a 'fair footing' (SE I 428). Supply and demand are not 'fair'. Support is essential if the market is to be made 'fair'.

Industry in Britain did not need premiums to be competitive. Industry in the catch-up countries is different: 'We should be justified in giving particular encouragement to manufactures in such countries as Poland and the southern parts of Siberia, and the same kind of encouragement to agriculture in England' (SE I 430n). The backward countries need to expand into the secondary sector. The workshop of the world needs to keep in good repair its agrarian base. Being 'fair' means being pragmatic. Circumstances are not always and everywhere the same.

Governments can protect the bi-sectoral balance by means of premiums. There are bounties and tariffs. There are the Corn Laws. Chapter 7 jumps through the hoops in the light of Malthus's recommendation that any equilibrium had to be 'fair': 'It may not appear impolitic artificially to maintain a more equal balance between the agricultural and commercial classes by restricting the importation of foreign corn, and making agriculture keep pace with manufactures' (SE II 65).

To benefit one sector is to harm the other. It is 'fair'. When England imports cheap grain from Poland, it enriches a poorer country. Free trade is aid: the world's wealth 'will not only be more rapidly increased but more equably diffused' (SE I 410). Free trade is interest: having sold cheap grain to England, agrarian Poland is better able to purchase industrial England's manufactured exports. The Corn Laws constrict the gains from free trade. Agriculture wins but industry loses. The tariff is not even-handed but still it is 'fair'. There has to be balance. There has to be food.

It is the same with the taxes levied to finance the bounties. Both sectors pay in but only the grain exporters take out. Taxes reduce purchasing power and therefore domestic demand. It is not a total loss. Diminished demand at home is counterbalanced by increased demand abroad. The manufacturers sell less because disposable income has been reduced at home. The farmers sell more because the taxpayers are subsiding their grain. It is 'fair'. There has to be food.

The agricultural surplus is the strategic hub of balanced growth. The landed classes still have a role to play. Primogeniture and entailing preserve the estates that fund employment-creation through unproductive consumption. It is a bi-sectoral economy. Even in the era of individualism, material sacrifices must be still be made in the national interest and for the collective good.

References

By T. R. Malthus

(1798 [1970]). *Essay on the Principle of Population, as It Affects the Future Improvement of Society, with Remarks on the Speculations of Mr. Godwin, M. Condorcet, and Other Writers* (abbreviated as FE), ed. by A. Flew. Harmondsworth: Penguin.

(1803 et seq. [1989]). *An Essay on the Principle of Population: Or a View of Its Past and Present Effects on Human Happiness, with an Inquiry into Our Prospects Respecting the Removal of the Evils Which It Occasions* (2nd edition, 1803; further editions in 1806, 1807, 1817, 1826) (abbreviated as SE I and SE II), 2 vols., ed. by P. James. Cambridge: Cambridge University Press.

(1814 [1986]). *Observations on the Effects of the Corn Laws, and of a Rise or Fall in the Price of Corn on the Agriculture and General Wealth of the Country*, reprinted in *The Works of Thomas Robert Malthus*, ed. by E. A. Wrigley and D. Souden. London: Pickering and Chatto, 7, 87–109.

(1815a [1986]). *An Inquiry into the Nature and Progress of Rent, and the Principles by Which It Is Regulated*, reprinted in *The Works of Thomas Robert Malthus*, ed. by E. A. Wrigley and D. Souden. London: Pickering and Chatto, 7, 115–145.

(1815b [1986]). *The Grounds of an Opinion on the Policy of Restricting the Importation of Foreign Corn*, reprinted in *The Works of Thomas Robert Malthus*, ed. by E. A. Wrigley and D. Souden. London: Pickering and Chatto, 7, 151–174.

(1820 [1989]). *The Principles of Political Economy* (abbreviated as PR), ed. by J. Pullen. Cambridge: Cambridge University Press.

(1827 [1986]). *Definitions in Political Economy, Preceded by an Inquiry into the Rules Which Ought to Guide Political Economists in the Definition and Use of Their Terms, with Remarks on the Deviation from These Rules in Their Writings* (abbreviated as DEF), reprinted in *The Works of Thomas Robert Malthus*, ed. by E. A. Wrigley and D. Souden. London: Pickering and Chatto, 8.

(1836 [1989]). *The Principles of Political Economy: The Alterations to the First Edition* (abbreviated as PR II), ed. by J. Pullen. Cambridge: Cambridge University Press.

Arthur Young Papers, British Library, Additional Manuscript Collection, 35.155.

Secondary Literature

Lewis, W. A. (1954). Economic Development with Unlimited Supplies of Labour. *Manchester School, 22*, 139–191.

Marx, K., & Engels, F. (1848 [2011]). *The Communist Manifesto*. London: Penguin Books.

Pullen, J. R. (1981). Notes from Malthus: The Inverarity Manuscript. *History of Political Economy, 13*, 794–811.

Ricardo, D. (1821 [1951–1955]). Principles of Political Economy and Taxation. In P. Sraffa & M. Dobb (Eds.), *The Works and Correspondence of David Ricardo* (11 vols., I). Cambridge: Cambridge University Press.

Semmel, B. (1965). Malthus: 'Physiocracy' and the Commercial System. *Economic History Review, 17*, 522–535.

Smith, A. (1776 [1961]). *The Wealth of Nations* (E. Cannan, Ed., 2 vols.). London: Methuen.

Spence, W. (1807). *Britain Independent of Commerce*. London: W. Savage.

7

Tariffs and Bounties

Britain had a large agricultural sector and a large landed aristocracy. It was still Mucky Billy and the Lord of the Manor even as it was Spinning Jenny and Stephenson's Rocket. Britain had a dual economy. Malthus, both a traditionalist and a moderniser, wanted to keep it that way.

Malthus was not calling for a gradual transition so much as he was speaking out for balanced growth. The sheep and the grain, the iron and the steel, all have a role to play so long as the proper proportions are maintained. We build on what we have and on what we are.

Balanced growth might be the free gift of natural law. It is automaticity and not intervention that leads the butcher, the brewer and the baker to maximise their nation's wealth even as they target their individual well-being. As it is at home, so it is abroad. The 'great general rule' can only be global freedom of trade: 'Each nation should purchase its commodities wherever they can be had the cheapest' (SE I 410).

The general rule is freedom. The real world, however, is what it is: 'It is not true that the tastes and wants of the effective demanders are always, and necessarily, the most favourable to the progress of national wealth' (SV 246). Even 'the most liberal political economist' (SE I 409) must accept that sometimes the national interest can only be assured

D. Reisman, *Thomas Robert Malthus*, Great Thinkers in Economics,
https://doi.org/10.1007/978-3-030-01956-3_7

through 'forcing some part of the industry of the country into a channel less advantageous than that in which it would run of its own accord' (SE I 428). Manufacturing can normally look after itself. Agriculture, however, is a thing apart. Food is too important to be left entirely to supply and demand.

To Malthus, the long-term ideal must be 'the most perfect freedom of trade in corn, as well as in every other commodity' (SE II 74). The practice in the imperfect here-and-now is beggar-thy-neighbour, 'essentially unsocial' (SE II 74). For the world as a whole, barrier-free exchange is the proper road to wealth and happiness. For each individual State, however, the national interest may lie not with the invisible hand but with taxes and subsidies, tariffs and bounties. Perfect freedom of trade, like Smith's Oceana or Utopia (Smith 1776 [1961]: I 493), 'can never be realized' (SE II 74). It is most of all a problem in the world market for food.

Grain 'forms one of the very few exceptions to the policy of a general freedom of trade' (letter from Malthus to Prévost, 1818, in Zinke, 1942: 177). Writing to Macvey Napier in 1821, Malthus said that the Corn Laws 'must be allowed to be an exception to the general rules of Political Economics' (letter from Malthus to Macvey Napier, 1821, Macvey Napier Papers, 2.ff.445). Free trade in food would be a recipe for disaster: 'The ruin of our agriculture would be certain' (SE I 403). Balanced growth is unlikely to survive without restriction. The natural order can let the nation down. Intervention is preferable to automaticity if the alternative is to starve.

Malthus was torn between freedom and food. Throughout the whole of his career, he seems to have been ambivalent and vacillating. His multiple and conflicting loyalties are visible in his four pamphlets on the factor land, in the successive editions of the *Essay* and in the two editions of the *Principles*. The question seems to be the same. The answer seems to evolve.

At the end of his life, Malthus may have been on the point of declaring that it had all been a will-o'-the-wisp. He may have been about to state that, food or pins, freedom of exchange is the wonder drug that keeps all the doctors away. Or he may have remained a yes-but liberal who believed to the end that food was a thing apart.

7.1 Investigation of the High Price of Provisions (1800)

In 1800, after the first *Essay* in 1798 and his visit to Scandinavia the following year, Malthus published a pamphlet entitled *An Investigation of the Cause of the Present High Price of Provisions*. Still anonymous, he is described as the author of the *Essay* and a disinterested 'lover of truth' (1800 [1986]: 6). He is said to be free of bias towards any single class.

Grain was scarce, and the price was high. The reason, Malthus said, had not been opportunistic speculation in essential staples. Corn dealers and middlemen, 'accused unjustly', are in truth 'absolutely necessary' (1800 [1986]: 6). Individual interest and social interest are the same when merchants take grain off the market in the expectation of a rise: 'The man who refuses to send his corn to market when it is £20 a load, because he thinks that in two months' time it will be at £30, if he be right in his judgement, and succeed in his speculation, is a positive and decided benefactor to the state' (1800 [1986]: 11). If he be right, he will, as Adam Smith had observed, have prevented a dearth from turning into a famine (Smith 1776 [1961]: II 38). If no corn had been withheld, the scarcity price might have risen not to £30 but to £50.

Speculation was not the disease but the cure. As for the suspension of the specie standard in 1797, it is premature to blame the banks. The depreciation of paper relative to gold is in its nature 'slow and gradual' (1800 [1986]: 16). It could not, in three years, have produced the 'sudden and extraordinary' (1800 [1986]: 16) rise in the price of necessaries that had been observed. The banks in making loans might only have been accommodating a pre-existent need. Higher prices create a need for more currency. Money issue was the effect of inflation. It was not the cause.

The real reason why grain was high was unsatisfied demand. A rise in disposable incomes was pulling up the price. It was the downside of an increase in 'the riches of the country' (1800 [1986]: 6). It was also the unwelcome consequence of ill-considered humanitarianism. Not just money wages but parish allowances were being put up in line with the cost of grain.

Morally speaking, the allowances reflect honour on 'the humanity and generosity of the higher and middle classes of society' (1800 [1986]: 9). The prosperous were willing to pay more in poor rates in order to spread the hardship more evenly. It was good morals but bad economics. The stock of grain, augmented by imported supply, was simply not able to meet the demand: 'All the provisions of the country would be consumed: and all the people would starve together' (1800 [1986]: 13).

Britain needs more grain to feed its geometrically increasing population: 'Of late years, even in the best seasons, we have not grown corn sufficient for our own consumption' (1800 [1986]: 17). It is the great advantage of high prices that they make consumers more economical in their use of grain and farmers better motivated to increase supply. The Corn Laws, by restricting imports, would have stimulated the home supply. They contribute in that way to the sustainable subsistence of the poor.

Tariffs were protecting manufactured goods. Artificially inflating the profit rates in industry, they were depriving the agricultural sector of capital. The Corn Laws would correct the inter-sectoral imbalance. It is less clear if they would arrest the rise in price. While diminishing returns are implicit in his arithmetical ratio of 1798, in the 1800 *Investigation* there is no real discussion of increasing costs on marginal land. Grain prices were rising not because of cost-push but because of demand-pull. The abolition of the Corn Laws would presumably augment the supply from abroad. On balance, however, Malthus in 1800 was neither for nor against the existing policy on grain.

7.2 Observations on the Corn Laws (1814)

In 1814, there was the *Observations on the Effects of the Corn Laws.* As in 1800, Malthus was trying to avoid any bias. Writing in 1814, he sums up the arguments 'on both sides of the question….with the strictest impartiality' (1814 [1986]: 87, 88). He then says that the best policy will always depend on the merits of the case: 'Wealth, population and power are, after all, only valuable, as they tend to improve, increase, and secure the mass of human virtue and happiness' (1814 [1986]: 101).

New in the *Observations* was the exploration, one year before Ricardo in 1815, of diminishing returns. There had been some recognition of non-constant yields in the analysis of America in 1798, but no serious exploration of the implications. Hollander says that Malthus's first clear analysis of the marginal plot came in 1813, in a letter to Francis Horner (Hollander 1997: 717, 820–821). In the *Observations* a year later he first applied the doctrine of falling yield to the case for protection.

The liberalisation of the Corn Laws, Malthus suggests, might deliver lower grain prices but not without 'throwing much poor land out of cultivation' (1814 [1986]: 96]. Domestic production would shrink and agricultural improvement wither: 'It is only by keeping the price of corn up, very considerably above the average of the rest of Europe, that we can possibly be made to grow our own consumption' (1814 [1986]: 99).

Old countries expand into less-fertile plots. Imports are an easy alternative to marginal soil: 'Few things seem less probable, than that Great Britain should naturally grow an independent supply of corn.... It would incontestably answer to us to support a part of our present population on foreign corn' (1814 [1986]: 97). As for the argument that domestic production keeps prices more stable, Malthus retorts that the contention is 'obviously not tenable': 'A free trade in corn would in all ordinary cases not only secure a cheaper, but a more steady, supply of grain' (1814 [1986]: 99). Oscillations and cobwebs can begin at home. Imported supplies can contain the amplitude of the domestic fluctuations.

In terms of comparative cost, Britain's advantage lies with manufacturing. Agriculture has 'cultivated all its good soil' (1814 [1986]: 95). It is retreating on to 'poor land, to provide for the demands of an increasing population': 'The growing price of corn therefore....is probably higher than that in the rest of Europe' (1814 [1986]: 107, 108). It does not make sense. Economically, and in line with 'the general principles of political economy', we should 'buy all our commodities where we can have them the cheapest' (1814 [1986]: 98). We should source our grain in world markets. We should shift the margin of cultivation to fertile Poland that has an absolute advantage in cheap grain. We should abandon our marshes and our barren mountain tops. Foreign is best. Our margin does not pay its way.

Free trade in grain would arbitrage the prices. It would also put money in the hands of corn-exporting nations. Buyers as well as sellers, they 'would evidently have their power of purchasing our commodities increased, and would thus contribute more effectually to our commercial and manufacturing prosperity' (1814 [1986]: 99). Trade goes both ways. Foreign suppliers are fully aware of Britain's 'extraordinary skill, capital and machinery' (1814 [1986]: 105). In order to buy, however, they must first sell. Agricultural protection is counterproductive. A decline in trade affects our economy as a whole—'in which case our agriculture itself would soon suffer' (1814 [1986]: 106).

It is straightforward market economics: 'No purchase is ever made, either at home or abroad, unless that which is received is, in the estimate of the purchaser, of more value than that which is given' (1814 [1986]: 98). Everyone benefits from the freedom to exchange. The Corn Laws interfere with that freedom. All that remains is for Malthus to declare unambiguously that the Corn Laws like the Poor Laws must go. The reader of the *Observations* will wait in vain for that declaration. Malthus, no great admirer of the Corn Laws, knows that there are two sides to the coin.

Agriculture is not the whole of the economy and the Corn Laws not the sum total of its distortions. As in the *Investigations*, Malthus propounds a theory of second best. So long as manufacturing is protected, it would be inefficient and inequitable for agriculture to be deprived of its shield. In the absence of countervailing power 'an unnatural quantity of capital' would be 'directed towards manufactures and commerce and taken from the land' (1814 [1986]: 104). The agricultural sector would have to purchase the products of the industrial sector at 'a kind of monopoly price' (1814 [1986]: 104). It would have to sell its own output at whatever the traffic will bear. Political concessions will have selectively twisted the domestic terms of trade. Free trade ought to mean the 'natural level' and 'impartial justice' (1814 [1986]: 104). It should never be used as a lever 'to depress the cultivation of the land below other kinds of industry' (1814 [1986]: 104).

Internationally too, there is a need for a balance of distortion and a multilateral quid pro quo. It would not be a sensible move for Britain to abandon its protective Laws where its foreign partners were not responding with a bonfire of their own. The 'simple and obvious way of restoring things to their natural level' (1814 [1986]: 107) would be not to abolish the Corn Laws but rather to deploy the nation's taxes and subsidies in such a way as to prevent the foreigner from stealing market share. As Adam Smith says: 'When some tax is imposed at home upon any produce of [domestic industry]….it seems reasonable that an equal tax should be imposed upon the like produce of [foreign industry]' (Smith 1776 [1961]: I 487). The Corn Laws were not just a bulwark but a bargaining chip. Restrictions are in investment in the freedom of trade. They can be seen as a necessary step on the road to the invisible hand.

Economics aside, there is the nation. The *Observations* is concerned not just with a level playing field but with sovereign survival in troubled times. Population, exports and prices had all been going up. One cause had been the well-deserved 'success of our inventions for saving labour', but crucially, there had also been the 'unusual monopoly of the commerce of Europe, which has been thrown into our hands by the war' (1814 [1986]: 105). Britain as an island nation had been able to profit from the disruption abroad. The windfall would not last forever. The Corn Laws might be essential for the balance of payments once the warring states had reopened for trade.

Peacetime or wartime, the people must eat. The Corn Laws, by keeping prices high, directly encourage cultivation at home. The margin is a national treasure precisely because food security is more important than wealth. The French had already restricted food exports. A country which is dependent on food imports could be left without 'essential supplies….at the time of its greatest need' (1814 [1986]: 100). Even marginal land is better than that.

The danger is not imminent: 'Such a risk is not very great' (1814 [1986]: 100). Even Britain's enemies would not want to lose the revenues from exports. A country willing to pay 'would not be likely to starve' (1814 [1986]: 100). Yet statesmen, at home or abroad, are not always rational. History shows that governments frequently act from 'passion rather than interest', and that a 'wide-wasting calamity' (1814 [1986]: 100) can then be the result. The probability is low, but the loss would be catastrophic. Trapped in minimax, the Corn Laws would be the better bet.

Yet the fact remains that the grain prices are artificially inflated. Workers must pay more for their bread. Opponents of the Corn Laws said that the tariffs were a regressive tax on the lower classes and on the capitalists who employed them. Malthus replied that they were not a tax but a subsidy. It is the Corn Laws and not the Poor Laws that benevolent reformers ought to campaign to protect.

Living standards are unaffected once compensation is adjusted upward in line with food. The de facto indexation is not one-for-one: 'The whole of the wages of labour can never rise and fall in proportion to the variations in the price of grain.... Corn and labour rarely keep an even pace together' (1814 [1986]: 89, 90). Nonetheless, the price of corn has 'a powerful influence' (1814 [1986]: 98) on the corn wage that is paid. When the Corn Laws put up the price, the corn wage will ultimately follow it up.

Higher grain prices mean more jobs on the land. Sticky wages if anything expand the opportunities. The abolition of the Corn Laws would destroy openings because domestic agriculture would contract. The retention of the Corn Laws despite the rise in wages that it would occasion would deliver a knock-on benefit to industry. A thriving agricultural sector creates new demand for manufactured goods and for manufacturing labour. Where industry experiences increasing returns, the real wage goes up even if the money wage lags behind the artificially inflated price of wheat.

Bread is not the only consumable. As productivity rises and prices in the secondary sector fall, ordinary people will have higher real incomes to spend on 'conveniences and luxuries'. Middle-class living standards might lead to middle-class moral restraint. Higher real incomes might, of course, lead to earlier marriage. Since the food supply is simultaneously going up, the pressure of population is not an immediate threat.

The Corn Laws ought to stay. The Corn Laws ought to go. The *Observations* promised no more than 'a fair review of both sides of the question' (1815b [1986]: 151). Malthus made clear in 1814 that he was not planning to say 'on which side there is the greatest balance of good with the least alloy of evil' (1815b [1986]: 151, 152). Perhaps that was because he genuinely had not made up his mind. In 1815, he at last put his cards on the table. Doing so, Bernard Semmel says, he 'proclaimed the futility of making England the workshop of the world and the common carrier of the nations' (Semmel 1965: 533). Industry should not be allowed to crowd out the very real claims of land. It was Farmer Malthus. Protection to agriculture was not something on which even the industrial hegemon could afford to compromise. The Corn Laws had to stay.

7.3 Grounds of an Opinion (1815)

In 1815, there was *The Grounds of an Opinion on the Policy of Restricting the Importation of Foreign Corn*. Malthus said that the policy was good. Open markets, 'in the actual state of Europe', were not the answer: 'A system of restrictions so calculated as to keep us, in average years, nearly independent of foreign supplies of corn, will more effectually conduce to the wealth and prosperity of the country' (1815b [1986]: 160). As with the mercantilists' Navigation Acts, the national interest must be put before the private stake (1815b [1986]: 173). *We* comes before *I*. The consistent liberal is also a conservative.

The Corn Laws in 1815 were, more than virtually any other issue, what divided the classes and the ideologues. The Whigs wanted to open up. The Tories wanted to protect. Then, there was Malthus who in the *Grounds* declared himself 'in favour of some restrictions on the importation of foreign corn' (1815b [1986]: 160).

Malthus was careful not to reduce a complex of costs and benefits to a simplified either/or. If we opt for the unfettered admission of foreign corn, 'we must not be disturbed at the depressed state, and diminished produce of our home cultivation' (1815b [1986]: 172). If we retain our import restrictions, 'we must not be disturbed at a progressive rise in the price of grain' (1815b [1986]: 172). If our grain goes up, 'we must not be disturbed at the occasional loss or diminution of a continental market for some of our least peculiar manufactures, owing to the high price of our labour' (1815b [1986]: 172–173).

It is a well-worn conflict of objectives. Foreigners will always purchase non-replicable exports with a low price-sensitivity of demand. Our sellers can gouge a quasi-rent out of the inelasticity of supply.

A large part of a nation's output must, however, fight for market share in global competition. If prices rise, then exports fall. England as the leading industrial power would hold on to her customers even if the prices of her manufactured goods went up. The primary sector was more vulnerable. There was a strong case for the protection of Britain's agriculture lest Poland or France depopulates her countryside.

Protection is a stimulus to production and improvement. The resource cost per acre will fall since a higher reward to machinery and management is an incentive to boost total factor productivity: 'The quantity of additional produce would be immense' (1815b [1986]: 161). The population is rising. An increase in the supply of food will postpone the vice and misery of the arithmetical ratio.

The Corn Laws protect the quantity and stabilise the price. Capital and labour are retained on the land that might otherwise have migrated to manufacturing: 'No loss…affects the nation so deeply, and vitally' (1815b [1986]: 154). Some of the investment might even have gone abroad: 'The principal effect…..of low profits, is to dispose people to place their funds in other countries' (letter from Malthus to Prévost, 1818, in Zinke, 1942: 178). Farm labourers, thrown out of work, would be 'miserably poor' (1815b [1986]: 162). It would be different under the Corn Laws. Agriculture would enjoy an 'unimpaired' and 'steady' home demand (1815b [1986]: 166, 167). Fluctuations would be less. Food security would be assured. It would be worth paying a higher price for bread.

Malthus in the *Observations* had said that free trade could stabilise the market for grain. In the *Grounds*, he explained that he was still in favour of free trade but only in favour of trade that was '*really free*' (1815b [1986]: 156, emphasis in original). Britain's own policy is not enough. 'It is entirely out of our power….to obtain a free trade in grain' (1815b [1986]: 156).

Nice guys finish last. Foreign countries are obstructing their own exports and imports: 'It is not in the power of any single nation to secure the freedom of the foreign trade in corn' (1815b [1986]: 159). Genuinely free trade is the *optimum optimorum*, but protection is the best-*attainable* optimum so long as the nations cannot reach consensus on a common code. We cannot pursue our first-best principles—'I protest most entirely against the doctrine'—if there is not 'the concurrence of many others' (1815b [1986]: 158, 159). Bad neighbours are an argument in Britain's Corn Laws. The French are a pill at the best of times. Genuinely free trade is not possible so long as their grain exports cut off at a ceiling price. The French are making their own harvest failure into their neighbours' public bad. The Corn Laws are Britain's Great Wall against contagions like that.

Yet the fact is that French grain costs half as much as its British equivalent. Diminishing returns to marginal plots were only 'partially counteracted' by the 'prodigious increase of produce' (1815b [1986]: 160, 161n) that had been the consequence of high farming. Logically speaking, a country which has an absolute disadvantage in one line but an absolute advantage in another should specialise in the area of activity in which it excels. By that standard, Britain ought to become a net importer of grain because her second-rate home soils were no match for the foreigner's competitive price.

Malthus says that global prosperity would be at its maximum if 'every nation were to devote itself particularly to those kinds of industry and produce, to which its soil, climate, situation, capital, and skill, were best suited; and were then *freely to exchange* these products with each other' (1815b [1986]: 158, emphasis in original). The global division of labour would be the 'most efficacious mode' (1815b [1986]: 158). We, however, must start from here. Until the countries bargain collectively for multilateral free trade, each country must look after its own. The World Trade Organization was yet to come. At least for now, Malthus said, it would be wise to retain the Corn Laws.

Cheap grain, absolute advantage and the inter-sectoral allocation of capital are central to Malthus's legitimation of agricultural protection. By themselves, however, they are only the means to an end. The meta-principle had to be subjective utility, self-perceived. The Corn Laws ensure that 'the greatest portion of wealth and happiness may be steadily secured to the largest mass of the people' (1815b [1986]: 162). To a utilitarian like Malthus, that was enough.

If it could be shown that free trade is of especial advantage to the lower classes, 'I should consider the question as at once determined in favour of such a measure' (1815b [1986]: 162). In fact, the evidence points in the opposite direction: 'Very much the largest mass of the people, and particularly of the industrious orders of the state, will be more injured than benefited by the measure' (1815b [1986]: 171). The Corn Laws are the workers' choice. The Corn Laws are social democracy in action.

In a dynamic kaleidoscope, there will always be winners and losers. The libertarian may call it fair that the chips should lie where they fall. The utilitarian must rank the outcomes in terms of their utility coefficients. Malthus not only ranks the outcomes but also ranks the classes. There is sociology as well as psychology in his approach to the kaleidoscope of change. His multidisciplinary perspective is well illustrated by his discussion of a fall in price.

The deflation in the post-war recession was an indicator to him of what the repeal of the Corn Laws might entail. A fall in price, whether the effect is 'temporary' or 'lasting', has a 'powerful influence on the distribution of property' (1815b [1986]: 168). Deflation benefits fixed income recipients such as holders of the national debt. In that way, it skews purchasing power towards one class of citizens but victimises another: 'The stockholder would be benefited unfairly' (1815b [1986]: 169).

Talking statics, it is injustice. Talking dynamics, it is inefficiency as well. The creditor not only draws an unearned usufruct from falling prices but also does so 'at the expense of the industrious classes of society, and consequently at the expense of the wealth and prosperity of the whole country' (1815b [1986]: 169). The rentier scores a gain at the expense of the workers and the 'industrious middle orders' (1815b [1986]: 170). It is a gain that cannot be defended. As compared with the 'industrious classes', the interests of the debt-holders are 'not so closely interwoven with the welfare of the state' (1815b [1986]: 168). Just as important, the debt-holders who enjoy the utility are 'small in number' (1815b [1986]: 168). Even if their cardinal utility is considerably in excess of their headcount, a minority will not be missed.

The repeal of the Corn Laws will trigger a similar redistribution of income. One-half of all profit-earners in Britain are farmers or are dependent on farmers (1815a [1986]: 165). They will lose their capital if they have to sell on a falling market. There are the agricultural labourers whose jobs will be sucked abroad. There are the manufacturing labourers who depend for continued employment on demand generated in the primary sector. There are the landowners whose rents provide 'the most steady home demand for the manufactures of the country, the most effective fund for its financial support' (1815b [1986]: 167–168). It all adds up to a sizeable mass of utility that would be destroyed if the Corn Laws were to go.

Revolutions are always disruptive. 'The whole of the internal trade must severely suffer, and the wealth and enjoyments of the country be decidedly diminished' (1815b [1986]: 166). The subjective dimension should not be neglected: 'The transfer of wealth and population will be slow, painful, and unfavourable to happiness' (1815b [1986]: 167). Efficiency and utility speak with a single voice. The Corn Laws must stay.

7.4 An Inquiry into Rent (1815)

The *Inquiry into the Nature and Progress of Rent* was published in the same year as the *Grounds*. It was the same year as the *Essay on the Application of Capital to Land* by Sir Edward West, the *Essay on the External Corn Trade* by Robert Torrens and David Ricardo's *Essay on the Influence of a Low Price of Corn on the Profits of Stock* which, extended in 1817 in the *Principles,* became the central reference in the classical theory of rent. All the authors were building on Adam Smith and on James Anderson's *Enquiry into the Nature of the Corn Laws*, published the following year. Wartime food inflation had triggered a national debate on distribution and diminishing returns. It complemented but did not duplicate the ongoing discussion of imported grain as a safety valve and a solvent of tension.

7.4.1 Rents and Profits

Rent, Malthus says, is the difference between price and cost. It is 'that portion of the value of the whole produce which remains to the owner of the land, after all the outgoings belonging to its cultivation, of whatever kind, have been paid, including the profits of the capital employed, estimated according to the usual and ordinary rate of the profits of agricultural stock at the time being' (1815a [1986]: 115–116). Explicit costs like wages must be settled at the going market rate. Opportunity costs like profits must be covered. At the zero-rent margin, there will after that be nothing left. On the intra-marginal plot, there will be a surplus. That residual, that excess of price above cost, is retained by the landowner as rent.

The giants in the earth labour alongside the workers and the machines. Following in the footsteps of Smith and Anderson, Malthus traces the origin of rent to 'a most inestimable quality in the soil, which God bestowed on man – the quality of being able to maintain more persons than are necessary to work it' (1815a [1986]: 122). The giants in the earth are willing to support even those who have no direct link with the soil. The surplus is not alienation or theft but the gift of bountiful nature. It is 'quite unconnected with monopoly' (1815a [1986]: 119).

Nature is at the root of supply. Nature is also the cause of demand. When the subsistence is there, the population will expand. Malthus draws attention to 'that quality peculiar to the necessaries of life of being able to create their own demand, or to raise up a number of demanders in proportion to the quantity of necessaries produced' (1815a [1986]: 119).

Supply creates its own demand. Where there is a farm surplus, the census of consumers will go up. The effect in turn becomes the cause. As the population increases and the competition for food becomes more intense, the rising price of grain will give farmers a financial incentive to expand their production. They will do so both at the extensive margin, through 'bringing fresh land under cultivation', and at the intensive margin, by 'rendering the old much more productive' (1815a [1986]: 126). Sometimes opting for 'the progressive cultivation of new land' (1815a [1986]: 130), sometimes preferring the progressive improvement of 'what is already cultivated' (1815a [1986]: 128), farmers are faced with the challenge of mediocre crops on heterogeneous land. More means worse.

Plots are differentiated by soil and situation, access to infrastructure and proximity to markets. Returns vary because of the 'comparative scarcity of the most fertile land' (1815a [1986]: 119). Prices do not: 'There cannot be two prices for corn of the same quality' (1815a [1986]: 134). On the inferior plots, farmers' profits are just sufficient to retain them in agriculture. On the intra-marginal plots, there will initially be a super-normal jackpot. It will not last. In the long run, the leases will be renegotiated and excess profits absorbed into rent.

Differential rent is the economic reward that ensures a single rate of profit. It is a plastic catch-all that tracks but does not shape the outcome of demand relative to supply. In the 1803 *Essay*, Malthus had assigned an active role to rent: 'One of the principal ingredients in the price of British corn is the high price of land' (SE I 417). By the 1806 *Essay*, making rent not the cause but the consequence, he was asserting that land does no more than take what it is given: 'Universally, it is price that determines rent, not rent that determines price' (SE I 425). Differential rent in the *Inquiry* is no more than what differential demand throws up.

The growth in numbers and in incomes comes first. Rents are collected afterwards. On the least-productive land, they are not collected at all. Malthus in his evidence to the 1827 Committee on Emigration explained the causal sequence in the following way: 'The cultivating of poor lands is not the cause of the rise of rents; the rise of the price of produce compared with the costs of production, which is the cause of the rise of rents, takes place first, and then such rise induces the cultivation of the poorer land' (1827: 321).

Rents are adjusted upwards when the leases expire. In the short run, there is a windfall gain. When prices rise and rents are fixed, there is a redistribution of purchasing power to the farmer-capitalist. It is a form of forced saving. The delay will 'give a little time for the accumulation of capital on the land' (1815a [1986]: 143). A renegotiation lag stimulates investment and with it output: 'Temporary high profits are a more frequent and powerful source of accumulation, than either an increased spirit of saving, or any other cause that can be named' (1815a [1986]: 143–144). Landed aristocrats, relying on 'careless and uninterested bailiffs' (1815a [1986]: 143), risk ruin because they do not watch over their capital with care. Farmer capitalists are more likely to make improvements that increase the quantity and reduce the price of grain.

Some capital is attracted into agriculture from urban manufacturing and commerce. Even more has fallen close to the tree: 'By far the greater part is supposed to have been generated on the soil' (1815a [1986]: 128). High profits in the war years had 'afforded the means' for accumulation that had been both 'rapid' and 'advantageous' (1815a [1986]: 128). Long leases would give the farmers the security they need for long-term investment.

7.4.2 The Real Wage

Malthus in the *Inquiry* discusses the economics of the farmer-capitalists and of the landowning elite. There are, however, three classes on the land. There are also the agricultural labourers. Their fate too is closely linked to the price of grain. Their future too will be formed and deformed by the tariff on corn.

When the economy is stagnant, the average wage will be trapped at the subsistence minimum. Employment is capital-constrained. The population is multiplying to the limits of the positive checks. It is of little benefit to the labourer that the demand for grain is also stagnant and the price of grain correspondingly low: 'Among the labouring classes of different countries, none certainly are as wretched as those, where the demand for labour, and the population are stationary, and yet the prices of provisions extremely low' (1815a [1986]: 139–140). Cheap grain is not enough for a good life where capital is deficient and work is hard to find.

When the economy is growing, the position will be different. The increase in population and effective demand will be driving the production of food on to the intensive and the extensive margin. Incremental returns are becoming less. The price of grain is going up. Ceiling capacity at the stationary state is emerging as a real possibility: 'The high price of corn, occasioned by the difficulty of procuring it, may be considered as the ultimate check to the indefinite progress of a country in wealth and population' (1815a [1986]: 140).

The price of corn is high. It is not a hardship to the labourer but instead 'a positive and unquestionable advantage' (1815a [1986]: 138).

Corn is the staple food of the labourer. Without their basic provisions, the poor-in-work would be too debilitated to add value. Precisely because grain makes up such a large proportion of their budget, money wages are by custom and convention being adjusted upwards in line with the price of bread (SE II 83).

Only in a 'very rare case' (1815a [1986]: 127) will the uprating be instantaneous. Normally, there will be a 'period of some continuance' (1815a [1986]: 127) in which the agricultural capitalist will be able to pad his profits with yesterday's wage. The windfall claw-back is not a lasting transfer. The transition completed, the workers will be in receipt of full or at least partial compensation for diminishing returns in the growing of food.

It is compensation, but it is betterment as well. Urban or rural, the labourer is living in a bi-sectoral economy. Agriculture is cursed with the intensive and extensive margin. Industry, however, is blessed with economies of scale. Growing efficiency in the secondary sector tends to 'reduce the price of manufactured compared with raw produce' (SE II 41). The internal terms of trade turn against the factories and in favour of the farms.

Due to new technology and 'a more judicious division of labour', the real price in the secondary sector 'is almost constantly diminishing' (1815a [1986]: 126, 137). The living standards of the working classes are rising not in spite of but because of the tendency for 'each fresh addition to the raw produce of the country' to be 'purchased at a greater cost' (1815a [1986]: 135). The wage adjustment only partially reflects the basketful of commodities that is being consumed: 'The whole of a labourer's earnings is not spent in food' (SE II 24). The result, in the bi-sectoral economy, is that 'the condition of the labouring classes of society is the best' (SE II 24). Malthus can thus afford to be on the side both of the Corn Laws and of the working class. Even among capitalists, one-half of British profit-earners were farmers or the dependents of farmers (1815b [1986]: 165). After the workers, they were the largest single class. Protection means the greatest happiness of the greatest number. As he did in the *Grounds of an Opinion*, Malthus reaches the conclusion in the *Inquiry* that the Corn Laws are the working man's friend.

7.5 The *Essay on Population*

The market economy is built around supply and demand. Sometimes the self-regulating thermostat will not be enough. Where the market fails, it is the duty of the State to rescue its citizens from 'the most profitable employment of the national capital and industry' (SE II 62) that nonetheless leaves them hungry and insecure.

An essay on population must by necessity be an essay on subsistence. The first *Essay* concentrated on demand. By the second essay, Malthus was moving on to supply.

In the 1798 *Essay*, Malthus recognised that some countries in Europe were 'thinly populated', not yet 'extremely crowded and populous': 'Instead of doubling their numbers every twenty-five years they require three or four hundred years' (FE 89, 110). High wages and early marriages had not yet, by increasing the demand for food, depleted the domestic staple. The worst had not yet happened.

In the succeeding editions of his book, he returned repeatedly to the assertion that the geometrical ratio had not yet eaten its way through the grain. Britain, he said in 1817, had 'sufficient unexhausted fertility to allow of a very great increase in population' (SE II 68). The country could support not only its current population but 'double, and in time, perhaps even treble the number' (SE II 69). Agriculture in Britain, far from being cropped out, was already supporting 'a much larger portion of our population….than at any former period of our history' (SE II 71). While there are more diners, there is also more bread.

An exhausted nation would have 'no other means of increasing its population than by the admission of foreign grain' (SE II 68). The foreign margin is the reservoir in waiting: 'We see in almost every part of the world vast powers of production which are not put into production' (letter from Malthus to Ricardo, 1821, in Ricardo IX: 10). Imported grain can meet a future shortage. There is no lasting shortage at present. In Britain, due to steady improvement in per acre productivity, the physical limit is not in sight.

The betterment in farming is likely to continue 'for a considerable time', but the precondition is profit: 'New lands cannot be brought into cultivation, nor great improvements made on the old, without a high money price of grain' (SE II 69). Market demand is essential if the farmer-entrepreneur is to sink his savings in enhancement. In the *Inquiry* Malthus had said that, at least in 1815, scarcity prices were 'rarely found sufficient to balance the necessity of applying to poorer lands' (1815a [1986]: 137). A rising headcount and rising incomes did not by themselves provide an adequate incentive. A foreign vent was essential if food prices were to attract farmers on to the margin.

The export market gives 'a considerable stimulus....to every kind of improvement on the land' (1815a [1986]: 126). The reluctance to explore the intensive and extensive options, the knee-jerk propensity to farm even the most fertile land with 'inferior machines' (1815a [1986]: 134), would be 'greatly modified' (PR 194) if the market could be broadened so that the net revenues of the farmers could be driven up.

It is an argument for a tariff on imported grain. It is also an argument for an export bounty. Although it is not free market economics, a subsidy is simple common sense. It is 'a matter of the very highest importance, whether we are fully supplied with food': 'If a bounty would produce such a supply, the most liberal political economist might be justified in proposing it; considering food as a commodity distinct from all others, and pre-eminently valuable' (SE I 409). An inflated export demand would give domestic producers an incentive to expand their acreage.

Bounties, Malthus said in the 1803 *Essay*, were a form of insurance. They would lead to stockpiles of reserves, 'large public granaries' upon which a loss-averting nation could draw in time of need: 'It is impossible always to be secure of having enough if we have not, in general, too much....It must be a point of the first consequence to the permanent prosperity of any country to be able to carry on the export trade of corn' (SE I 407). It is minimax. To protect itself against a possible emergency, a nervous nation must plan for an over-supply. The foreign demand is the hedge that takes up the overhang.

The implicit assumption is that the foreigners will be ready and willing. Malthus in the 1817 *Essay* suggests two reasons why it might not be so. First, the safety valve presupposes that home and foreign harvests do not move in step. Malthus concedes that it will not be possible to dispose of an excess in a customer country if that country has an unwanted excess of its own (SE II 52). Second, there is an unrealistic assumption about the elasticity of demand. If the export price is reduced by the bounty, then the export quantity must increase at least in proportion in order to keep the nation's export earnings constant. Malthus says that this is something 'I very much doubt' (SE II 50).

Self-sufficiency to Malthus dictates a precautionary excess. The objective is to 'produce a growth of corn in the country considerably above the wants of the actual population' (SE I 410). Unneeded supply should be dumped abroad. Should there be a shortfall at home, the grain can be retained and the bounty itself immediately suspended.

The wily foreigner will be scheming to retaliate in kind. Foreign suppliers will seek to flood British markets when crops are good. They will hoard food at home when their own harvest is thin (SE II 68). It is not necessary to be a mercantilist to recognise the threat or to understand the remedy. A subsidy to exports backed up by a tariff on imports would improve Britain's bargaining position.

Bounties 'unquestionably encourage an increased growth of corn' (SE II 60). They also act as buffers to modulate the fluctuations in price. Inflated demand backed up by stable prices would have the downstream consequence of attracting 'a greater quantity of the national capital to the land' (SE II 56). Long-term investment would mean cheaper bread through improving the yields and offsetting the tendency to the margin. It was not just in industry but in agriculture that cost-cutting was taking place. Diminishing returns might give way to increasing returns once the drains and the crop-rotation had raised the productivity of the farms: 'There is even a chance....of a diminution in the real price of corn, owing to the extension of those great improvements' (1815b [1986]: 160–161). The price falls but the profit does not. It is a win-win scenario.

There are implications for the poor. The lower deciles, allowance made for the informal uprating in their pay, are particularly exposed to a rise in the price of food. There are implications for the rich. Landowners will devote land to food that they could have committed to pasturage or leisure. There are also implications for balanced growth. In a bi-sectoral economy that is developing its modern sector, unnecessary fluctuations in agriculture will have undesirable consequences for up-and-coming manufactures.

Ricardo had envisaged that England would exploit her comparative advantage in manufactures to pay for cheap grain from abroad.

Malthus was unwilling for his nation to put all its eggs in one basket. There were always trace elements of Physiocracy and a guarded respect for the landowning elite. There was always a war-seasoned awareness that Britain's food could not be bartered away for textbook nostrums. Malthus, more fundamentally, was never in sympathy with the dogmatic either/or. It is all a question of balance and mix. Britain must have a solid agricultural base. It must have its manufactures as well.

'Manufactures', Malthus says, 'cannot stir a single step without their agricultural pay-masters, either at home or abroad' (SE I 404). Unrestricted trade would leave prices and quantities at the mercy of foreign merchants answering to foreign statesmen: 'It is the height of folly and imprudence to have these pay-masters at a great distance' (SE I 404). Scarcity prices soak up purchasing power that in a bi-sectoral economy is required for industrial expansion. Bounties, working together with the Corn Laws, have implications for the level of total demand. They are more than a topic in farming economics alone.

Malthus was in favour of bounties. Adam Smith was not. Smith had no objection to public policy where the market was seen to underperform. He called the mercantilists' Navigation Acts, which had restricted British exports to more costly British ships, 'the wisest of all the commercial regulations of England' (Smith 1776 [1961]: I 487). He was not willing, however, to make an exception for export premiums. Tariffs distort trade but at least they amplify the tax take. Bounties both distort trade and draw down the exchequer reserve. Bounties, Smith complained, make our citizens pay higher taxes for a reduced supply (Smith 1776 [1961]: II 13). He could see no public interest in that.

Malthus in the *Essay* replied that Smith's argument was 'essentially erroneous' (SE II 53). Smith, he felt, had failed to appreciate that food is a thing apart. The people must be fed. They must be fed with staple foodstuffs grown principally by their fellow countrymen: 'Territories of a certain extent must ultimately in the main support their own population' (SE II 64).

Food is an exception. Taking the spillovers into account, the social optimum and the private optimum are not the same. The natural order is not enough. The State must get involved.

7.6 The Land and the *Principles*

By 1820, the story had largely been told. Sections from the *Inquiry* were carried forward into the *Principles*. The arguments in the *Essay*, the *Grounds* and the *Observations* were carefully explained but seldom altered. The *Principles* on land was consolidation and not radical change.

7.6.1 Free Trade in Grain

Food remained an exception. Adam Smith had asserted that a country's own farmers and landlords would not be injured by the free importation of primary produce from abroad (Smith 1776 [1961]: I 483). His argument was 'unquestionably too strong' (PR 218). Treating the unprecedented fall in grain prices in the early eighteenth century as the proof that grain is generally cheaper in rich countries, Smith had drawn 'inferences from actual appearances, not warranted by general principles' (PR 21). By the early nineteenth century, grain had become very expensive. Smith had been taken in by a freak coincidence. It had led to a serious underestimation of the danger from the open market. In Smith's time, imported grain was only 1/517th of total supply. In Malthus's time, it was 1/10th. Smith had not recognised the threat. Imported grain can 'essentially interfere with the home growth' (PR 22).

Were any fall to be prolonged, rents would also go down. Improvement would stagnate. Marginal plots would be abandoned. Capital would migrate to manufacturing. The nation would have nothing in reserve against bad harvests, political turmoil or the geometrical ratio which had not gone away.

As always, there was the rule and there was the exception. The rule was freedom of trade: 'Our commerce has been much impaired by unnecessary restraints….A much greater freedom might be given to foreign commerce' (PR 508). The exception was food. For reasons of 'health, happiness, or safety….we should permanently grow nearly our own consumption of food' (PR 508).

The 'natural course' (PR II 139) would have meant lower living standards and inadequate supplies. The artificial course had meant higher profits and improved yields. Governmental regulations, 'instead of impeding the progress of wealth and population....may have decidedly and essentially promoted it' (PR 223). Farming is the exception to the rule. Agriculture is 'the only considerable case where practically.... the interest of the individual and of the state are not proportioned to each other' (PR 218). Private profit does not capture the full social benefit. Tariffs and bounties—taxes and subsidies—divert the course of economic history into a channel where it would not, unaided, have gone.

7.6.2 Rise and Fall

The 'doctrine of the gradation of soil' must be 'modified and limited by other causes' (PR II 176). Improvements can 'overcome the effect of taking poorer land into cultivation' (PR 323). Although 'it would be quite impossible to say before hand', the amelioration is 'likely to be of frequent recurrence' (PR 324). It will proceed uninterrupted 'for a great length of time' (PR 336). Yield per acre might continue to rise 'for twenty or thirty' or even 'for hundreds of years' (PR 313, 332). Depleted land might be revivified into 'fresh land' (PR 170).

Farm machinery is costing less because the machine-makers are enjoying scale economies. The workforce is being trimmed: 'The last land taken into cultivation in 1813 did not require more labour to work it than the last land improved in the year 1790' or even in the year 1727 (PR 169, 324). Higher output per acre coupled with a lagged adjustment in rent is leaving the farmer capitalist with a short-run bonus that can be reinvested in manure and steam (PR 202). The evidence is all around. The economy has demonstrably not been forced on to the low-yield margin. The population is growing at a geometrical ratio. So, conceivably, is the supply of food.

Improvements in agriculture will not only 'prevent profits from falling' but will actually 'allow of a considerable rise' (PR 313). Technology may 'fully counterbalance, or even more than counterbalance, the difference of natural fertility' (PR 189). It has been so for the last hundred years when, an 'unquestionable fact' (PR 333), profits both in absolute terms and as a share of the national product 'have rather risen than fallen' (PR 208). It will be so for the next hundred years when, because of machinery and motivation, 'I should feel no doubt.... of an increase in the rate of profits' (PR 325).

It is the heavenly city. There is enough for the worker: 'Little or nothing has been taken from the wages of families' (PR 208). There is enough for the capitalist. Because of the 'skill and capital employed upon the land' (PR 208), there has been significant betterment in the position of the farmer. Profits in agriculture are both satisfactory in themselves and fully comparable to the competing rates in manufacturing and commerce.

There is also enough for the landlord: witness the 'very great increase of rents which have taken place in this country during nearly the last hundred years' (PR 208). The 'increased surplus from the diminished expenses of cultivation', the leases renegotiated, goes to 'increase the rents of the landlords' (PR 164). Ricardo had reservations about what he saw as a non-producer's surplus: 'The interest of the landlord is always opposed to that of the consumer and manufacturer' (Ricardo 1821 [1951–1955]: 335). Malthus did not. Uncompromisingly a three-class man, Malthus regarded the stake of the landlord as fully compatible with the well-being of the nation: 'No other class in the state is so nearly and necessarily connected with its wealth and power, as the interest of the landlord' (PR 225). Each of the two sectors, each of the three classes, had to have what it needed to contribute to the social whole. Manufacturing needed free trade. Agriculture needed tariffs and bounties. The *Principles* in 1820 did not deny that there was a role for protection. The people had to be fed.

For now, it is the heavenly city. At least for 'a very considerable duration' (PR 197), the march to the inferior margin has been arrested by an upward displacement in the diminishing fertility curve. It will, for 'some centuries to come' (PR 325), be possible to squeeze ever more grain from a fixed endowment of land because of technical improvement. It will be for 'centuries', but it will not be forever. Marshall's trees of the forest are born, attain adulthood and then die and decay (Marshall 1890 [1949]: 269). Nations, like trees and businesses, are trapped in a life cycle that imperils their productivity.

Cheaper bread, earlier marriages, more mouths to feed—given time, it will be as the first *Essay* had prophesied. Improvements 'cannot finally be sufficient to balance the necessity of applying to poorer land' (PR 197). The law of diminishing returns is 'always ready to act' (PR II 244). Potential economies, unlike those in manufacturing, will be exhausted. Profit rates will resume their fall. The powers in the soil, 'in the actual state of the earth', will have 'been tried to the uttermost' (PR 371). The population must and will 'press against the means of subsistence' (PR 164). The 'natural connexion' (PR 233) between the ratios and the checks will bring all the buses to a halt.

Progress, whether in decades or in centuries, will burn itself out. Any change for the better will only be 'of short duration' (PR 164). In the end, the increase in subsistence, even 'under the circumstances the most favourable to cultivation', will be 'finally stopped' (PR 371).

7.7 Towards 1836

Malthus died in 1833. The second edition of his *Principles* appeared three years later, in 1836. It had not been fully revised. Examining the existing corrections, the 1817 *Essay*, the *Quarterly review* of 1824, the correspondence with Nassau Senior in 1829, Thomas Chalmers in 1832 and Jane Marcet in 1833, Hollander has nonetheless concluded that Malthus in the last decade of his life was experiencing a crisis of faith: 'All this indicates a change in mood on Malthus's part that might be said to set the stage for the subsequent change in policy; by 1823, Malthus was beginning to see eye to eye with Ricardo' (Hollander 1997: 856). Had he completed his revisions, Hollander is suggesting, Malthus would probably have joined his fellow Whigs in proposing freedom of trade for primary produce and not just for manufactures.

The hints are there for detectives who, like Hollander, believe they can see the shadow on the wall. In the 1817 *Essay*, Malthus says that restrictions on foreign trade are 'essentially unsocial'. In the 1820 *Principles*, he declares that, because sufficient growth can be generated through manufacturing, grain exports are not decisive. In the *Quarterly Review*, he says 'it does not follow....that any forced encouragement should be given to agriculture'. In a letter to Mrs. Marcet he states 'I am for the removal of the restrictions' (all passages quoted in Hollander 1997: 847, 848, 849, 850, 855). In the *Principles* he does, of course, argue in favour of grain self-sufficiency (PR 508). It may be the exception that proves the rule. The passage occurs near the end of the book. Malthus was revising his text from the beginning.

The agrarian bias of Malthus's flirtation with Physiocracy had become more muted by the 1820s. A robust export market was making it less urgent for the rent-recipients to create effective demand. The folk memory of the Napoleonic Wars was being left behind by the Pax Britannica. The Reform Bill of 1832 was giving the manufacturers and the merchants a greater voice in Parliament. Possibly Malthus was moving with the times and becoming ever more of a Whig. He might have said in his second edition that the Corn Laws and the bounties had to go. But the evidence is not there.

References

By T. R. Malthus

(1798 [1970]). *Essay on the Principle of Population, as It Affects the Future Improvement of Society, with Remarks on the Speculations of Mr. Godwin, M. Condorcet, and Other Writers* (abbreviated as FE), ed. by A. Flew. Harmondsworth: Penguin.

(1800 [1986]). *An Investigation of the Cause of the Present High Price of Provisions*, reprinted in *The Works of Thomas Robert Malthus*, ed. by E. A. Wrigley and D. Souden. London: Pickering and Chatto, 7, 5–18.

(1803 et seq. [1989]). *An Essay on the Principle of Population: Or a View of Its Past and Present Effects on Human Happiness, with an Inquiry into Our Prospects Respecting the Removal of the Evils Which It Occasions* (2nd edition, 1803; further editions in 1806, 1807, 1817, 1826) (abbreviated as SE I and SE II), 2 vols., ed. by P. James. Cambridge: Cambridge University Press.

(1814 [1986]). *Observations on the Effects of the Corn Laws, and of a Rise or Fall in the Price of Corn on the Agriculture and General Wealth of the Country*, reprinted in *The Works of Thomas Robert Malthus*, ed. by E. A. Wrigley and D. Souden. London: Pickering and Chatto, 7, 87–109.

(1815a [1986]). *An Inquiry into the Nature and Progress of Rent, and the Principles by Which It Is Regulated,* reprinted in *The Works of Thomas Robert Malthus*, ed. by E. A. Wrigley and D. Souden. London: Pickering and Chatto, 7, 115–145.

(1815b [1986]). *The Grounds of an Opinion on the Policy of Restricting the Importation of Foreign Corn,* reprinted in *The Works of Thomas Robert Malthus,* ed. by E. A. Wrigley and D. Souden. London: Pickering and Chatto, 7, 151–174.

(1820 [1989]). *The Principles of Political Economy* (abbreviated as PR), ed. by J. Pullen. Cambridge: Cambridge University Press.

(1827). Evidence to the Select Committee on Emigration (Third Report), in *Parliamentary Papers.* London: House of Commons, 5, 311–327.

(1830). *A Summary View of the Principle of Population* (abbreviated as SV), in FE, supra.

(1836 [1989]). *The Principles of Political Economy: The Alterations to the First Edition* (abbreviated as PR II), ed. by J. Pullen. Cambridge: Cambridge University Press.

Macvey Napier Papers, British Library, Additional Manuscript Collection, 2.34.612.

Zinke, G. W. (1942). Six Letters from Malthus to Pierre Prévost. *Journal of Economic History*, 2, 174–189.

Secondary Literature

Hollander, S. (1997). *The Economics of Thomas Robert Malthus*. Toronto: University of Toronto Press.

Marshall, A. (1890 [1949]). *Principles of Economics*. London: Macmillan.

Ricardo, D. (1821 [1951–1955]). *Principles of Political Economy and Taxation*, in Ricardo, infra, 1.

Ricardo, D. (1951–1955). *The Works and Correspondence of David Ricardo* (abbreviated as Ricardo) (P. Sraffa with M. Dobb, Eds., 11 vols.). Cambridge: Cambridge University Press.

Semmel, B. (1965). Malthus: 'Physiocracy' and the Commercial System. *Economic History Review, 17,* 522–535.

Smith, A. (1776 [1961]). *The Wealth of Nations* (E. Cannan, Ed., 2 vols.). London: Methuen.

8
The Circular Flow

There is production: land, labour and capital are combined in such a way as to generate final output where previously there had been only promise and potential. There is realisation: consumption, investment, government expenditure and net exports are national expenditure that finds the national product a home. A nation wants sustainable growth in its productive capacity without wasteful over-heating, underperformance or stagnation. A nation does not always get what it wants.

Malthus was the spiritual heir to Adam Smith on self-sustaining growth. Yet he was also the witness to wars, disruptions, downturns and unemployment. If the population mechanism did not condemn honest men and women to vice and misery, then the circular flow might itself leave them hungry and poor.

8.1 Wealth

Today, the definition is different. In the shadow of great economic statisticians like James Meade, Richard Stone and Simon Kuznets (Reisman 2017: 20–24), the national product is defined to be the sum

D. Reisman, *Thomas Robert Malthus*, Great Thinkers in Economics,
https://doi.org/10.1007/978-3-030-01956-3_8

of new value added in a nation in a reporting year. Wherever possible it is measured through revealed preferences and subjective satisfactions rather than through the accountant's paid-out costs or physical quantities. No distinction is made between goods and services. Primary, secondary or tertiary, if it crosses the frontier from firms to households it is a part of the national income.

Today, every student has been schooled in the standard catechism. Things were different in the crucible years. The Physiocrats defined the real wealth of the nation to be the net primary surplus. Smith said it was 'the annual produce of its land and labour' (Smith 1776 [1961]: I 267). Lauderdale made it 'all that man desires as useful and delightful to him' (Lauderdale 1804: 57). Malthus followed Smith when, most of all in his *Principles* in 1820 and his *Definitions* in 1827, he sought to isolate the characteristics of the vital aggregate that, by growing larger, makes all members of the community better off.

8.1.1 Goods

Malthus knew that there was no consensus on the appropriate rubric. The cacophony of usages was introducing the 'utmost confusion' (PR II 16) into public debates. Malthus proposed that the meaning should be confined, as Smith had done, to material objects 'capable of accumulation and definite valuation' (PR 28): 'I should define wealth to be the material objects necessary, useful, or agreeable to man, which are voluntarily appropriated by individuals or nations' (PR II 25). In the first edition of the *Principles*, there had been no mention of voluntary appropriation (PR 28). The amplification came later to make explicit the negotiated swap. Following Adam Smith, Malthus uses the term wealth as a synonym for income. Wealth is not used in the modern sense to indicate the stock while income means the flow. It is a linguistic convention.

Wealth must be tangible. Susceptible to accumulation, it has the inter-temporal dimension of 'some degree of duration' (PR 44). Wealth must also lend itself to 'definite valuation' (PR 46) in non-ego units accessible to an independent observer. Since wealth must be 'voluntarily appropriated', the inference is that the non-ego units should be the market prices of place and time.

Quantification through market prices implies 'scarcity and difficulty of production' (DEF 107). The air, the sun and the rain are not wealth. They are free goods 'in unlimited abundance' (DEF 10). They have not 'required some portion of human exertion to appropriate or produce' (DEF 107). There is no reservation price that proxies the utility. There is no purchase or sale that stamps a number on the transfer. Wealth is 'the exchangeable value of the whole' (PR 422). The air has no such value and nor do unsold stocks. If an inventory is unsold, it will 'lose both its use and its value, and cease to possess the character of wealth' (PR 370). Unwanted output gathering dust on the shelves is not a part of the national product. It vanishes from the data. It does not exist. Malthus's usage is different from the convention adopted in more modern national income accounts. It is a point of view.

Utility is 'the quality of being serviceable or beneficial to mankind' (DEF 107). Consumption is the precondition for the reliable reproduction of wealth. Want-satisfaction is 'convenient and agreeable' (1824 [1963]: 175). That is a good thing, but not in itself wealth: 'All wealth is necessarily useful; but all that is useful is not necessarily wealth' (DEF 107).

Wealth is goods: 'A country will….be rich or poor according to the abundance or scarcity with which these material objects are supplied' (PR 29). Those economists who have ventured beyond material things have fallen into 'contradictions and inconsistencies' (PR II 20) that could have been avoided if they had adopted the everyday definition of wealth. It is not just Smith and Malthus but most ordinary people who see the wealth of the nation as commodities packed in boxes.

8.1.2 Services

Wealth must be material. Services are not material and are therefore not wealth. Satisfaction from 'intellectual attainments', 'personal qualities', 'religious and moral knowledge', 'a lecture on chemistry' (PR II 16, 17, 24), even if they could be marketised and in that way quantified, can never be accumulated. Invisible and intangible services are unable even to reproduce the wage capital that feeds them. In the words of Adam Smith, they 'perish generally in the very instant of their performance' (1776 [1961]: II 196). 'Opera-singers and opera-dancers' have utility. Utility is not enough.

Labour is not wealth but it is related to wealth. Malthus divides the factor labour into three categories. Each is defined by its proximity to the generation of time-travelling things.

First, there is productive labour that embodies itself in the final output of the primary or secondary sector. Workers who 'supply the demands of society for material products' (1824 [1963]: 176) are 'directly productive of wealth' (DEF 107). Their labour should not be double-counted as final output in itself. Because material wealth is the endstate, their contribution is a productive one nonetheless.

Second, there is unproductive labour that produces no wealth. The evanescent exertions of cooks, clerks, grooms and menials, because they are 'not directly productive of material objects' (PR II 275), leave nothing but memories behind. It would be 'strange and incorrect' (PR II 19) to include the tertiary sector in the statistic on wealth when, however 'useful and important', it 'does not realize itself on any object which can be valued or transferred without the presence of the person performing such service' (PR II 26). Bygone utility is irrelevant. Satisfaction cannot make a service into wealth when quite clearly it does not survive.

Third, there is the mixed case of service labour that facilitates material activity but only does so at one remove. Teachers inculcate relevant skills and lawyers process the contracts. On-the-job training 'gratifies the wants of man by means of material objects' (PR 49) but is itself neither industry nor agriculture. Analogous to quasi-money, it is quasi-production. A complement and even a precondition, still it is not material. It is not wealth.

Everything depends on everything else. A concert is a non-material source of happiness but it is also a relaxing investment in future productivity (PR II 33). A concert ticket, interpreted as 'spending with a view to future production' (DEF 248), may be seen as a first step in the direction of value added. So may an afternoon spent at the dog-track: 'Walking, riding, driving, card playing, etc., may all be, indirectly, causes of producing' (DEF 48). Such reasoning is dangerous. Because everything depends on everything else, the logical deduction is that there can be no real distinction between material tradeables and tradeable services, between productive and unproductive labour. There would be no framework but only the open-ended ad hoc. To pluralise, the flow would make the line of demarcation 'quite indistinct' (PR II 22).

As a scientist, Malthus recognised that a borderless commons was bound to introduce 'the greatest confusion into the science of political economy' (DEF 48). A line had to be drawn. Malthus knew that his distinctions were artificial but he also believed that there had to be a constitution. Even if the individual clauses could be disputed, the rules themselves were the necessary fixed points that allow the economist to conceptualise the circular flow.

8.2 Value

Wealth must be defined. It must also be quantified. A crude enumeration is the silent roll call of the heterogeneous availabilities. It is necessary but it is not sufficient. For the *what* to be used as the basis for comparison and aggregation, it must first be converted into the *how much* of a common metric. Malthus knew that valuation was the *sine qua non.* He also knew that there was no consensus on the metric that should be employed.

Language is a part of the story. Malthus was pedantic about words. He wrote a whole book on *Definitions*. In the *Principles,* he points out that even profits can be called labour by an 'unphilosophical' use of language: 'We might just as correctly call rent labour' (PR II 79). He, therefore, advises against propositions that 'defeat all the useful purposes of a useful nomenclature, and....create confusion in the ordinary language of political economy' (PR II 78).

The measure of value is central to the economic system. It is essential that it be defined with 'distinctness and precision': 'It is not a little discreditable to a branch of knowledge which claims to be called a science that the meaning of a term which is constantly met with in every work on political economy, and constantly heard in every conversation on the subject, should not yet be settled' (PR II 128). Discreditable or not, the fact is that 'the most correct and useful definition of it, is still open for discussion' (PR II 128).

Adam Smith had recognised the need for a 'definite meaning' that avoids 'much indistinctness and unnecessary circumlocution' (PR II 129). There had to be a constant measuring rod, an 'ultimate and real standard by which the value of all commodities can at all times and places be estimated and compared' (Smith 1776 [1961]: I 37). Smith was the great pioneer upon whose shoulders the whole of the economic tradition has sought to stand. It has not been easy. Smith seems to have identified at least two separate standards of value.

The objective measure is labour embodied. The toil and trouble expended in hunting a deer is the irreducible element that determines what that deer will be worth relative to a beaver that embodies a different real cost (Smith 1776 [1961]: I 53). Ricardo in 1817 took sunk labour to be the natural origin of wealth: 'The value of a commodity, or the quantity of any other commodity for which it will exchange, depends on the relative quantity of labour which is necessary for its production' (Ricardo 1821 [1951–1955]: 11). So, in 1867, did Karl Marx.

The subjective measure is labour commanded: 'Every man is rich or poor according to the degree in which he can afford to enjoy the necessaries, conveniencies, and amusements of human life' (Smith 1776 [1961]: I 34). In this second measure, the focus shifts from producing to spending, from supply to demand. The operative variable becomes not historical exhaustion but expected utility. More to the point, labour is the single yardstick, 'the only accurate measure of value' (Smith 1776 [1961]: I 41).

W. S. Jevons (1871), Carl Menger (1871), and Léon Walras (1874, 1877) in the 1870s were to argue that value is all in the mind and that the market-clearing price is its real-world avatar. Their marginal revolution was not created in a day. Heretics such as Richard Whateley (1831) and Mountifort Longfield (1834) had been preaching the gospel even in the age of Ricardo, Malthus and Marx. Malthus knew about Bentham. He also knew about Bailey.

Samuel Bailey in 1825 in his *Critical Dissertation* had dismissed Ricardo's labour embodied as yesterday's account book that lacked a current next-best foregone. A better measure, Bailey said, would be 'the esteem in which any object is held. It denotes, strictly speaking, an effect produced on the mind': 'A thing cannot be valuable in itself without reference to another thing' (Bailey 1825: I 5). Value is in essence a unique individual's unique perception. Always relative, never absolute, when we compare two objects for purposes of exchange, 'we appear to acquire the power of expressing our feelings with precision' (Bailey 1825: I 3).

Malthus knew that he had to choose between the objective valuation of the Ricardian mainstream and the subjective introspection of the fringe and the marginal. He had been forced to do so when he began to explain the origins of rent. In the 1803 *Essay*, he was on the side of cost. It is labour: the price of produce 'is necessarily regulated by the wages of labour' (SE I 401). It is land: 'One of the principal ingredients in the price of British corn is the high rent of land' (SE I 417). By the 1806 edition, he had changed his mind: 'Universally, it is price that determines rent, not rent that determines price' (SE I 425). Rent had become the effect. It was not the cause. In the *Definitions* in 1827, he made it all clear. Value is 'the relation of one object to some other, or others in exchange, resulting from the estimation in which each is held' and 'the object which measures it' (DEF 107).

Value is desiredness but it is also supply. Smith's 'value in use' (Smith 1776 [1961]: I 32) 'rarely occurs in political economy' (DEF 107). Although water is a necessity, diamonds in comparison a luxury, there is no external measure of a unique individual's utility differential. Smith's 'value in exchange' (Smith 1776 [1961]: I 32) is more useful. It gives 'a most correct definition of wealth' (1827 [1986]: 323). Value in exchange is 'the state of the supply compared with the demand' (DEF 109). It is what ordinary people mean when they speak of value.

Jevons was unidimensional. He stated that 'final degree of utility determines value' (Jevons 1871 [1970]: 77). Ricardo, also monocausal, deduced that value is determined by 'the quantity of labour realized in commodities' (Ricardo 1821 [1951–1955]: 13). Ricardo said that it was subjective satisfaction that was the icing on the cake. It was Alfred Marshall who, unifying the two blades of a single pair of scissors, restored peace by declaring that there was equal value in each perspective. It was not demand *or* supply that determined the equilibrium price but, like two pillars of an arch, both together that were needed to do the work (Marshall 1890 [1949]: 290).

Malthus's *Principles of Political Economy* looks forward seventy years to Marshall's *Principles of Economics.* As Malthus saw it, there were reservation prices on both sides of the market. The value of a commodity is the compromise that is struck: 'The prices of commodities do not depend upon their intrinsic utility, but upon the supply and the demand' (PR 80). Hidden in demand is the desire to possess. Hidden in supply is the sunk cost of production. The price expressed in money is the balance of force.

The price expressed in money is 'an accurate and unexceptional measure of value at the same place, and nearly at the same time' (PR II 39). Money is the common language. Money is 'universally considered as a correct measure of value' (PR II 43). Money, however, is specie: 'Nominal value in exchange, or price....may be defined to be the value of commodities estimated in the precious metals' (PR II 44). Commodities are compared against the benchmark of treasure. Yet treasure itself is a commodity. The market price and the mint price need not be the same. Specie speaks in two different languages at once.

Malthus knew that the value of every economic tradeable can vary in time and space. The precious metals are not exempt from fluctuations in availability and taste. In the last analysis, there will never be a perfect indicator of general purchasing power. William Empson paraphrases Malthus's search for the ideal that does not exist in the following way: 'There are but few things in life of which we have a perfect measure. Where we have not, we shall only aggravate our disadvantages by acting or reasoning as if we had' (Empson 1837 [1963]: 232). Perfection is impossible. What is possible is a fully serviceable second best: 'Money makes a much better measure of value than any other *commodity*' (PR II 95, emphasis in original).

Money is the best attainable measure of the national wealth. Aware, however, of its imperfections, Malthus never ceased to experiment with alternatives. He was always searching for 'a correct measure of the power of purchasing generally' (1823 [1986]: 181). In the *Measure of Value*, written three years after the *Principles* and four years before the *Definitions*, he declared that he had found a bedrock absolute: 'The labour which commodities will command may be considered as a standard measure of their value' (1823 [1986]: 207).

In 1820 and 1827, Malthus said that the price expressed in money tracks the relative wealth. In 1823, he said that a more constant standard would be the labour commanded: 'The best practical measure of the relative wealth of different countries would be the quantity of common labour which the value of the whole annual produce of each country would enable it to command at the actual price of the time' (1823 [1986]: 208). The value of specie varies with bullion flows, new mines and precautionary uncertainties. The value of corn is trapped between the short-run harvest cycle and the long-run margin of cultivation. A weighted index of both specie and corn would be the worst of both worlds. Intrinsic value is a chimera. Labour commanded is better placed to serve as the measuring rod.

Malthus said what he meant in two papers to the Royal Society of Literature. In his first paper, in 1825, he said that labour commanded alone can 'represent and measure the natural and necessary conditions of the supply of commodities' (1825 [1986]: 301). In his second paper, in 1827, he said that 'the ordinary quantity of labour which a commodity will command in any country....will measure correctly the natural and necessary conditions of its supply in that country' (1827 [1986]: 322). The common denominator is the labour of an unskilled agricultural worker. The sacrifice is assumed to be relatively stable. Labour alone, 'never varying in its own value' (Smith 1776 [1961]: I 37), is the best achievable measure of wealth. The canonical Adam Smith had said it was.

It is labour commanded. It is not labour embodied. Malthus's writings on the labour standard date from the last decade of his life. Neither before nor after did he adopt the hard-line Ricardian interpretation of value as cost expended: 'The cost of production only influences the prices of commodities as it regulates their supply' (PR 77).

Ricardo focused on labour cost to the exclusion of profit or rent. Malthus could see no sense in that: 'The exchangeable value of commodities is scarcely ever proportioned to the quantity of labour employed upon them' (PR 109). Ricardo neglected the intensity of desire of the would-be purchaser. Ricardo failed to see that value is never free-standing but always in relation to an opportunity foregone. Ricardo made no allowance for speculative activity 'if a large supply is soon expected' or 'a future scanty supply is looked forward to' (PR II 45). Ricardo references no real-world experience of labour embodied: 'There is no stage of society in which it will be found correct' (PR 86). In all of these ways Ricardo was 'greatly wide of the truth' (PR II 84).

Malthus never said that labour was the sole source of value or that historic cost should be included in wealth even 'if it exists in a great excess above the wants of those who are to use it' (PR 186). Labour commanded is not a theory of production but of indexation: 'The labour which commodities will command or purchase, is used entirely as a measure' (PR II 250).

Sometimes Malthus used labour as the *numéraire*. More often he used money. Always, however, it was the interaction between supply and demand in conditions of scarcity that set the ratio of exchange. Wealth is given its value through the 'higgling and bargaining' (Smith 1776 [1961]: I 36) of infinite dyads. The market price is the foundation of the circular flow.

8.3 Say's Law

Outputs and inputs are in limited supply. Scarcity of resources means that authentic human needs are not being satisfied. New wealth transcends the shortfall. Dynamic efficiency pushes outward the capacity-for-happiness frontier. Production is validated by consumption. The circular flow always circles.

Demand can be constrained by supply. However hungry or cold, people cannot meet their urgent wants with marketfuls of commodities that do not exist. What is more debatable is whether supply can also be constrained by demand. Microfailures are the essence of decentralised decision-making where producers supply apples when consumers are demanding nuts. Without microfailures, there would be no competition and no search. Macrofailures are, however, the black hole. There can be a shortfall of demand in the single market for apples. Can there also be a shortfall of demand in all micro-markets at once? Can there be a general glut?

Malthus defines across-the-board oversupply in the following terms: 'A glut is said to be general, when, either from superabundance of supply or diminution of demand, a considerable mass of commodities falls below the elementary costs of production' (DEF 113). A 'considerable mass' of consumables can only be sold at a loss. The implication is that in the next marketing period they will not be produced. That way lies recession, depression and even the breakdown of the market economy.

Adam Smith could not see any reason for a deficiency in total demand: 'What is annually saved is as regularly consumed as what is annually spent, and nearly in the same time too; but it is consumed by a different set of people' (Smith 1776 [1961]: I 359). His French disciple, Jean-Baptiste Say, proclaimed in his *Treatise* of 1803 that to supply is in its nature to demand: 'A product is no sooner created, than it, from that instant, affords a market for other products to the full extent of its own value' (Say 1803 [1971]: 134). Supply creates its own demand: 'It is production which opens a demand for products' (Say 1803 [1971]: 133). Precautionary balances in normal circumstances will be regarded as irrational and wasteful: 'Money performs but a momentary function....When the transaction is finally closed, it will always be found, that one kind of commodity has been exchanged for another' (Say 1803 [1971]: 134). No one but a miser will hoard idle potential. It was Smith's suggestion but it is known as Say's Law. A partial glut is the invisible hand. A general glut is a theoretical impossibility.

David Ricardo, continuing the tradition of Smith and Say, made clear where he stood: 'No man produces, but with a view to consume or sell, and he never sells, but with an intention to purchase some other commodity, which may be immediately useful to him, or which may contribute to future production' (Ricardo 1821 [1951–1955]: 290). Whoever has commodities has both the power and the intention to spend: 'There cannot, then, be accumulated in a country any amount of capital which cannot be employed productively' (Ricardo 1821 [1951–1955]: 290).

Mismatches occur, mistakes happen and estimation is imperfect. A specific imbalance must not, however, be confused with an aggregate deficiency. To produce is to consume: 'Productions are always bought by productions' (Ricardo 1821 [1951–1955]: 291). Whether in the barter system or in a monetary economy with an inter-temporal store of value, the rule is the same. So long as the resources derived from a sale are spent on consumables or lent on to strangers for a return, in either case demand is the direct consequence of supply.

James Mill in his *Elements of Political Economy* in 1844 perpetuated the message: 'Production can never be too rapid for demand. Production is the cause, and the sole cause, of demand. It never furnishes supply, without furnishing demand, both at the same time, and both to an equal extent' (Mill 1844 [1963]: 237). It is true *ex ante*: 'A man produces, only because he wishes to possess' (Mill 1844 [1963]: 228). It is true *ex post*: 'Every commodity is always, at one and the same time, matter of demand, and matter of supply' (Mill 1844 [1963]: 228). It is true by definition.

In his *Commerce Defended*, Mill had already stated categorically that 'production creates a market for produce' (Mill 1808: 92). A general excess is a theoretical impossibility: 'Whatever be the additional quantity of goods therefore which is at any time created in any country, an additional power of purchasing, exactly equivalent, is at the same instant created; so that a nation can never be naturally overstocked either with capital or with commodities' (Mill 1808: 81).

A general glut, Mill said, would never occur. Since commodities are produced with a view to exchange, one half of the nation will always furnish the demand for the other half: 'A nation's power of purchasing is exactly measured by its annual produce' (Mill 1808: 81). The circular flow always balances.

Smith, Say, Ricardo and Mill had maintained that effective demand was never more than the simple offer of one good for another. Malthus was the outlier. He concluded that their doctrine was 'utterly unfounded' (PR 353). The circular flow could be disrupted by demand as well as supply. He criticised the Panglossian optimists behind Say's Law for parroting that the proportions between the micro-markets must have been miscalculated 'at a period, when all the merchants of our own country, and many in others, find the utmost difficulty in employing their capitals' (DEF 58). It is like an assertion 'that it *cannot* rain, when crowds of people are getting wet' (DEF 59, emphasis in original). It is in direct opposition to 'general experience' (DEF 59). It discredits the science. It has to go.

History is, however, what it is. By the end of the 1820s, it was deficient demand that had disappeared into the intellectual underworld where before Keynes no one but outsiders like Marx, Silvio Gesell, John

Hobson and Major Douglas chose to go: 'The great puzzle of effective demand with which Malthus had wrestled vanished from economic literature. You will not find it mentioned even once in the whole works of Marshall, Edgeworth and Professor Pigou' (Keynes 1936 [1973]: 32). Ricardo was 'stone-deaf to what Malthus was saying' (Keynes 1936 [1973]: 364). Keynes, of course, was not.

8.4 Oscillation and Trend

Everyone knows that things can go wrong. Malthus was not deviating from Smith, Say, Ricardo and Mill when he appealed to 'general experience' to show that the national wealth had not been increasing at a stable rate. What was unorthodox was his prediction that the downswings can be permanent as well as transitory. Even the free market might not be able to revive the saw-toothed cycle once it had followed the trend into an underperforming equilibrium.

8.4.1 The Fluctuations

Harvest failures, blockades and the suspension of convertibility are exogenous shocks. Random and unpatterned, they are qualitatively different from the endogenous disruptions that arise within the ongoing process of wealth creation. Such disturbances are not the enemy outside. Rather, they are the cause and effect of a single country's circular flow.

In the upswing, there is an unanticipated rise in prices. Supernormal profits generate both the ability to save and the incentive to invest. Since money wages are only adjusted upward after a lag, the employers take advantage of cheap labour and forced redistribution to expand their workforce.

The slack is increasingly absorbed. The population does not immediately rise in response to the need. As the ploughmen and mill-hands become increasingly scarce, so the competition among the employers bids up the wage. Rising incomes encourage earlier marriage and with it larger families.

More mouths to feed pushes the farmers ever further into diminishing returns. Recourse to inferior land becomes economically attractive because of the increasing price of grain. The insight into the economics of poor countries is sometimes termed the 'Malthusian trap'. More people are the cause of more food. More food, however, is the precondition for more people: 'The increase in population is necessarily limited by the means of subsistence' (SE I 304). It is circular causality. It is in the spirit of the circular flow.

In the short run, there is a shortage of labour. In the long run, there is the lagged response. The parents have already bred their reserve army. Delayed by 'ten or twelve years together' (SE I 346) or perhaps even by 'sixteen or eighteen years' (PR 357), the next generation inexorably pushes the insiders and the newcomers alike into 'severe distress' (SE I 346).

Money wages are cut as the labour force expands. Grain prices fall because purchasing power is less. Employers dismiss workers because so much of their output is 'absolutely useless' (PR 368). Capital is withdrawn. Marriages are postponed. Childbearing is rationed. Positive checks set in which decimate the labour force. They are the working man's friend. Unions and statutory floors are not needed so long as epidemics, wars and infanticide are restoring the seller's market.

Positive checks are not the end but the beginning. Unfilled vacancies and rising wages lead to earlier marriages and new births. They prolong the life expectancy of the economically active: 'An extraordinary healthiness generally succeeds any very great mortality' (SE I 207). It is a good time to be a worker. As with any hog-cycle or expanding cobweb, however, it will not last. The population multiplier has made the return of hard times inevitable. Given ten years or perhaps even eighteen years, the low-income trap will be the reaction that follows the stimulus until it in turn sets in motion the next sequence of automatic correctives.

It is population and subsistence that are at the root of the periodicity. The bunching of industrial investments, the mismatch of the consumer and the capital subsectors, the regular sunspots that cut disposable income, none figure in Malthus's theory. It is preponderantly the primary sector that explains why it is that 'the same retrograde and progressive movements with respect to happiness are repeated' (FE 77).

Perpetual oscillations are the four seasons. They are built-in stabilisers on a par with Sir James Steuart's coiled spring (SE I 23n). It is all a matter of dammed-up interdependence and unsynchronised mutuality. Not timeless equilibria but internally generated deflections, what is clear is that the imbalance is only a '*temporary* glut' (PR 461, emphasis added). No lasting damage will be done to the national wealth so long as each short-term resting place produces its own successive turning point.

Fluctuations are the four seasons. The trend is different, Smith anticipated unlimited betterment. Marx warned of a permanent downswing from which the capitalist system has no inbuilt capacity to recover.

8.4.2 The Trend

The laws of population and of diminishing returns to labour on the land have an obvious and irremediable 'degree of permanence' (PR 371). Moral restraint and agricultural improvement may postpone for many centuries the upward bound when nature will have 'been tried to the uttermost' (PR 370) and the stationary state sets in. They cannot put it off forever. Assuming it is a robust prediction and not simply a tendency law, the future is bleak. Although it may take a thousand years or more, the growth and the betterment in every 'well-peopled territory' (SE I 261) will grind to a halt.

Prediction or tendency, Malthus says that population struggling for subsistence may be regarded as imposing a ceiling limit to sustained development. There is more. Even if the childbearing is restrained and the margin extended, still there is a third spectre at the feast that might bring the festivities to a close. That spectre is thrift: 'The employment of a capital, too rapidly increased by parsimonious habits, may find a limit, and does, in fact, often find a limit, long before there is any real difficulty in procuring the means of subsistence' (PR 469).

It is a fact. Parsimony, too rapidly increased, is pulling the trend line down. The imbalance between spending and saving is not just a possible but 'a probable occurrence' (PR 478). Long before the population has bred itself into distress, long before high farming has reached its final frontier, the national wealth will have settled into a permanent state of inertia. There is no lower turning point to reverse a trend that has hit rock-bottom.

The shortfall is not a downswing oscillation but a long-lived new normal. There will be 'a marked depression of wealth and population permanently' (PR 369). There will be 'a permanent want of employment and the most abject poverty, in consequence of retrograde and permanently diminished wealth' (PR 456). There will be a 'permanent diminution of production' (PR 466). There will be a 'permanent' level of activity that will never go up so long as worrisome frugality keeps down 'the demand for further product' (PR 441).

The accumulation of capital would be 'perfectly futile' (PR 370). If demand is deficient, there will be no reason for the businessmen and the farmers to expand supply: 'No nation can *possibly* grow rich by an accumulation of capital, arising from a permanent diminution of consumption' (PR 370, emphasis in original). If saving and consuming are properly aligned, the advance to the possibility frontier occurs automatically and in 'no great length of time' (PR 426). If saving remains permanently in excess of consuming, the correction will occur only after 'the lapse of many thousand years' (PR 426). 'Many thousand years' is another way of saying that economic underperformance is more than 'a temporary period of want of employment' (PR 456). Rather than a passing recession in the short-term slump of the business cycle, it is an underemployment equilibrium which is made to last.

The producers, unable to expand their sales, will cap their workforce. The mercantile classes, starved of business, will not 'continue extending their concerns, and realizing their profits' (PR 466). The supply side will 'slumber for ages' in the underemployment equilibrium of 'an uncultivated soil' and 'a scanty yet starving population' (PR 440). The demand for 'material luxuries and conveniences' will 'very soon abate' (PR II 205). Even the demand for basic necessaries will require 'effective encouragement' (PR II 206).

The nation as a whole is not spending enough. The 'wants of the society' are not 'clamorous for a supply' (PR 467). Without the opportunity to earn, the deprived are forced on to charity or sacrificed to the positive checks. It is market failure. There may nonetheless be a happy end.

8.5 The Golden Mean

It is an apocalypse waiting to happen. Adam Smith treated deferred gratification as essential for the national wealth: 'Capitals are increased by parsimony, and diminished by prodigality' (Smith 1776 [1961]: I 358). Evaluated by their respective contribution to the growth effort, 'every prodigal appears to be a public enemy, and every frugal man a public benefactor' (Smith 1776 [1961]: I 362).

Smith believed in abstention because investment was the high road to affluence. Yet he also saw the need for indulgence. Just as Quesnay had warned that his *Tableau Economique* could lose its equilibrium, so Smith had recognised that his own circular flow would not be sustainable if there were not a 'balance of the annual produce and consumption' (Smith 1776 [1961]: I 523). Spending and not spending were two pillars of a single arch.

It is all in Adam Smith. What is not in Adam Smith is the trend that spirals downward into the perpetual trough. Parsimony in proportion is an integral part of economic growth. Parsimony in excess is the permanent glut.

Malthus had seen the threat to effective demand from a permanent rise in saving as early as the second *Essay* in 1803 (SE I 350–352). In 1820, in the *Principles* he explained in detail what the 'extra saving' could cost. Where 'the demand for commodities was not such as to afford fair profits to the producer', where 'the capitalists were at a loss where and how to employ their capitals to advantage', there the effect of still further saving would be 'still further to distress the capitalists' (PR 372). The principle of saving, 'pushed to excess, would destroy the motive to production' (PR 8).

In some circumstances, a penny saved will be a penny earned. In some circumstances, a flourishing economy will 'certainly be ruined by extravagance' (PR 369). It is, in short, not unbending absolutes but 'the circumstances of the period' that will dictate whether extra saving will be a 'national benefit' or a 'national disadvantage' (PR 517).

Nothing in macroeconomics is good or bad in itself: 'No general rule can be laid down respecting the advantage to be derived from saving, or the division of property, without limitations and exceptions' (PR 10). Malthus says that his 'main doctrine' throughout 'the whole range of nature and art' (PR 269, 515) is the philosopher's Golden Mean: 'This tendency to extremes is exactly what I consider as the great source of error in political economy' (PR 352n).

The optimal balance between saving and spending depends upon the due proportion of the parts (PR 426). Required is 'some happy medium' (PR 266), some 'intermediate point' where, 'taking into consideration both the power to produce and the will to consume, the encouragement to the increase of wealth is the greatest' (PR 9). The most suitable mix is crucial if an economy is to avoid the twin pitfalls of *too much* and *too little* that always threaten 'the happiness of the great mass of society' (PR 522).

At one extreme, there is *too much*: 'If consumption exceed production, the capital of the country must be diminished, and its wealth must be gradually destroyed from its want to produce' (PR 9). If current demand is in excess of current supply, the nation is depleting its existing asset-stock and doing nothing to replace the loss. Abstention is the precondition for accumulation. Without abstention, it is the slippery slope: 'Every succeeding period will see the society worse supplied' (PR 34). Smith was right. Without parsimony today, there will be no national wealth tomorrow.

At the other extreme, there is *too little*: 'If production be in a great excess above consumption, the motive to accumulate and produce must cease from the want of will to consume' (PR 9). If current output is plentiful but current consumption low, the nation is stockpiling an endowment which its frugal citizens are refusing to buy: 'It might as well be thrown into the sea' (PR 364). Smith was right: 'Consumption is the sole end and purpose of all production' (Smith 1776 [1961]: II 179).

One person's expenditure is another person's livelihood. The precondition for prosperity is 'that consumption which is necessary to give the proper stimulus to production' (PR 480). If national spending is damped, there will be 'no adequate motive to the proprietors of land to cultivate well', no pecuniary incentive for manufacturers to grow 'the wealth derived from conveniences and luxuries' (PR 9). Investors will not convert their revenue into capital: 'undue' proportions having pushed out the 'due' proportions, there will be 'no adequate demand for the products of such capital' (PR 375). Workers would be unemployed (PR 266). The wealth of the nation would 'come to a stand long before the soil had been well cultivated' (PR 9).

Nothing but the 'simplest food, the poorest clothing, and the meanest houses' (PR 8) would be supplied. There would be 'a general want of demand, both for produce and population' (PR 365). Households, recognising that saving for one's family is 'a most sacred private duty' (PR 517), would be cutting their spending. What one can do, all cannot. The paradox of thrift has the effect of 'aggravating instead of alleviating our distresses' (PR 505). Moral values destroy jobs. The economy is burdened with a larger pool of loanable funds 'than is consistent with the most effective encouragement to the growth of public wealth' (PR 517). There is no way out. It will be permanent. It will be the stationary state long before the marginal plot of land has been exhausted.

There are the two extremes of *too much* and *too little*. In between, there is the 'intermediate point'. It is not easy in the real world to triangulate the optimum: 'The resources of political economy may not be able to ascertain it' (PR 9). Lack of knowledge 'throws a kind of uncertainty over the science of political economy' (PR 515). Malthus knew that he did not know the precise coordinates. What he did know was that an 'intermediate point', varying in time and space, is a structural necessity. Proportion is all.

John Pullen observes that, because Malthus was reluctant to make unsupported generalisations, his doctrine of proportions had to be left 'non-operational' (Pullen 1982: 282). Niggardly nature was not willing to reveal all its secrets. Situated on the intellectual middle ground, it was bounded indeterminacy, neither philosophical nihilism nor overconfident Say's Law. It was second best. We do what we can.

Oskar Lange was one of many to have regarded Malthus's approach to the saving optimum as the best attainable theory when first-best refuses to share: 'No underconsumption theorist ever has shown what this optimum is and how it is determined. The problem, however, was put forward with unsurpassed clarity already by Malthus' (Lange 1938: 24). Lange was attracted by Malthus's idea of a macroeconomic Golden Mean. He was less attracted by the razor's edge that irreversibly triggers a permanent recession. Perhaps he saw that, alongside the dystopia of over-saving that lasts for 'many thousand years', Malthus also put forward a less apocalyptic vision of a self-stabilising mechanism that would, given time, eventually restore the trend line to ceiling growth.

8.6 Restoring the Balance

Imbalance is *too much* or *too little*. The aim is to get the balance right: 'All the great results in political economy, respecting wealth, depend upon *proportions*' (PR 432, emphasis in original). Desired supply must be matched by desired demand. Desired withdrawals must be accompanied by desired injections.

Market economists look in the first instance to the invisible hand to restore the equilibrium. They, 'for the most part, trust to the inclinations of individuals in this respect' (PR 479). They anticipate that calculative rationality and private self-interest will normally be enough to correct an excess or a deficit. High wages produce children. High profits produce capital. Pins or oranges, children or capital, the thermostat restores the balance: 'The laws which regulate the rate of profits and the progress of capital, bear a striking and singular resemblance to the laws which regulate the rate of wages and the progress of population' (PR 370).

Oscillations around the trend are self-righting. They generate their own turning points and built-in stabilisers. It is only the trend itself which is pulled down by over-saving into a permanent ice age. Market economists will find this counter-intuitive. The economic calculus, they will say, will generally be sufficient to restore the proportions: 'The great laws of demand and supply….will generally direct us into the right course' (PR 516).

Malthus was a market economist. Like other market economists, he believed that the devolved response was the best one: 'Individual interest needs no extraneous assistance' (PR 517). It was as true for macroeconomic aggregates as it was for single commodities. Malthus said that 'the whole question of saving' can safely be left to 'the uninfluenced operation of individual interest and individual feelings' (PR 517). That makes it all clear. Malthus said the imbalance was permanent. Then, he said it was not.

Malthus shows that injections and withdrawals are subject to financial incentives. Rational actors make a dispassionate comparison of their next-bests foregone. If they choose to defer their gratification, the reason must be the reward that they expect. The upward-sloping schedule leads him to the prediction that, because profits have a secular tendency to rise over time; therefore, the rational actor will rank jam tomorrow above jam today: 'When profits rise, the motive to accumulation will increase, and there will be a tendency to spend a smaller proportion of the gains, and to save a greater' (PR 516). It is a theory of saving but not a theory of stagnation. What is saved for a return is immediately invested for a return. Malthus seems to be espousing a form of Say's Law that is somewhat different from his more usual acknowledgement of sub-capacity equilibrium. Total demand is safe. Demand cannot be deficient where what is taken out of the circular flow is subsequently put back.

It is a schedule. Rather than a 'permanent diminution of consumption' (PR 370), there is a continuous recalibration of cost and benefit. When profits rise the rational invest. When profits fall, they opt for current consumption instead: 'Whenever capital increases too fast, the motive to accumulation diminishes, and there will be a natural tendency to spend more and save less' (PR 516). The market-clearing profit acts as the in-period regulator. Accomplishing *ex post* what can never be estimated *ex ante*, it teases out the 'intermediate point' at which the excess of saving will be slimmed down to the level of investment. So long as the gravitational pull of the 'intermediate point is not 'interrupted by bad laws or unwise exhortations', the free market will 'more frequently attain' the 'just mean' (PR 516). National wealth and full employment are safe. The 'permanent diminution' is a paper tiger.

Rising profits trigger investments which offset savings. Falling interest rates might be expected still further to boost the level of aggregate demand. Households would save less. Firms would borrow more. The price of savings would in that way shepherd the flows into their proper proportions.

Malthus regarded profit rates as a balancing force. Interest rates were less significant. In the eighteenth century, despite the generally low price of grain, 'the *natural* rate of interest' in Britain fell from 4 to 3% (PR 318, emphasis in original). The Pope had had a similar experience a century before. It suggests that the supply of loanable funds was increasing more rapidly than the borrowers' demand. What is counter-intuitive is that businesses seem not to have arbitraged interest-bearing savings into higher-profit real investment. Cheap money is an invitation to leverage capital. The response seems nonetheless to have been sluggish.

Profit was going up and interest was going down. Each was the opportunity cost of the other. Market signalling had evidently not solved the inconsistency. Malthus may have attributed the perverse response to 'bad laws and unwise exhortations', to the Usury Laws which capped interest at 5% and the reluctance of the commercial banks to lend long term. Assuming that profit rates were in excess of interest rates, there may have been unexploited gains from trade because of a deficiency in economic rationality.

Banking failure does not intrinsically discredit the free market. Malthus was a market economist. He said that a country has 'the means of gradually recovering itself from any shock' (PR 488). He said that 'remedial processes' are in play which 'prevent the continuance of excess or defect' (DEF 62). He said that economic counterweights 'act powerfully to prevent the permanence either of glut or scarcity' (DEF 62). In the long run, it will be progress without end. It is hard to believe that this was the same man who wrote of a 'permanent diminution' and predicted that the permafrost would last for 'many thousand years'.

There is no contradiction in Malthus's economics. The confusion arises because of his choice of words. 'Permanent diminution' and 'many thousand years' were never intended to be taken at face value. Days, weeks, months, years—it is all a question of time. An oscillation to Malthus is a short-run fluctuation. The trough of the trend is a long-run fluctuation. A depression is no more than a sticky stopping place that does not, 'for a time' (PR 417), bounce back to the trend. There are 'periods of greater or less prosperity, and sometimes of adversity' (letter from Malthus to Ricardo, 1817, in Ricardo VII: 122). Nothing in economics is ever permanent. Semantics lets Malthus down.

The good times will always return. In the transition, it will be a veil of tears: 'It is undoubtedly true, that every thing will ultimately find its level, but this level is sometimes effected in a very harsh manner' (SE I 410–411). It rather alters the argument. The patient can be cured but the cure is harsh. The market can solve the problem. What Malthus is asking is whether it should be allowed to do so. It is an entirely different debate.

Adjustment is harsh. It is especially harsh for the lower classes who have little to cushion themselves against the adversity and distress of long-term unemployment. Healing crises of 'eight or ten years, recurring not infrequently, are serious spaces in human life' (PR 521–522). Protracted downturns add up to 'a serious sum of happiness or misery' (PR 521). The 'mercantile classes' can 'realize fortunes' (PR 521) in bad times by betting against the odds The 'great mass of society' makes losses in a recession that will never be compensated through subsequent gains in the boom (PR 52 l).

Transitions are stressful. Theorists of equilibrium states do wrong to neglect the misery caused by a recession that can last a decade. Transitory oscillations are perhaps acceptable. Permanent oscillations are perhaps not. Morally speaking, Malthus is saying, no utilitarian should write off the sacrifice made in the present in order that future generations might encash the reward. Stalin's kulaks lived on cold turkey. Some of them died. Their children went to university and the ballet.

A *tâtonnement* that lasts for a decade is harsh. At least the demand-deficient 'diminution' will not be 'permanent'. Nature is good. In the long run, the word 'permanence' will be returned to the dictionary where it belongs.

References

By T. R. Malthus

(1798 [1970]). *Essay on the Principle of Population, as It Affects the Future Improvement of Society, with Remarks on the Speculations of Mr. Godwin, M. Condorcet, and Other Writers* (abbreviated as FE), ed. by A. Flew. Harmondsworth: Penguin.

(1803 et seq. [1989]). *An Essay on the Principle of Population: Or a View of Its Past and Present Effects on Human Happiness, with an Inquiry into Our Prospects Respecting the Removal of the Evils Which It occasions* (2nd edition, 1803; further editions in 1806, 1807, 1817, 1826) (abbreviated as SE I and SE II), 2 vols., ed. by P. James. Cambridge: Cambridge University Press.
(1820 [1989]). *The Principles of Political Economy* (abbreviated as PR), ed. by J. Pullen. Cambridge: Cambridge University Press.
(1823 [1986]). *The Measure of Value Stated and Illustrated, with an Application of It to the Alterations in the Value of the English Currency Since 1790*, reprinted in *The Works of Thomas Robert Malthus*, ed. by E. A. Wrigley and D. Souden. London: Pickering and Chatto, 7, 179–221.
(1824 [1963]). Political Economy, review of J. R. McCulloch's *Essay on Political Economy, Quarterly Review*, 1824, reprinted in *Occasional Papers of T. R. Malthus*, ed. by B. Semmel. New York: Bert Franklin, 171–230.
(1825 [1986]). On the Measure of the Conditions Necessary to the Supply of Commodities (1825), *Transactions of the Royal Society of Literature*, 1/1, reprinted in *The Works of Thomas Robert Malthus*, ed. by E. A. Wrigley and D. Souden. London: Pickering and Chatto, 7, 301–311.
(1827 [1986]). *Definitions in Political Economy, Preceded by an Inquiry into the Rules Which Ought to Guide Political Economists in the Definition and Use of Their Terms, with Remarks on the Deviation from These Rules in Their Writings* (abbreviated as DEF), reprinted in *The Works of Thomas Robert Malthus*, ed. by E. A. Wrigley and D. Souden. London: Pickering and Chatto, 8.
(1827 [1986]). On the Meaning Which Is Most Usually and Most Correctly Attached to the Term Value of a Commodity, *Transactions of the Royal Society of Literature, 1/2*, reprinted in *The Works of Thomas Robert Malthus*, ed. by E. A. Wrigley and D. Souden. London: Pickering and Chatto, 7, 315–323.
(1836 [1989]). *The Principles of Political Economy: The Alterations to the First edition* (abbreviated as PR II), ed. by J. Pullen. Cambridge: Cambridge University Press.

Secondary Literature

Bailey, S. (1825). *A Critical Dissertation on the Nature, Measures, and Causes of Value*. London: Hunter.
Empson, W. (1837 [1963]). Life, Writings and Character of Mr. Malthus. *Edinburgh Review*, 64 (Reprinted in *Occasional Papers of T.R. Malthus*, pp. 231–268, by B. Semmel, Ed., New York: Bert Franklin).

Jevons, W. S. (1871 [1970]). *The Theory of Political Economy* (R. D. C. Black, Ed.). Harmondsworth: Penguin Books.
Keynes, J. M. (1936 [1973]). *The General Theory of Employment, Interest and Money*. In *The Collected Writings of John Maynard Keynes*. London: Macmillan.
Lange, O. (1938). The Rate of Interest and the Optimum Propensity to Consume. *Economica, 5,* 12–32.
Lauderdale, J. M. (1804). *An Inquiry into the Nature and Origin of Public Wealth*. Edinburgh: Archibald Constable.
Longfield, M. (1834). *Lectures on Political Economy*. Dublin: Richard Milliken & Son.
Marshall, A. (1890 [1949]). *Principles of Economics*. London: Macmillan.
Menger, C. (1871 [1950]). *Principles of Economics* (J. Dingwall & B. F. Hoselitz, Ed. & Trans.). Glencoe: The Free Press.
Mill, J. (1808). *Commerce Defended*. London: C. and R. Baldwin.
Mill, J. (1844 [1963]). *Elements of Political Economy* (3rd ed.). New York: Augustus M. Kelley.
Pullen, J. R. (1982). Malthus and the Doctrine of Proportions and the Concept of the Optimum. *Australian Economic Papers, 21,* 270–286.
Reisman, D. A. (2017). *James Buchanan*. London: Palgrave Macmillan.
Ricardo, D. (1821 [1951–1955]). *Principles of Political Economy and Taxation,* in Ricardo, infra, I.
Ricardo, D. (1951–1955). *The Works and Correspondence of David Ricardo* (abbreviated as Ricardo) (P. Sraffa with M. Dobb, Eds., 11 vols.). Cambridge: Cambridge University Press.
Say, J.-B. (1803 [1971]). *A Treatise on Political Economy* (C. R. Prinsep, Trans.). New York: Augustus M. Kelley.
Smith, A. (1776 [1961]). *The Wealth of Nations* (E. Cannan, Ed., 2 vols.). London: Methuen.
Walras, L. (1874, 1877 [1954]). *Elements of Pure Economics* (W. Jaffé, Trans.). London: George Allen & Unwin.
Whateley, R. (1831). *Introductory Lectures on Political Economy*. London: B. Fellowes.

9

Circular Flow and Social Class

There must be effective demand. The circular flow is purchase as well as production. Farmers and manufacturers will only supply if their explicit and opportunity costs are being covered by money changing hands. In a trough or in a boom, what is wanted is 'an effective demand for commodities, that is, a demand by those who are able and willing to pay an adequate price for them' (PR 372–373). It is *effective* demand because it *effects* the continuation of supply 'without a fall of profits not required by the state of the land' (PR II 279). It is made up of consumption, investment, public expenditure and a net export market. Without effective demand, there will be no national wealth.

Adam Smith regarded the workers, the capitalists and the landowners as the 'the three great, original and constituent orders of every civilized society' (Smith 1776 [1961]: I 276). Ricardo made the relative shares of the three great factor payments 'the principal problem of Political Economy' (Ricardo 1821 [1951–1955]: 5). Malthus built on the class-based sociology that was in the air to explain the social stratification of national expenditure. The circular flow is not numbers without a pulse. It is human beings layered into social classes. It is not discrete

D. Reisman, *Thomas Robert Malthus*, Great Thinkers in Economics,
https://doi.org/10.1007/978-3-030-01956-3_9

individuals making one-off choices but rather broad categories of individuals whose choices are scripted for them by their economic function.

The macroeconomic problem is socially patterned. Each class makes a different contribution to the whole. The real imperative is whether the national income 'is distributed in such a manner between the different parties concerned as to occasion the most effective demand for future produce' (letter from Malthus to Ricardo, 1821, in Ricardo IX: 10). Distribution does not stop at social justice or allocative efficiency. It affects growth and employment as well.

9.1 The Working Class

Adam Smith, looking bottom-up at the pyramid of hierarchy, had said that national felicity will always fall short of its maximum so long as the footmen, the ploughmen and the common labourers, 'the far greater part of every great political society', are excluded and forgotten, 'poor and miserable' (Smith 1776 [1961]: I 88). Malthus continued the theme that the broad base at the bottom cannot be treated simply as a business asset and a burden on relief. The lower orders are 'the most numerous class in every nation' (SE I 380). They make a major contribution to value added and to aggregate demand. They are also, 'from their numbers, unquestionably of the greatest weight, in any estimate of national happiness' (1815b [1986]: 162).

William Paley and Adam Smith had said it. Malthus knew that they were right. Utility is the end. Affluence is only the means: 'The labouring classes should be well paid, for a much more important reason than any that can relate to wealth; namely, the happiness of the great mass of society' (PR 472). Precisely because the labouring classes form 'the largest part of the nation', it follows from the head-counting Benthamism of one-treated-as-one that 'their general condition is the most important of all' (1827: 317). The maximand is the greatest happiness of the greatest number. The labouring classes are the greatest number. They are all around.

All the classes should go up with growth. The least advantaged should go up the most. It would bring the utility scores of the fellow citizens that much closer together: 'It is the spread of luxury, therefore, among the mass of the people, and not an excess of it in a few, that seems to be the most advantageous, both with regard to national wealth and national happiness' (SE II 193). The manual classes are an end in themselves. They are more than the malleable means to another serving end: 'If a country can only be rich by running a successful race for low wages, I should be disposed to say at once, perish such riches!' (PR 236).

9.1.1 The Population Constraint

It is *too much* and too *little* again. It is a matter of degree, balance and proportion.

Population in excess of subsistence degenerates into vice and misery. Consider stationary China where, in Adam Smith's description of famine and failure, a starving surplus is reduced to eating the carcase of any carrion, 'a dead dog or cat, for example, though half putrid and stinking' (Smith 1776 [1961]: I 81). Consider slow-growing Poland where, in Malthus's own account of wage capital that lags behind, living standards are only marginally better: 'In all those countries, such as Poland, where, from the want of accumulation, the profits of stock remain high, and the progress of cultivation either proceeds very slowly, or is stopped, the wages of labour are extremely low' (1815a [1986]: 124).

The workers live badly in stagnant Poland. Progress is being held back by lack of demand. A wage cut is no guarantee of a job where, even if labour is cheap, 'there is neither the power nor the will to employ it all': 'The commodities which those labourers would produce are not in such request as to ensure tolerable profits' (PR 495). The immediate problem is not the supply of subsistence but the demand for output. Final demand is low. Derived demand is low. The working class is poor not because labour is being exploited by capital but because capital itself is in short supply.

Adam Smith had believed that continuing economic growth would upgrade the material well-being of all the social classes. Malthus in 1798 had said that the historical record was far from encouraging:

'The increasing wealth of the nation has had little or no tendency to better the condition of the labouring poor' (FE 186). By 1817 he had decided that Smith, adjustment made for headcount, had been right: 'A rapid increase of wealth….will always, caeteris paribus, have a desirable effect on the poor' (SE II 86). In America, the accumulation of capital is outpacing the supply of job seekers: 'Profits cannot be low, and labour for some considerable time remains very high' (1815a [1986]: 124). Profits are high. Labour cannot be low. Life in a growing economy is a plus-sum game.

9.1.2 Earning and Spending

On the side of production, labour is 'both a positive good in itself, and absolutely necessary to a further increase in the annual produce' (SE I 439). On the side of consumption, it validates the increase in supply that made possible its wage: 'That a permanent increase of population is a powerful and necessary element of increasing demand, will be most readily allowed' (PR 347).

The charity hard cases and the House of Lords consume. So, importantly, do the rest of us: 'It is by no means necessary that the rich should be excessively luxurious, in order to support the manufactures of a country….The best, and in every point of view the most advantageous manufactures in this country, are those which are consumed by the great body of the people' (SE II 193). The commodities targeted at the super-rich elite 'are trivial on account of the comparative smallness of their quantity' (SE II 193). For sustainable growth, there is no substitute for mass consumption.

Henry Ford envisaged a productive system in which every Ford worker would drive to work in a new Ford car. Karl Marx had a different business model that depended on low wages for high profits. Malthus could see the advantages both of a luxury wage and of a starvation wage. For the individual enterprise, pay is unquestionably a cost: it tends to 'lower profits, and diminish or destroy the motive to accumulate' (PR 472). For the economy as a whole, in contrast, pay is the godsend that keeps high the level of demand: 'Those who live upon the wages of labour, unproductive as well as productive, receive and expend much the greatest part of the annual produce' (PR 423).

The working class is a consuming class: 'The home demand of the country depends very much upon the condition of the labouring classes; that is, that the extent of the effectual demand for the manufactures and commodities consumed at home, depends essentially upon the good conditions of the labouring classes' (1827: 317). A country cannot be more than 'partially prosperous' (1827: 317) which does not draw upon the demand of its working class. Henry Ford was right. Karl Marx was wrong. Business prospers when it pays its workers handsomely so that they can spend.

The conflict of objectives is always there. Higher wages 'at the expense of profits' (PR 370) will gnaw at the per unit return of an individual enterprise. Paradoxically perhaps, higher earnings are also what is required to spend an economy into sustained economic growth. The microeconomics and the macroeconomics do not always point in the same direction.

Malthus concedes that higher wages could 'impede the growth of wealth more by diminishing the power of production, than they could encourage it by increasing the demand for produce' (PR 477). It would be a risk in a recession. Early capitalism was a stew of atomistic price-takers. No perfect competitor 'will ever employ capital merely for the sake of the demand occasioned by those who work for him' (PR 471). Each is more likely to act the free rider on the spillover demand which he hopes his fellow businessmen will create.

Things would be different if the level of total demand were already buoyant: 'Wages and profits very often rise together. When the value of the whole commodity rises from the state of the supply compared with the demand, there is a greater value to divide between the capitalist and the labourer' (1827: 317). The total is rising. Growth is feeding growth. In a self-reinforcing upward spiral, there is more than enough for both factor incomes in absolute terms to be going up.

Money wages rise when the accumulation of capital is shifting outward the demand for labour. Even if the money wage is flat, the purchasing power of the workers may still be going up. Manufactured goods are becoming cheaper. Potatoes are being substituted for grain.

There is also the participation rate. Household incomes—'the earnings of a whole family' (PR II 216)—are being augmented by the labour, often through part-time 'task-work', of women and children (SE I 434).

Women were a part of the labour force. Malthus in the 1798 *Essay* hints that he may have been on their side: 'One half the nation appears to act as Helots to the other half' (FE 82). He will certainly have known of Mary Wollstonecraft's *Vindication of the Rights of Women*, recently published in 1792. Malthus never returned to the topic of women's rights. Had he done so, he would have had to resolve the problem of the deterrent that is also a stimulus. The opportunity cost of women's paid employment acts as a preventive check to early marriage. By augmenting the household budget, however, the second income facilitates discretionary childbearing even where the principal breadwinner's wage is flat.

9.1.3 Informal Indexation

The relatively deprived are the most exposed to fluctuations in food. Frederick Morton Eden in 1797, generalising from regional surveys, had shown that 40% of the median labourer's income was being spent on bread, with a further 20% being devoted to top up foodstuffs like milk and meat (Eden 1797: I 491–589). A rise in the price of cereals would make serious inroads into a household income that was already low.

The custom had been adopted to uprate the money wage in line with the price of grain. It was discussed in Chapter 7. The logic was fairness but it was also expediency. A well-fed worker is more productive than one who is undernourished and infirm. Malthus in the *Observations*, the *Inquiry*, the 1817 *Essay* and in the *Principles* confirmed that wage rates were commonly adjusted upward in line with the price of bread. He had authority on his side: 'Adam Smith has clearly and correctly stated that the money price of labour depends on the money price of provisions, and the state of the demand and the supply of labour' (SE II 83). The 'paramount regulator' (PR 241) will always be the reservation wage. The standard of living will nonetheless be the silent partner.

Fine-tuning takes place but the reaction is delayed. Price signals do not adapt instantaneously, as if guided by an omniscient auctioneer. When grain prices rise in advance of a lagged wage correction, the forced saving which results will boost profits at the expense of the lower-class spend. The workers will have to tighten their belts. It is a built-in stabiliser that limits the rise in price. Since grain is a necessity, there is unlikely to be much room for manoeuvre. Charity may be the last refuge.

When grain prices fall the stakes will be reversed. So long as the price of labour has not fallen, or not fallen in proportion, the result of the delay will be a boost to total employment and to aggregate demand. A transitory mismatch rather than a permanent integer, the artificial stimulus will only survive until such a time as 'labour has adjusted itself to the new level of prices' (PR 446). The workers in the interim will be overcompensated.

Unplanned redistribution in favour of a spending estate leans against the recessionary tendencies of a becalmed economy that has unsold stocks to clear (SE I 401–402n). Imperfect indexation buffers the downturn. By delaying a market-clearing cut in pay it gives windfall purchasing power to the wage-earning community: 'The money price of labour never falls till *many* workmen have been *for some time* out of work' (letter from Malthus to Ricardo, 1821, in Ricardo IX: 10, emphasis added). The incidence of the 'many' and the 'for some time' falls on the quantity of employment and not the price per worker. It is not an unmixed blessing. Sticky wages for the insiders may be costing the outsiders their chance (PR 418).

There is a further way in which imperfect adjustment can have a stimulatory effect on the economy. Pay is put up in line with bread. Following Eden, however, Malthus notes that only 40% of the household's income is actually earmarked for bread (1814: 89). Total consumption is not grain alone but a bundle of 'necessaries, conveniences, and luxuries of life' (PR 240). Some 60% of the household's income is spent on commodities of which the price does not go up with the price of bread. In some cases, the price goes down.

A part of the indexed compensation will be allocated to 'other necessaries' (SE II 44) such as housing and fuel. A part will be exchanged for 'conveniences and luxuries' such as soap, candles, tea, sugar and clothing (1814: 89). Some of these consumables will lie above the physical maximum. Being in line with 'the habits of the people' (PR 556), they are socially prescribed quasi-necessities nonetheless. It is the breadline but it is not the breadline. When incomes rise in step with bread, socialised households will be able to devote more than half of their discretionary adjustment to the props and costumes of their social role.

Prices in the primary sector may have a long-term tendency to rise. The prices of manufactures are more likely to move in the opposite direction. Economies of scale create a macroeconomic spillover in that they free up disposable income for additional purchases. Informal indexation in a dual economy can create employment and income for the victims in a slump. Wage adjustment in line with bread is a 40% solution. It is unintended overkill which helps the economy to spend itself out of bad times.

Good times or bad times, it will never be enough. Working-class consumption by itself will never be sufficient to push the economy to its frontier: 'No power of consumption on the part of the labouring classes can ever....alone furnish an encouragement to the employment of capital' (PR 471). Despite the sheer force of numbers, 'population alone cannot create an effective demand for wealth' (PR 350). The workers are not the whole of aggregate demand. They are, however, a sizeable part. The labouring classes are already enjoying 'an increased command over the necessaries of life' (PR 324). They are diversifying at the margin into conveniences, amusements and luxuries. It is the mass market and the affluent worker. It is Henry Ford. It is not Karl Marx.

9.1.4 Capital and Labour

Business is a sequence. The capitalist finances this year's production with last year's retentions in the hope that he will multiply his profits still further when, next year, his value added will be realised. In the veil of tears, the capitalist must reinvest last year's surplus in this year's inventories, this year's machines and this year's wages bill. The worker must be grubstaked today: 'The funds for the subsistence of the manufacturer must be advanced to him before he can complete his work' (SE II 30). The capitalist will recoup his investment if and when today's product is disposed of at a profit tomorrow.

Saving is the precondition for investment. Profusion squanders valuable resources that might have been embodied in fixed plant or deployed as wage capital to fund the shop floor. So does wasteful hoarding which immobilises economic potential that might have become effectual demand for output and input alike: 'The avaricious man….locks up his wealth in a chest and sets in motion no labour of any kind, either productive or unproductive' (FE 176).

The miser locks away sterile gold that could have been total demand. His irrational choice is not for all seasons: 'No political economist of the present day can by saving mean mere hoarding' (PR 32). The miser will be making a greater contribution to the creation of new wealth if he shifts the fruits of his abstention into consumption or investment instead. His savings could have been placed in 'the effectual funds for the maintenance of labour' (FE 186). There is much to praise in 'the superior wealth and usefulness of the character who employed the poor' (FE 181). Even luxuries create jobs. They relieve decent working men more effectively than Speenhamland handouts or Mr. Whitbread's cottages. The capitalist is the true friend of the poor. His factory has the function of a charitable foundation that gives work to the needy. Adam Smith had said so (Smith 1776 [1961]: I 359).

A growing economy is a dynamic support system. So long as more income is generating more saving which is facilitating more employment, a growing population will be more likely to escape the China trap. Where the demand for labour does not keep pace with the supply, 'the real wages of labour will sink till they are only just sufficient to maintain a stationary population' (SE II 27). China speed is misery and vice. Where, however, economic growth is the effect and cause of further saving, a growing labour force is less likely to be out of work: 'The faster the value of the annual produce increases, the greater will be the power of purchasing fresh labour' (PR 261).

The labour force is multiplying in an unstoppable ratio. The supply of wage capital must be increasing at least as fast: 'The progressive increase of capital, and of the funds for the maintenance of labour, is the great cause of a demand for labour, and of high corn wages' (SE II 40). Income, saving and investment must all be on an upward trend. The fund devoted to the payment of wages must be going up: 'On the state of this fund, the happiness, or the degree of misery, prevailing among the lower classes of people, in every known state, at present chiefly depends' (SE I 325).

9.1.5 Jobless Growth

Man 'cannot really multiply and prosper unless his labour be wanted' (SE I 101). Capital accumulation means that his labour will continue to be wanted. It will be the proletarian paradise. It will be a chicken in every pot.

Or will it? Total capital is the sum of inanimate plant plus circulating capital destined for the input with a pulse. Adam Smith did not entertain the possibility that what Marx called the 'organic composition of capital' (quoted in Meek 1953: 80) might be twisted in favour of innovations that 'substitute machinery for manual exertions' (PR 402) and away from the wage capital that keeps human labour in work. Malthus did: 'The funds for the maintenance of labour do not necessarily increase with the increase of wealth, and very rarely in *proportion* to it' (SE II 77, emphasis in original). The language reveals the dystopia. In spite of his 'not necessarily', in the spirit of his 'very rarely', what Malthus may have feared is that Smith's China was not dead but only sleeping.

The nation is growing rich. Capital is being accumulated. The sequence by itself may not be enough. The workers depend upon a 'steady and continued demand for labour' (SE II 24–25). In the downswing, the demand will become slack. What Malthus is saying is that even in buoyant times the slack might persist. Machinery might displace the human input. Growth and accumulation might not be able to prevent fixed capital from encroaching into circulating capital just as Thomas More's sheep had done when pasturage ate up the redundant ploughmen (More 1516 [1978]: 26).

John Barton in his *Observations* in 1817 had said that it had to happen: 'As the arts are cultivated and civilization is extended, fixed capital bears a larger and larger proportion to circulating capital' (Barton 1817 [1934]: 17). Automation is revolutionising the proportions. The wages fund may not be cost-effective: 'It is easy to conceive that under certain circumstances, the whole of the annual savings of an industrious people might be added to fixed capital, in which case they would have no effect in increasing the demand for labour' (Barton 1817 [1934]: 18). Competition from the robots keeps the remuneration low. It is little comfort that it may also keep the birth rate down.

Ricardo, after reading Barton, revised his own views on Smith's smooth transition from growth to saving and then on to the wages fund. In the 1821 edition of his *Principles*, he conceded that the demand for labour was not inevitably a rising function of national wealth: 'The same cause which may increase the net revenue of the country, may at the same time render the population redundant, and deteriorate the condition of the labourer' (Ricardo 1821 [1951–1955]: 388). Much later there would be Marx: 'In proportion as capital accumulates, the lot of the labourer, be his payment high or low, must grow worse' (quoted in Meek 1953: 103).

There was also Malthus, who in his own *Principles* called Barton's *Observations* 'an ingenious pamphlet on the condition of the labouring classes' (PR 261n). Malthus agreed that the coefficients between fixed and wage capital very rarely stayed the same. Substitution was taking place. It was an evolution but not a cause of unemployment: 'There is little reason to apprehend any permanent evil from the introduction of machinery' (PR 412).

Technology was less likely to create a Marxian reserve army in a dynamic economy where one capital can complement the other: 'In general….the use of fixed capital is extremely favourable to the abundance of circulating capital' (PR 262). Fixed capital tends to increase the gross product. It makes possible still more saving and still more investment. It creates new openings for an expanding workforce.

The effect would be greater still if Malthus had explicitly recognised the multiplier expansion. The subsequent rounds may or may not have been visible in embryo in the call for public spending of earlier economists like William Petty. It may have been implicit in Petty's suggestion in 1662 that there should be 'entertainments, magnificent shews, triumphal arches' and 'useless pyramid-building on Salisbury Plain' in order to demand-pull an economy out of a recession (Petty 1662 [1997]: I 31). Bernard Corry is critical of Malthus for selling his own argument short: 'There is no suggestion of any secondary or "multiplier" effects accompanying the process. In fact, there is not even any clear suggestion of a link between income and consumption – i.e. no consumption function' (Corry 1962: 119). There was scope for Malthus to strengthen his case. Yet the case as it stands is strong. Machinery, Malthus contends, is expanding and not suppressing the supply of jobs.

On the land, equipment facilitating the exploitation of marginal plots had to be operated by living labour. In the cotton industry, and 'notwithstanding the increasing use of fixed capital' (PR 263), the demand for workmen had actually gone up. The proportions will change. It is no reason to fear that people will be pushed out by things. 'The most usual effect' is that the 'value of the whole mass of goods made by the new machinery greatly exceeds their former value; and, notwithstanding the saving of labour, more hands, instead of fewer, are required in the manufacture' (PR 402).

The bias towards fixed capital 'will lead to a great extension of wealth and value' (PR 412). Particularly, will this be so if the restructuring of capital involves not just the replication of embodied know-how but Schumpeter-like 'creative destruction' (Schumpeter 1942 [1976]: 81) that necessitates unanticipated retooling. In the 1817 *Essay*, Malthus had written of 'ingenuity in machinery' (SE II 34) as if it were a once for all transition. In the 1826 *Essay*, he amended his message to 'no ingenuity in machinery *which was not continually progressive*' (SE II 34n, emphasis added). The growing wealth of nations perpetuates the continuing wealth of persons. It protects workers' jobs even if the coefficients are mutating towards iron and steel.

Domestic markets are being widened as the cause and effect of mechanisation: 'Accumulation ensures effective demand' (PR 365n). In spite of that, the circular flow can still be interrupted. One threat to employment is satiety. The 'cheapness of domestic commodities occasioned by machinery' might then lead to 'increased saving rather than to increased expenditure' (PR 412). Another threat relates to the very nature of capital intensity itself: 'Whenever the introduction of fixed capital has for a time the effect of diminishing the demand for labour, it will generally be found that the value of the whole annual produce is at the same time diminished' (PR II 206).

There is production but there must also be sale. If there were to be a swing against labour, then it might not be a sustainable one. Artificial intelligence does not have effective demand. While cheaper consumables made with better machines will have a stimulatory effect on real income, the inducement will not go far if the workers displaced are left without adequate purchasing power to complete the circular flow. Essential is a working class able and willing to buy. If internally generated limits to growth are to be avoided, then the machine intensity of the capitals must not exceed a demand-determined Golden Mean.

9.2 The Middle Class

At the bottom, there are the wage earners. At the top, there are the landowners. In the middle, there are the commanding heights of industry and trade who are the drivers of the new economic order: 'A taste for material objects, however frivolous, almost always requires for its gratification the accumulation of capital, and the existence of manufacturers or merchants, wholesale dealers and retail dealers. The facc of society is thus wholly changed. A middle class of persons, living upon the profits of stock, rises into wealth and consequence' (PR 35).

The new industrial age is the age of discovery. As well as inspiring 'a taste for conveniences and comforts among the labouring classes', the kaleidoscope of capitalism will by its very nature 'excite invention, encourage science and the useful arts, spread intelligence and spirit' (1814 [1986]: 102). Competition is challenge. Aspiration develops the mind and character. Better people are both the cause and the effect of the revolution in taste and technique.

The new industrial order tends to 'infuse fresh life and activity into all classes of the state' (1814 [1986]: 101). It tends to upgrade men's activities even as it satisfies their wants (Marshall 1890 [1949]: 76). Manufacturing and commerce open doors and equalise life chances. They 'afford opportunitics for the inferior orders to rise by personal merit and exertion, and stimulate the higher orders to depend for distinction upon other grounds than mere rank and riches' (1814 [1986]: 101). Social stratification becomes more fluid, the social structure less ossified. The class at birth becomes less important than the class that is achieved. Interclass mobility gives 'a new and happier structure to society' (1814 [1986]: 101).

Some go up and some go down. The industrial order puts a monetary value on the ambitious worker who has what it takes for a seat on the board. At the same time, the economic transformation is weakening 'the pernicious power of the landowners' (PR II 84). Rent as a share in the national income is falling. Erstwhile dependents are reinventing themselves as 'merchants, manufacturers, tradesmen, farmers, and independent labourers' (PR II 84). As the workers are levelled up and the aristocracy is levelled down, economic evolution is producing a bulge in 'the proportion of the middle classes' (1814 [1986]: 102). It has far-reaching consequences. The middle classes are 'the body on which the liberty, public spirit, and good government of every country must mainly depend' (1814 [1986]: 102).

Embourgeoisement is a cause of moral restraint. Unaffordable births are becoming less common while improvements in farming are postponing 'for several centuries' the margin of exhaustion. The ratios are not an imminent barrier to sustained growth. With rising real incomes, however, an internal contradiction is emerging which has no precedent in the pre-affluent productive system. The middle classes are parsimonious. Parsimony can go too far.

The middle class is a saving class. It is in the nature of the businessman that he pares down current consumption in order to ensure 'future wealth and enjoyment' both for himself and for 'those to whom he means to leave his property' (PR 360). The businessman is working and saving not just for himself but for his family: 'The desire to realize a fortune as a permanent provision for a family is perhaps the most general motive for….continued exertions' (PR 471). It is altruism as well as egotism that keeps him late in the office. Market capitalism is duty even as it is licence.

Saving is also self-advertisement. Abstention is the means to an end where self-made men are struggling to put their economic success on public display. The intergenerational business dynasties were yet to come. Malthus was living at a time when fresh-faced entrepreneurs were fighting for scarce position. It was Darwin's survival of the fittest and Marx's perfect competition. Small firms had not given way to long-lived monopolies.

Determined to earn and to retain their status, the *nouveaux riches* treat parsimony as a social and not just an economic investment in 'bettering their condition' (PR 363). They have neither the time nor the will to plunge their economic power into luxury consumables. Veblen's leisure class advertises itself through 'conspicuous consumption' (Veblen 1899 [1970]: 85). Marshall's business élite treats the expansion of capital as the status symbol supreme (Marshall 1890 [1949]: 190). It is all in Marshall. Earned status is business status. Profit must be made a stepping stone towards still greater success.

The saving class is in that way driven to be an investing class as well. The world is underdeveloped: 'There is hardly a country in the four quarters of the globe where capital is not deficient' (PR 372). No growth in wealth, global, national or individual, would be possible without the 'conversion of revenue into capital' (PR 352). Farmers make agriculture into a business: improving their technology, the result has been an 'increase of wealth on the land' (PR 35). Industrialists reinvest in fixed and circulating capital: their motive is to equal or improve upon 'ordinary remuneration in the shape of profits' (PR II 67). Saving is not immobilised in idle hoards. It is quickly reinvested in machines and men.

There is, however, a proviso. There must be demand sufficient to dispose of the final product. In a retaining culture, that demand might not be forthcoming. Businessmen produce largely, consume sparingly, and save too much: 'Almost all merchants and manufacturers save, in prosperous times, much more rapidly than it would be possible for the national capital to increase, so as to keep up the value of the produce' (PR 465). Thence the internal contradiction. The middle classes need to save. The middle classes also need to spend. Threatening the economic balance, additional withdrawals would have the effect of 'aggravating instead of alleviating our distress' (PR 505).

Both saving and spending are essential if the circular flow is not to sink into excess supply and contraction. The middle class is a spending class: 'There is nothing so favourable to effectual demand as a large proportion of the middle classes of society' (PR II 261). The problem is that they as a class are not spending enough: 'The capitalists cannot continue the same habits of saving. They must either consume more, or produce less' (PR 466). Since exertion is onerous and the 'mere pleasure of present expenditure' not something that Malthus's middle classes value above security, family and return, 'the probability is that a considerable body of them will be induced to .... produce less' (PR 466).

The future of the new business civilisation is under threat. Oversaving and not the Marxian proletariat is the wolf at the door. The business-based middle classes are not making a market for each other's goods. The non-commercial middle classes have neither the desire nor the ability to fill the gap. Prices will fall below the cost of production. Profits will turn into losses. New investment will cease. There would be no 'immediate and pressing demand for capital' because there would be no 'immediate and pressing demand for commodities' (PR 491). Adam Smith had praised parsimony. Keynes was to warn that parsimony could turn malign: 'There has been a chronic tendency throughout human history for the propensity to save to be stronger than the inducement to invest' (Keynes 1936 [1973]: 347). In the long run, it will be the downward spiral. The invisible hand will not correct the decline.

Parsimony is an essential component of economic growth. Pushed, however, beyond 'a certain point', it would make the nation 'poor, and comparatively unpeopled' (PR 363). Lord Lauderdale in 1804 had already inveighed against 'this baneful passion for accumulation, that has been falsely denominated a virtue' (Lauderdale 1804: 218). The 'creation of a quantity of capital more than is requisite' must inevitably lead to unsold stocks because of inadequate demand: 'The finest palaces in the world stand empty at Delhi, unoccupied and undesired' (Lauderdale 1804: 220, 221). The same fate would befall the finest warehouses at Manchester if the false God of abstinence were allowed to drain away the national wealth.

The proper response, Lauderdale said, is neither abstention nor indulgence but a sensible balance, within 'due bounds': 'Parsimony, when pushed beyond a certain extent....must be fatal to the progress of public wealth' (Lauderdale 1804: 220, 271). Malthus knew Lauderdale personally but, before the *Principles*, had said little in print about parsimony turned malign. Already in 1814, however, in his correspondence with Ricardo, he was acknowledging that demand might be in deficit: 'A nation must certainly have the power of purchasing all that it produces, but I can easily conceive it not to have the will' (letter from Malthus to Ricardo, 1814, in Ricardo VI: 132). By the *Principles* in 1820, he had made up his mind.

Malthus felt that Lauderdale had gone too far in deprecating thrift just as Smith had gone too far in deprecating prodigality (PR 351–352). It was a matter of emphasis rather than direction. On the core issue of balance, the two authors were in agreement. There should neither be *too much* nor *too little*. A lack of expenditure would discourage production. Malthus was concerned that the economy was at risk from a lack of expenditure. Unable to rely on effective demand from the working and the middle class, Malthus knew that an alternative source of effective demand had to be found.

9.3 The Landowners

The landowners make a double contribution to effective demand. Firstly, they spend where the working classes lack the means and the middle classes lack the will. The landowners purchase the unwanted residual which otherwise would not have found a home. Second, they provide employment for the subclass of unproductive labour. Only material goods figure in the nation's wealth. The landowners, spending disproportionately in the service sector, prevent 'great numbers of the labouring classes from being starved for want of work' (PR 487).

9.3.1 A Spending Class

Farmers are agricultural capitalists whose factor income is profits. They are not rent-recipients but own-account tradesmen whose maximand is the competitive return. Landlords are different. Passive rather than active, the aristocracy reaps where it never sowed. It enjoys an unearned income that is the unplanned outcome of diminishing returns and an unstoppable increase in population.

When grain prices fall, and after the leases have been renegotiated, the national income is redistributed away from the rent-recipients. When grain prices rise, the long-term effect is to favour the landowning estate: 'The greater is the value of the rent, the less is the value of the labour and profits' (PR II 59). The national income is unaffected. The national expenditure, however, receives a boost. The capitalists are a retentive class. Not so 'the retainers of a court and an overgrown aristocracy' (PR 34). They have no reason not to run down a surplus that renews itself automatically.

The landowning class contributes to the profits of capital and the wages of labour. It does this on the side of demand and not of supply. Writing to Ricardo at a time when trade was 'exceedingly slack', Malthus said that the fall in prices and incomes on the land was having a recessionary effect in the market for manufactured goods: 'The main cause of the present slackness of trade is the diminished incomes of the Landlords and Farmers' (letter from Malthus to Ricardo, 1815, in Ricardo VI: 303). A rise in grain prices would have increased the incomes of the rent-spending class. So would agricultural protection that raised grain prices and with them the rents.

The landowners are a spending class. Eschewing self-denying frugality, they devote their income to 'material conveniences and luxuries', 'a few splendid foreign commodities' and to personal services which 'neither require nor generate capital' (PR 35, 378). While the satisfaction of their basic needs for mansions, clothing and carriages will be subject to the law of diminishing utility, it is unlikely that their incremental demand for fashions and frivolities will ever exhaust itself into satiety. After allowing for the skewness of their choice set, it is a welcome truth that the rent-recipients are affording a 'steady home demand for the manufactures of the country' (1815b [1986]: 167). A steady home demand is all to the good when the alternative is unsold goods and out-of-work manpower.

It is easy to dismiss the descendants of the feudal warlords as an anomaly and a survival. Malthus argues the opposite, that even a class which adds nothing to total wealth can be an integral part of modern capitalism. Rather than a functionless curiosum, the landowners make a valuable contribution to the extent that they provide market demand for the wealth that has been added by others: 'Though they do not so actively contribute to the production of wealth....there is no class in society whose interests are more nearly and intimately connected with the prosperity of the state' (1815b [1986]: 167).

William Spence had maintained that the landowners, receiving their rents in acknowledgement of agricultural produce, played an essential role in the circular flow: 'It is clear, then, that expenditure, not parsimony, is the province of the class of land proprietors, and that it is on the due performance of this duty, by the class in question, that the production of national wealth depends' (Spence 1807: 36). Spence believed that the class of land proprietors had a function approaching a duty to 'expend the greater part of the revenue which they derive from the soil': 'So long as they perform this duty, every thing goes on in its proper train' (Spence 1807: 33). Should they not exchange their income for manufactures and services, then there can be no doubt but that 'the machine of society must be broken up' (Spence 1807: 36). Malthus followed Spence. The rents had to be spent. The land proprietors were keeping modern capitalism afloat.

It was the circular flow but it was not secure. The effective demand of the landlords is even now 'insufficient' (PR 466) to stabilise total demand in a recession. Their contribution will decline still further as industry expands in the towns while agrobusiness in the villages succeeds to knee-jerk inertia. Rents are already being crowded out by profits. Between 1780 and 1820, rents had fallen from 'a fourth or a third' to 'a fifth of the gross produce' (PR 214). In the feudal period, the share of rent in the national wealth was 40%. By 1815, it had fallen to 25% (1815b [1986]: 167), to 20% (1815a [1986]: 130), or perhaps even less.

The share is less but the absolute amount is more: 'The landlord has a less *share* of the whole produce, yet this share, from the very great increase of the produce, yields a larger quantity' (1815a [1986]: 130, emphasis added). The landlords retain a presence in the recycling of the material flow. Their share in the national expenditure must nonetheless 'diminish, owing to the increasing number and wealth of those who live upon a still more important surplus – the profits of stock'

(1815a [1986]: 142). The cherry orchard is increasingly being shared with the capital-owning class. It is crowding into the rent-recipients' room at the top.

Both in industry and agriculture, the ascendancy of profits can only be a good thing. The capitalists are 'beyond all question, the main source of accumulation' (PR 199n). The gain-maximising ethos is invading the countryside. Despite continuing primogeniture the estates are being divided and sold. Menials are being replaced by productive labourers. Landlords are investing for bottom line. Prodigality is giving way to parsimony. It is the concomitant of the 'increase of wealth on the land as well as elsewhere' (PR 35). The landowners of tomorrow may not think like the landowners of today. Even the landowners might always not prove a luxury-loving, free-spending bulwark against a dearth in total demand.

9.3.2 Unproductive Consumption

The stationary state is never far away. The geometrical ratio in the increase of population will be arrested by a lasting deficiency in aggregate demand even before the margin of subsistence has been fully cropped: 'If the effectual demand for necessaries were fully supplied, and an adequate taste for unproductive consumption, or personal services had not been established, no motive of interest could induce the producers to make an effectual demand for this greater number of labourers' (PR II 251).

Malthus says that there will be 'no occasion for unproductive consumers, if a consumption sufficient to keep up the value of the produce takes place among those who are engaged in production' (PR 464–465). The need arises because the workers and the capitalists do not, taken together, generate adequate demand to absorb the material product and the landlords, absorbing some of the material surplus, do not absorb enough (PR 466, 475). The balance must be put right: 'This certain proportion of unproductive consumption….is absolutely and independently necessary to call forth the resources of a country' (letter from Malthus to Ricardo, 1821, in Ricardo IX: 19).

The service sector fills the gap: 'Menial servants are absolutely necessary to make the resources of the higher and middle classes of society efficient in the demand for material products' (PR II 278). Service workers and factory workers, Malthus believed, are two sides of the same coin: 'It is absolutely necessary that a country with great powers of production should possess a body of unproductive consumers' (PR 463). A 'body of demanders' (PR 464) is the sine qua non for sustained activity. It must, however, conform to the rule of 'adequate proportion' (PR 463).

There must not be *too much*. Where personal services predominate, 'capital and wealth are comparatively deficient' (PR II 27). Adam Smith had cautioned that overexpansion would not 'leave a sufficiency for maintaining the productive labourers, who should reproduce it next year' (Smith 1776 [1961]: I 364). Malthus saw Smith's threat to reproduction as a warning not to go too far: 'If the neat revenue of a country could only be employed in the maintenance of menial servants and soldiers, there is every reason to think that the stimulus to production in modern states would be very greatly diminished' (PR II 205).

There must not be *too much*. Nor, however, should there be *too little*. Even if the total capital stock is increasing, still 'a rapid conversion of unproductive into productive labour' (PR 463) could be a self-negating tendency. The nation needs factory hands to produce material output but it also needs opera-singers to take it off the market. Both the productive and the unproductive are needed if the nation is to grow in wealth and population. Here as elsewhere, it is important that the variables should gravitate into 'the most favourable proportions' (PR II 206). Here as elsewhere, 'the wealth of nations depends upon the proportion of parts' (PR 479).

The doctrine of proportions 'meets us at every turn' (PR II 278). Balance is important not just in political economy 'but throughout the whole range of nature and art' (SE II 269). Science is not in a position to identify the precise optimum: 'What the proportion is....the resources of political economy are unequal to determine' (PR 464). Logically speaking, however, it must exist. Public policy must do what it can to stabilise the equilibrium. The search for the Golden Mean has implications both for public spending and for the social structure.

In the case of spending, the spectre of inadequate demand must lead even a conviction liberal to advocate public services funded through taxation and debt. Soldiers, teachers, civil servants of all kinds are spending income that could have been devoted to capital and wealth. It is a meaningless either/or. Malthus was led by his rejection of Say's Law to the unexpected conclusion that State payments for non-productive labour may be creating essential demand that keeps the economy on course (PR 463–464).

In the case of society, the theory of balance legitimates the indolence of the landowners. The 'great laws of nature', Malthus says, 'have provided for the leisure of a certain portion of society' (PR 463). It would do harm to economic progress if this 'beneficent offer' were not accepted by 'an adequate number of individuals' (PR 464). Beyond some 'intermediate point' it is the self-indulgence of a backward-looking aristocracy and not the self-denial of the rational, the calculative and the alert that must be smoothing the road to material wealth. The past must be marching alongside the future.

Ricardo was not sure that Malthus's argument made sense: 'Will the taking 100 pieces of cloth from a clothiers manufactory, and clothing soldiers and sailors with it, add to his profits? Will it stimulate him to produce? – yes, in the same way as a fire would' (Ricardo 1820 [1951–1955]: 425). Advocates of social welfare, less sympathetic to decaying feudalism, would say that Malthus might have defended the Poor Laws with the same argument that relief transfers resources to a class that will spend. Income replacement or unproductive labour, both have the potential to reverse a recession into a boom.

References

By T. R. Malthus

(1798 [1970]). *Essay on the Principle of Population, as It Affects the Future Improvement of Society, with Remarks on the Speculations of Mr. Godwin, M. Condorcet, and Other Writers* (abbreviated as FE), ed. by A. Flew. Harmondsworth: Penguin.

(1803 et seq. [1989]). *An Essay on the Principle of Population: Or a View of Its Past and Present Effects on Human Happiness, with an Inquiry into Our Prospects Respecting the Removal of the Evils Which It Occasions* (2nd edition, 1803; further editions in 1806, 1807, 1817, 1826) (abbreviated as SE I and SE II), 2 vols., ed. by P. James. Cambridge: Cambridge University Press.

(1814 [1986]). *Observations on the Effects of the Corn Laws, and of a Rise or Fall in the Price of Corn on the Agriculture and General Wealth of the Country,* reprinted in *The Works of Thomas Robert Malthus,* ed. by E. A. Wrigley and D. Souden. London: Pickering and Chatto, 7, 87–109.

(1815a [1986]). *An Inquiry into the Nature and Progress of Rent, and the Principles by Which It Is Regulated,* reprinted in *The Works of Thomas Robert Malthus,* ed. by E. A. Wrigley and D. Souden. London: Pickering and Chatto, 7, 115–145.

(1815b [1986]). *The Grounds of an Opinion on the Policy of Restricting the Importation of Foreign Corn,* reprinted in *The Works of Thomas Robert Malthus,* ed. by E. A. Wrigley and D. Souden. London: Pickering and Chatto, 7, 151–174.

(1820 [1989]). *The Principles of Political Economy* (abbreviated as PR), ed. by J. Pullen. Cambridge: Cambridge University Press.

(1827). Evidence to the Select Committee on Emigration (Third Report), in *Parliamentary Papers.* London: House of Commons, 5, 311–327.

(1836 [1989]). *The Principles of Political Economy: The Alterations to the First Edition* (abbreviated as PR II), ed. by J. Pullen. Cambridge: Cambridge University Press.

Secondary Literature

Barton, J. (1817 [1934]). *Observations on the Circumstances Which Influence the Condition of the Labouring Classes of Society* (J. H. Hollander, Ed.). Baltimore: Johns Hopkins Press.

Corry, B. (1962). *Money, Saving and Investment in English Economics 1800–1850.* London: Macmillan.

Eden, F. M. (1797). *The State of the Poor* (3 vols.). London: J. Davis.

Keynes, J. M. (1936 [1973]). *The General Theory of Employment, Interest and Money.* In *The Collected Writings of John Maynard Keynes.* London: Macmillan.

Lauderdale, J. M. (1804). *An Inquiry into the Nature and Origin of Public Wealth*. Edinburgh: Arch. Constable.

Marshall, A. (1890 [1949]). *Principles of Economics*. London: Macmillan.

Meek, R. L. (Ed.). (1953). *Marx and Engels on Malthus*. London: Lawrence and Wishart.

More, T. (1516 [1978]). *Utopia*. London: J. M. Dent.

Petty, W. (1662 [1997]). *A Treatise of Taxes and Contributions*. In C. H. Hull (Ed.), *The Economic Writings of Sir William Petty* (2 vols.). London: Routledge and Thommes Press.

Ricardo, D. (1820 [1951–1955]). *Notes on Malthus*, in Ricardo, infra, II.

Ricardo, D. (1821 [1951–1955]). *Principles of Political Economy and Taxation*, in Ricardo, infra, I.

Ricardo, D. (1951–1955). *The Works and Correspondence of David Ricardo* (abbreviated as Ricardo) (P. Sraffa with M. Dobb, Eds., 11 vols.). Cambridge: Cambridge University Press.

Schumpeter, J. A. (1942 [1976]). *Capitalism, Socialism and Democracy*. London: George Allen & Unwin.

Smith, A. (1776 [1961]). *The Wealth of Nations* (E. Cannan, Ed., 2 vols.). London: Methuen.

Spence, W. (1807). *Britain Independent of Commerce*. London: W. Savage.

Veblen, T. (1899 [1970]). *The Theory of the Leisure Class*. London: Unwin Books.

10

Society and State

Economics is about passion. Every undergraduate knows that. There is the passion for spending: 'An adequate passion for consumption may fully keep up the proper proportion between supply and demand, whatever may be the powers of production' (PR 365). There is the passion for not spending: 'A passion for accumulation must inevitably lead to a supply of commodities beyond what the structure and habits of such a society will permit to be consumed' (PR 365). The passion for the immediate plus the passion for the deferred add up to the national income. Every statistician knows that.

A balance sheet always balances. Desired economic parameters provide no such reassurance. The passion for spending is Say's Law. It ensures that whatever can be produced will also be sold. The passion for not spending is Lauderdale's law. It is a warning that saving in excess of its optimum can lead to surplus product that no one wants to buy. This much is clear. The two passions should not be grouped together 'as if they were of the same nature' (PR 366). In terms of their impact and their consequences, they are not.

The production possibilities of land, labour and capital are necessary but not sufficient. For growth to be sustainable, there must also be total

D. Reisman, *Thomas Robert Malthus*, Great Thinkers in Economics,
https://doi.org/10.1007/978-3-030-01956-3_10

demand. It must be appropriately distributed between the immediate and the deferred, between the classes that save and the classes that spend, between the private sector and the public sector that does what it can to smooth out the oscillations. Effective demand should not be *too much* or *too little*. It should be in keeping with the need.

This chapter continues the discussion of the three classes and the circular flow that was begun in Chapter 9. It confirms that the landowners tend to be a spending class but also shows that, spending or saving, a compulsory reallocation of their property rights can never be an option. There is more to social stability and constitutional democracy than effective demand alone. A shift upward in the national expenditure function is a more promising strategy. Effective demand is the willingness to spend and not just the ability to do so. If demand remains stubbornly in deficit, then the answer might have to be the State.

10.1 The Distribution of Land

Malthus was not a conviction egalitarian in the spirit of William Godwin or Tom Paine. He was, however, a cautious moderate who believed that economic disparities should know their bounds: 'All the great results in political economy, respecting wealth, depend upon *proportions*' (PR 432, emphasis in original) It was an application of his theory of balance: 'The wealth of nations depends upon the relation of parts' (PR II 278). The distribution of endowments should confine itself to the middle ground: 'It is from overlooking this most important truth, that so many errors have prevailed in the prediction of consequences' (PR 432).

10.1.1 Distance and Demand

Excessive inequality in the ownership of land, neither necessary or useful, is wrong: 'A better distribution of landed property might exist than that which actually prevails in this country at present.…To make it better, the distribution should be more equal' (PR 439). Marx believed the lion in the path was up-and-coming capital. To Malthus, it was the commanding heights of land.

In Europe in the Middle Ages, 'a most unequal and vicious division of landed property was established' (PR 429). It survives to the present day in the form of self-replicating institutions and out-of-date entitlements. Malthus, writing as an economist and a liberal, believed that it was essential to reconsider the social utility of the long-lived estates in the light of the post-feudal economic revolution.

Landlordism perpetuates inefficiency: 'It is not probable that the soil should be properly cultivated' (FE 198). Short leases and undercapitalised tenants had led to 'a slack kind of cultivation' (PR 429) that, in the language of the ratios, was depriving the growing population of essential food. It contrasts badly with the situation in North America where there were no sitting proprietors to stifle the owner-operators' productivity. The lesson seems to be that greater equality 'would encourage further production' (PR 439).

Production is too low. So is aggregate demand. Small farmers on large *latifundia* do not have the incomes that would spend the economy into affluence: 'A very large proprietor, surrounded by very poor peasants, presents a distribution of property most unfavourable to effective demand' (PR 429). It was the South as well as the North. Spanish America had been held back more by 'want of demand than want of capital' (PR 393).

The landowners themselves are, of course, a spending class. Rural England 'possesses a very large class of effective demanders' (PR 436). Rent-recipients are unproductive consumers whose outgoings and those of their sterile dependents provide a market for the material sector. They consume but they do not create. It is a strong argument for an absentee elite but it is also a building that is not made to last. Marginal utility might decrease as total consumption goes up. Incremental cravings might beyond a point be weak and unpredictable. A surfeit of consumables might cause the satiated to call a halt.

A love of finery might reach a ceiling limit. The prosperous landowner, 'after he had furnished his mansion or castle splendidly, and provided himself with handsome clothes and handsome carriages, would not change them all every two months, merely because he had the power of doing so' (PR 430). New goods might or might not reinvigorate his jaded palate. Nor might he see any need to extend his roll of unproductive servants and retainers who perform vicarious consumption on his behalf. The ambitious capitalist has a rational reason to save and invest. The rich landowner might keep his fortune idle because the man who has it all has no further need to spend.

The genuine plutocrat might not fulfil his macroeconomic function. At least the moderately prosperous are not yet on strike: 'The excessive wealth of the few is in no respect equivalent, with regard to effective demand, to the more moderate wealth of the many' (PR 431). It is a sound reason for a guarded reallocation of property in favour of middle-ranking noblemen who have not lost their propensity to consume: 'Thirty or forty proprietors, with incomes answering to between one thousand and five thousand a year, would create a much more effective demand for wheaten bread, good meat, and manufactured products, than a single proprietor possessing a hundred thousand a year' (PR 430).

Redistribution is needed because the billionaire oligarchs, always a minority, are shopped-out and bored: 'No instance has ever been known of a country which has pushed its natural resources to a great extent, with a small proportionate body of persons of property, however rich and luxurious they might be' (PR 431). The 'greatest powers of production' are rendered useless by a 'want of effective demand' (PR 432). A pragmatic correction of excessive shares should be regarded as an argument in the production function and a cause of further growth.

A proper distribution of landed property and with it the flow of rent is 'as necessary to the continued increase of wealth as the means of producing it' (PR 482). The ideal would be redistribution, but with the proviso that the changes should not go too far: 'Beyond a certain extent, they would impede the progress of wealth as much as they had before accelerated it' (PR 431). Landlords would not be able to contribute to their farmers' improvements: 'The progress of wealth would be checked by a failure in the powers of supply' (PR 432). An 'antagonist principle', sooner or later, would 'interfere with the power of production' (PR 439). Demand goes up but supply goes down. It is not a good way to promote the continued increase of wealth.

10.1.2 Land and Law

France following the revolution undertook a 'fearful experiment' (PR 433). The large estates of feudal Europe had been 'most unfavourable to liberty and good government' (SE II 84). After 1789, there had been a new law under which landed property was to be divided equally between the children.

The lot of the peasantry had been 'decidedly improved' (SE I 246). It would not last. Within less than a century, Malthus predicted, the 'too great division of lands' (SE I 240) would be the cause of 'extraordinary poverty and distress' (PR 434). Subdivision would 'diminish surplus produce' (SE I 240). It would turn loose the population multiplier. Larger families would cancel out the gains. It was not a model which England could safely adopt: 'We should probably be more populous than we are at present; but, as a nation, we should be extremely poor' (SE I 240).

England did not practise subdivision. It had laws of primogeniture (which specified that the eldest son inherits all) and of entailing (which prevented large estates from being broken up). Concentration had gone too far. French-style parcelling out did not, however, go far enough. It was a question of proportion, and the invisible hand might be able to fine-tune the correction. If there were a free market in land, then the properties, equal or unequal, would gravitate to their economic size. It would be the economist's contribution to the broader debate on the optimal social distance.

Malthus was opposed to 'the vices of the government and the structure of the society' that, perpetuating quasi-feudal practices, were limiting 'the free division and alienation of land' (SE II 28, 49). It might have been expected that he would have called for the repeal of laws that treated land as something other than an economic commodity like pins. Malthus, however, was his own man. He came down in favour not of free trade but of primogeniture and entailing. The land laws, he declared, were good laws. They were supporting a going concern.

Perhaps he felt that the estates would level themselves in time. Land was already changing hands. Even without the abrogation of existing laws, the 'natural extinction' and the 'natural imprudence' of some great families had already brought landed property on to the market (PR 435). New blood was coming in. Old blood was going out. The younger sons of the landed classes, unable to share in the inheritance, were joining the upper middle classes. The crossover was reducing 'the distinctions founded on rank and birth' (PR 436). It was extending the impact on social life of 'personal merit' (PR 436). It was infusing into business and the professions the wealth-creating 'energy and activity' (PR 436) for which there had been little outlet in their older brother's stately home.

The economic market was already widening its presence on the land. It will, be a slow transition, lagged by the chains of its history. Even if primogeniture and entailing were formally to be abolished, 'past habits' (PR 438) would still stand in the way of early subdivision. Landed property might still be handed on by bequest and convention. Ingrained norms might still dilute the impact of gain-seeking rationality.

A free market in land could have an unexpected feedback on the new industrial sector. The business classes maximise their profits in order to better their condition. It is not just consumer utility that accounts for their work ethic but also the opportunity to put their success on public display.

Vertically, and as a class, the business interest is driven by 'the motive of competition with the landlords' (PR 438). It is a quasi-Marxian class struggle which derives hegemony from the ownership of a valued factor of production. Horizontally, and as discrete individuals, the new classes are driven to promote themselves into a more prestigious status group. Large estates make even a small man look big. Small estates, on the other hand, simply water the currency: 'If there were few estates of above a thousand a year, the mercantile classes would ....be induced to moderate their exertions in the acquisition of wealth' (PR 438). It is not rational to invest in a positional good if the good, widely diffused, is not positional at all. A nation that values economic activity would be well advised to limit access to the more glittering prizes. The merchants and bankers are already making limited inroads into the estates. The inroads should remain limited. The aristocracy should remain a class apart.

10.1.3 Land and Politics

It would be rash to say that the liberalisation of the law would contribute positively to economic growth. Even, moreover, if it did, 'there are higher considerations to be attended to than those which relate to mere wealth' (PR 437). Primary among these is the stability of the political order.

The British constitution 'has practically given a better government, and more liberty to a great mass of people for a longer time than any which history records' (PR 437). It is the conviction of the conservative that a system which has stood the test of time must have the balance of advantage of its side: 'It would be most unwise to venture upon any.... change as would risk the whole structure' (PR 437). Fanciful blueprints come and go. Radical revolutions always fail. The search for something better—although 'it is not perhaps easy to say'—is more than likely to end in defeat: 'The chances are so dreadfully against our attaining the object of our search' (PR 438).

A country which wishes to perpetuate its going constitution will have no choice but to perpetuate the social structure upon which that constitution is built. In Britain, the constitutional order is 'mainly due to a landed aristocracy' (PR 437). It is a strong contention and a defence of the status quo. Even if greater efficiency did result from a more equal distribution of land, yet the aristocracy cannot 'be supported in an effective state but by the law of primogeniture' (PR 437).

The free economic market must give way to the greater public good. Stability must be ranked above prosperity. There is more to a nation than individualism, atomism and the present day. Liberalism, as Edmund Burke emphasised so strongly, must be situated in the time-hallowed 'partnership not only between those who are living, but between those who are living, those who are dead, and those who are to be born' (Burke 1790 [1968]: 194–195). The consistent liberal must also be a conservative. Malthus, like Burke, believed that tried-and-tested institutions must not be crowded out by exchange.

Without the rents, there would be no economic and cultural advance. Without the role models, social interaction would remain rude and crude (PR 150). Without, above all, the unequal power that is conferred by unequal wealth, there would be no intermediate locus that countervails the ever-latent pressure from the top and from the bottom. Property has a 'natural influence' to 'check at once the power of the crown and the violence of the people' (PR 434). A balanced constitution presupposes a balanced society. The marketisation of land would disturb the equilibrium. That would be a risk. Economically, culturally and politically, the balanced society has stood the test of time.

If landed property were to become fragmented and atomistic, there would be no sizeable middle to defend the interests of the vast majority against 'the tyranny of despotic rulers' on the one side, 'the fury of a despotic mob' (PR 439) on the other. The landed interest is the bulwark between Hobbes's Leviathan who wants to enslave and Burke's common people that does not know its own mind.

If landed property were to be made freely marketable but then subsequently engrossed, there would be a different aberration. The classes that have made their fortunes in business might grow their fortunes still further through land. Their economic dominance would put teeth into their 'political ambition' (PR 438). In the end, the merchants and manufacturers would be the 'only persons who could possess great influence in the state; and the government of the country would fall almost wholly into their hands' (PR 438). It could all go badly wrong. Their interests 'do not always prepare them to give the most salutary advice' (PR 439).

Smith recalled that the mercantilist State had been in the pocket of the trading class (Smith 1776 [1961]: II 160). Marx declared that 'the executive of the bourgeois State is but a committee for managing the common affairs of the whole bourgeoisie' (Marx and Engels 1848 [2011]: 66). Malthus knew what might happen if the three great classes were to collapse into two. He said: 'It may by no means be wise to abolish the law of primogeniture' (PR 439). Read as a warning against the encroachment of money politics, it is a Marx-like, Smith-like admonition against economic trends which would make it difficult for 'our present constitution [to] be maintained' (PR 438).

Yet proportion is essential. Without it, the constitutional order might give way to the military junta: 'The army might easily be made the richest part of the society' (PR 435). To prevent the collapse of democratic checks and balances, the landed interest must retain its wealth but the other two classes must acquire new wealth of their own. In that way, through the inexorable progress of acquisitive individualism, a true triangle of forces would emerge. Vice and misery are the recipe for revolt. Widespread poverty, as history shows, threatens the 'existence and duration of....a well-constituted republic' (PR 434). Moral restraint and the accumulation of capital have political as well as economic implications. The workers and the capitalists must move upward with the wealth of the nation. Their move upward has nothing to do with the abolition or retention of primogeniture.

At the same time, the business classes must be given the opportunity to 'contend in wealth with the great landlords' (PR 436). Industry and trade lead to an 'increase in the proportion of the middle classes of society, which the growth of manufacturing and mercantile capital cannot fail to create' (PR 431). Levelling up rather than levelling down, it nonetheless is an equalising tendency which recalibrates the balance of power. The House of Commons is friendly to business activity. Business activity strengthens the House of Commons.

The economic basis is the foundation for the political transformation. In the words of David Hume: 'The lower house is the support of every popular government; and all the world acknowledges, that it owed its chief influence and consideration to the encrease of commerce, which threw such a balance of property into the hands of the commons' (Hume 1752b [1755]: 29). Adam Smith, looking backwards, saw that capitalism and democracy had gone hand in hand: 'Commerce and manufacture gradually introduced order and good government, and with them, the liberty and security of individuals' (Smith 1776 [1961]: I 433). Industrialisation emancipates 'the great body of society from a dependence on the landlords' (SE II 84). Luxury tempts the aristocrats to dissolve their private armies. 'Protection to property' (SE II 40) provides the security that business requires to chance its capital. Profits, reinvested, become 'both the cause and effect of increasing riches' (SE II 84). Servitude gives way to plurality once the state has 'freed itself from the worst parts of the feudal system' (SE II 40). It all adds up to a more balanced society in which the middle classes come to share political power but the landowning class remains the firm hand on the tiller. It is 'a change of prodigious advantage to the great body of society, including the labouring classes' (SE II 84).

The labouring classes in Malthus's lifetime were not within sight of the vote. The middle classes were. Malthus regarded the 1832 Reform Bill which widened the franchise as a step in the right direction. It placed Parliament 'upon a much broader and more solid base than ever' (PR II 270n). Premature reforms of a 'sudden and extensive nature' are never advisable but the inclusion of the middle classes would clearly bring 'the practical working of the constitution nearer to its theory' (PR II 270n). The reformed Commons would defend property and oppose turbulence. Both in the Commons and in the Lords, however, the landed interest would retain a veto power. For political balance as well as effective demand, the rights and privileges of the landed class should not be infringed.

10.2 Habits and Conventions

The rich might become jaded and replete. Marginal futilities might no longer lure the great landowners into the shopping centres. It can happen to the rest of us.

Adam Smith had not anticipated that the fire would burn itself out: 'The desire of food is limited in every man by the narrow capacity of the human stomach; but the desire of the conveniencies and ornaments of building, dress, equipage, and household furniture seems to have no limit or certain boundary' (Smith 1776 [1961]: I 183). Smith denies that satiety will ever set in: 'Some workmen....when they can earn in four days what will maintain them through the week, will idle the other three. This, however, is by no means the case with the greater part. Workmen, on the contrary, when they are liberally paid by the piece, are very apt to overwork themselves' (Smith 1776 [1961]: I 91). Aspiration springs eternal. The mission is never accomplished.

Smith did not anticipate a post-economic nirvana in which relentless craving would be stilled at last. John Kenneth Galbraith was more sceptical about the future of consumer demand. Beyond some critical point, he said, 'the marginal utility of present aggregate output, *ex* advertising and salesmanship, becomes zero' (Galbraith 1958 [1973]: 154). Malthus was writing about hunger and poverty in an underdeveloped country where only the grandest of the grandees could be said to have satisfied the sum total of their wants. In spite of that, Malthus felt that the income elasticity of demand was not on the side of demand itself: 'Most men place some limits, however variable, to the quantity of conveniences and luxuries which they will labour for' (PR 406). Targeted utility once secured, they will see no need to generate effective demand so as to keep other men in work. Moving limits will become set in their ways.

Necessity is the mother of assiduity: 'It is the want of *necessaries* which mainly stimulates the labouring classes to produce luxuries' (PR 379, emphasis in original). In order to consume their own necessaries, the labouring classes are impelled to produce necessaries and luxuries for solvent paymasters in all the social groups. Were the stimuli of need to be removed, 'there is every reason to think that less time would be so devoted' (PR 379). *Manaña* is another day.

Discretionary consumption is not worth the toil and trouble. If the labourer can support himself and his family by two or three days' labour, he will thereafter 'indulge himself in many hours or days of leisure' (FE 95). Once he has secured his traditional basketful of 'conveniences and comforts' (SE II 85), he will have no incentive to repress his 'natural tendency to idleness' (PR 395). He will see no need to sacrifice his free time in order to secure 'the luxury of improved lodging and clothing' (SE II 85) that meets no more than a marginal need. The low-income trap holds no terror for him. Malthus saw it every day in his study tour of Ireland. The Irishman is contented with 'loitering about' (PR 397). The Irishman's 'wants are few' (PR 399). The Irishman has a low aspiration level. The Irishman does not want to better his condition. The Irishman does not regard manufactured consumables analogous to the washing machines and motor vehicles of modern capitalism as hard-earned complements to leisure. Being backwards is very much to the Irishman's taste.

It was not brute numbers struggling for basic subsistence that accounted for the 'poor clothing and worse lodging of the Irish labourer' (PR 396). Rather, it was an unwillingness to imagine a more satisfying choice set. Potatoes were cheap. Expensive grain was not the staple. The amount of land and labour required to maintain a family was 'unusually small' (PR 394). Indolence was the Irishman's consumer choice. The consumer is king. The supply curve of labour bends back. A nation that wants higher productivity should cut the Irishman's wages. The Irishman's wages should certainly not go up.

It was true in New Spain and it was true in the South Pacific. Malthus's cases studies are drawn from a variety of regions. Pre-industrial territories are poor because the locals see no need to do more in order to buy more. The under-achieving indulge their 'love of ease' because they have no desire for the creature comforts of which they 'are almost destitute' (PR 358, 384). If people prefer indolence to consumption, less will be demanded and less will be supplied. Consumer sovereignty will be holding them back. Their circular flow will have settled into a rut.

Self-replicating customs are an important reason why even after a 'lapse of ages' fertile territories remain 'poor and thinly peopled': 'Lands which might be made capable of supporting thousands of people, may be left to support a few hundreds of cattle' (PR 384, 390). Output fails to reach its productive potential because social habits, 'such as they are at present', are inconsistent with the 'providence, energy, and self-command' (PR 398) that are the cause and effect of economic discipline. Land, labour and capital can be found to support a larger population. The bottleneck is not the resources so much as the motivation. It is psychology and not economics that is keeping the consumption function down.

Capitalist enterprise, affording 'regular and constant work' (PR 397–398), builds up the new habits of reliability and rational conduct. Supplanting the indolence of the voluntarily underemployed (PR 398), they are the staging post for the economic take-off. It is not smooth sailing. The done thing has deep roots. An economy is 'a plant of slow growth' (PR 359). *Natura non facit saltum.* A change in attitudes takes time.

There must be a general upgrading in the willingness to work. That is on the side of supply. It must be matched by a shift outward in the desire to demand. Disposing of the increment is the trickier problem. If the demand is not there, the business sector will stagnate.

Needed is a new capitalist man who is willing to play his part as a consumer and not just a producer: 'If every person were satisfied with the simplest food, the poorest clothing, and the meanest houses, it is certain that no other sort of food, clothing, and lodging would be in existence' (PR 8). Without 'such a taste as will properly stimulate industry' (PR 359), the frontiers of demand would not be expanding to accommodate economic growth. The maximisation of utility as seen by the maximisers themselves would point to a steady state.

A work ethic and disposable income on their own are not enough: 'It is unquestionably true that wealth produces wants; but it is a still more important truth, that wants produce wealth' (PR 470). While supply and demand inevitably react upon each other, nonetheless 'the order both of precedence and of importance, is with the wants' (PR 470). Wants, however, are sluggish. The greatest of all difficulties is to inspire the great mass of the people 'with the wants best calculated to excite their exertions in the production of wealth' (PR 470). If total demand does not keep pace with total supply, continuing growth will sink into arrested development that will not be able to feed the rising census.

Wants create wealth. They are the first mover in the sequence: 'The actual check to produce and population arises more from want of stimulus than want of power to produce' (letter from Malthus to Ricardo, 1817, in Ricardo VII: 123). Writing to Ricardo in 1817, Malthus expressed his concern that the supply side was robust but that the demand side was fragile: 'You seem to think that the wants and tastes of mankind are always ready for the supply; while I am most decidedly of opinion that few things are more difficult, than to inspire new tastes and wants' (letter from Malthus to Ricardo, 1817, in Ricardo VII: 122). Yet inspired they must be if the 'permanent tastes and habits of the people' are ever to generate 'an adequate degree of consumption' (PR 446). Without an adequate degree of consumption, it might be the 'check to production' that itself becomes 'permanent' (PR 447).

New wants must be created and then be created anew. It is the 'grand difficulty' (PR 356) in the way of economic growth. In a letter from 1814, Malthus made the lack of interest in the shifting frontier the primary cause of stagnation in an advanced economy: 'When capital is abundant it is not easy to find new objects sufficiently in demand.

When capital is scarce nothing is more easy' (letter from Malthus to Ricardo, 1814, in Ricardo VI: 131).

A rich country cannot easily find new consumables to satisfy new wants that do not exist. If consumers are 'satisfied with simple clothing' (PR 363) and staple foodstuffs, there will be no home market for ribbons, laces and velvets, for sugar, grapes and tobacco. Activity would slacken. Prices would be flat (PR 448). Involuntary idleness would be widespread (PR 361). 'Vast powers of production', in 'almost every part of the world', will not be 'put into action' (letter from Malthus to Ricardo, 1821, in Ricardo IX: 10). The economy would grow at a snail's pace.

It could be decline. It could be fall. If so, then the final consumer, traditional and unadventurous, would be to blame: 'Without an expenditure which will encourage commerce, manufactures, and unproductive consumers….a country such as our own, which had been rich and populous, would, with such parsimonious habits, infallibly become poor' (PR 362–363). The future is almost upon us. The marginal consumables that Malthus calls luxuries are even now 'heavy of sale' (PR 359). The jaded landowners are the harbingers of what is to come.

Ricardo's reply was that it was all a *non sequitur*. New departures cannot correct a deficiency in total demand precisely because the unwanted consumables will not in the first instance have been produced: 'There could be no adequate motive to push production to this length, and therefore it would never go so far' (letter from Ricardo to Malthus, 1821, in Ricardo IX: 16). Ricardo's reply is in line with Say's Law. Even a lesser circular flow always circles. It does not, however, directly address Malthus's contention that statics is just a game but that dynamics is fraught with risk. Lack of imagination is capable of driving a great nation into the ground.

The sticking point is that standards of living are always sticky. Commodity consumption is always buffered by 'the countervailing luxury of indolence' (PR 468). We are all Irish peasants at heart. For sustained progress, it is incumbent upon us nonetheless to escape from our comfort zone. Discretionary luxuries are 'the most distinguishing characteristics of civilization' (SE I 430n). It would be 'a most important error' (PR 359) to neglect the mould-shattering impact of the new. Without the never-ending superfluities of the 'mechanical arts', Hume had said, 'men sink into indolence, lose all enjoyment of life, and are useless to the public' (Hume 1752b [1955]: 22, 24). Malthus had absorbed the message of Hume. It is never good to slumber too long under a tree. Least of all should one slumber under a tree when the population is increasing, subsistence must be found and effective demand is unreliable.

Yet the inertia is always there. Deep-seated attitudes and handed on customs are, Malthus saw, a glacier of conservatism which is resistant to upstart new challenges: 'To change long-existing habits is of all enterprises the most difficult' (SE II 105). Difficult or not, the cake had to crumble. Malthus does not say precisely how to awaken the sleeping giant of demand-led novelty. He does, however, suggest that foreign trade can play a part. Foreign trade is, quite literally, an exogenous shock. It is 'Wonder' in the sense of Adam Smith (Smith 1795 [1967]: 50). Globalisation has a bracing cold demonstration effect. It forces people to think.

A 'commerce with strangers', Hume had said, has the attractive feature that it stuns and amazes: 'It rouses men from their indolence; and.... raises in them a desire of a more splendid way of life than what their ancestors enjoyed' (Hume 1752a [1955]: 14). The demonstration effect is a cultural revolution. Economic development begins in the mind. Malthus saw the jolt to knee-jerk shopping as one of the chief benefits that a nation derives from the globalisation of choice.

Foreign trade, Malthus said, is 'an almost necessary ingredient in the progress of wealth' (PR 470). Going beyond absolute and comparative advantage, building on the 'adequate extension of the market' (PR 402) that is the precondition for scale and scope, foreign trade has the path-breaking capacity 'to inspire new wants, to form new tastes, and to furnish fresh motives for industry' (PR 470). Novelty is education. Trade is a 'principle which prompts to expense' (PR 468). Expence is a principle which prompts to expansion: 'More fresh labour will be set in motion every year, and the increase of wealth will be certain and rapid' (PR 443). If saving is excessive, then imported luxuries pare down the surplus. Trade shakes things up. It is not simply the adaptation of supply to an inherited demand.

Malthus says less about the bracing cold shower that has its origin at home. Writing in the country of the flying shuttle and Crompton's mule, he is nonetheless aware that British entrepreneurs are not passive pace-takers whose intellectual property is being copied from a vanguard abroad (PR 402). Rather than catch-up, he saw that they were relying on local knowledge to satisfy a focused need.

Innovations, Malthus says, tend to be consumer-led. They are mainly marketed 'when there is a decided demand for them' (PR 401). Importantly, the demand might not be a revealed preference for an existing product. It can also be a latent demand for a new breakthrough that promises 'a better adaptation....to the tastes, wants and consumption of the society' (PR 356). The ingenuity of man, called forth by his wants, will 'seldom greatly exceed those wants' (PR 402). The ingenuity of the businessman is to unlock existing wants that have not yet been formulated or articulated. The entrepreneur in the sense of Malthus does not pull a new product out of the void so much as market a pacifier that fills an empty niche. It is market research rather than manipulation and producer sovereignty that drives on the process of change.

Effective demand might be reinvigorated by foreign luxuries and home-based alertness. There is also social status. Malthus's 'man of liberal education', when he sets out to 'better his condition', is concerned not just with calorie consumption but relative standing. He wants to rank himself with gentlemen and not with farmers or 'the lower class of tradesmen' (FE 90). Betterment for the socially mobile is invidious comparison even as it is houseroom and nutrition. Place is the antidote to indolence. No one wants to be left behind.

Economic growth widens the horizons. Malthus knew that aggregate demand could be a snowball as more and more people are empowered to spend their way into a higher reference group. The rich landowner already has all the trophies. The Irish peasant or the man of liberal education is still on the way up. Mobility makes it less likely that the nation will experience a 'general want of demand' (PR 365) because its satiated citizens have become replete.

Robert Wallace had welcomed the new manufacturing age because of the more palatable trough that would entice the sleepy savage, 'lazy and indolent', back into work: 'This awakens ambition, kindles emulation, quickens industry, and engages men to labour, that they may procure the tempting objects they desire' (Wallace 1753: 28). Wallace was, four decades before Malthus, predicting that 'mankind would increase so prodigiously, that the earth would at last be overstocked' (Wallace 1761: 114). He was understandably relieved to predict a stimulus on the side of demand that would prime the pump of economic growth.

Malthus was less confident: 'There is much more reason to fear that the working classes will consume too little for their own happiness, than they will consume too much to allow of an adequate increase of wealth' (PR 473). In Glasgow, the cottons that the workers produce are in surplus but the workers themselves are in distress. The solution is in their own hands. They should 'alter their wants and tastes' (PR 443). They should earn more money and spend more money. They should opt for what Wallace had recommended. They should move on from the low-consumption plateau.

Discretionary consumption is the locomotive that pulls the train. There is no way that a growing economy can do without the incentive of indulgence. For all that, it might be a mixed blessing. It is essential. But is it good?

Malthus was a man of simple tastes. He knew that Adam Smith had dismissed superfluous luxuries as 'trinkets and baubles….fitter to be the playthings of children than the serious pursuits of men' (Smith 1776 [1961]: I 439). He agreed with Adam Smith that, morally speaking, a rat race within a squirrel wheel had no inherent logic but to keep itself in motion. Luxuries 'only tend to gratify the vanity of a few rich people' (FE 194). Such a misallocation of resources is not in the interests of 'the society in general' (FE 195)—save in one important respect. Even the indulgences that austere puritans castigate as 'trivial', 'useless', and sometimes 'pernicious' (SE I 333) have the beneficial property that they create employment for the great mass of the people. A gold-plated mousetrap does more than catch mice.

Adam Smith had denied that unlimited consumption would bring true happiness. Basic needs once satisfied, Smith had said, economic man will find it 'proper….to sit still and to be contented' (Smith 1759 [1966]: 211). It is *too much* and *too little* again. Malthus could see that, while people should not be emaciated, nor should they be obese.

Morally speaking, he felt, there is likely to be a point at which discretionary consumption will have served its purpose. At that critical cut-off, the age of growth at all costs could reasonably give way to a less frenzied pursuit of wealth that allows for 'a greater degree of relaxation from severe toil' (PR 473). Diversifying into leisure, more time would be available for 'innocent amusements and useful instruction' that would develop the neglected dimensions of men's potential: 'I should consider it as very cheaply purchased, by the sacrifice of a portion of the national wealth and populousness' (PR 473–474).

It is Zeno the Stoic. It is Keynes's on the 'Economic possibilities for our grandchildren' (1930 [1972]). It is also an abstract ideal that will never be more than a philosopher's pipe dream: 'I see no probability, or even possibility, of accomplishing this object' (PR 474). The population is rising. Effective demand must rise in step. The alternative is China, or Poland, or India where as early as the first *Essay* Malthus made clear what under-consumption could mean: 'It is probable that the very frugal manner in which the Gentoos are in the habit of living contributes in some degree to the famines of Indostan' (FE 115–116). The subcontinent is plagued by famine because the Hindus like Weber's Puritans practise asceticism when what Mother India requires is spend-spend-spend.

10.3 State and Demand

First principles point to *laissez-faire*. In the national economy as in the micro-market for pins, the government should trust to the natural order: 'No one could think of interfering with it, even in its caprices': 'In leaving the whole question of saving to the uninfluenced operation of individual interest and individual feelings, we shall best conform to that great principle of political economy laid down by Adam Smith which teaches us a general maxim, liable to very few exceptions, that the wealth of nations is best secured by allowing every person, so long as he adheres to the rules of justice, to pursue his own interest in his own way' (PR 517–518).

The best course is '*not* to interfere' (PR 18, emphasis in original). There are exceptions. Profits and markets do not inevitably stabilise the level of aggregate demand. Where saving is excessive and consumption is inadequate, State spending may be needed to restore temporary balance to the circular flow (PR 480).

10.3.1 Spending and Taxing

In normal times, the workers and the capitalists will not be generating sufficient demand: 'Though there may be the power, there is not the will; and it is to supply this will that a body of unproductive consumers is necessary' (PR 489). Unproductive consumption is necessary to lean against the prevailing shortfall. Landlords and other persons of property play their part by paying for service workers who consume but do not produce. There is also the State. The government employs politicians, bureaucrats, judges and other non-producing dependents who flesh out the total. Without State-sector hangers-on, much of material output would be 'comparatively useless': 'They ensure that consumption which is necessary to give the proper stimulus to production' (PR 480).

In normal times, the State will employ some service labour. Infrastructure is essential for domestic trade and the single price. Legislation is a public good that must be publicly provided. In a cyclical downturn, such as Britain experienced after 1815 the State should be even more active in job creation. 'Public works, the making and repairing of roads', on top of the 'tendency among persons of fortune to improve their grounds and keep more servants', are 'the most direct means within our power of restoring the demand for labour' (PR 591).

Public works do not detract from material wealth. In a recession, both labour and capital are in surplus. The incremental services provided by demobilised soldiers and out-of-work manuals do not compete with private capital or 'come for sale into the market' (PR 511), already overstocked. Wealth creation aside, public works are an investment in social capital. Employment keeps labour active. Make-work prevents backsliding into the bad moral effects of habitual idleness.

Public works are downward redistribution. The principal beneficiaries are the working class. As with poor relief, however, the artificial stimulus has a perverse effect on marriage, family-size and, in time, the level of pay. 'Concealing too much the failure of the national demand for labour', work projects might 'prevent the population from gradually accommodating itself to a reduced demand' (PR 511). Summing the pluses and the minuses, the workers at the end of the day might not really be better off: 'I think it relieves them for a short time, but leaves them afterwards in a condition worse than before' (1827: 321).

Counter-cyclical public works restructure the labour force from private to public, goods to services. At the same time, new hires obtain new incomes which they will spend almost entirely on private tradeables: 'Instances have practically occurred of national wealth being greatly stimulated by the consumption of those who have been supported by taxes' (PR 481). Even without the full multiplier expansion of Keynesian economics, it is clear that the initial injection will contribute 'powerfully to distribution and demand' (PR 479–480). Properly calibrated, it will lead to the 'full play' of the nation's 'physical resources' (PR 478). It will create a market for stock that would have otherwise remained unsold.

Taxation in a recession is a stabiliser that hastens the recovery. Malthus's contention is unexpected and idiosyncratic. Malthus believed that a rise and not a fall in taxes would be the more likely to unleash an expansion. A reduction is a false God. Tax cuts that return income to the private sector only make a bad situation worse. The prosperous would save when they ought to spend. The unemployed would not be demand-pulled into work: 'No taking off of taxes, nor any degree of cheapness of corn, can compensate a want of demand for labour' (PR 521). The downward ratchet will not be reversed: 'The evil occasioned by imposing a tax is very rarely compensated by the taking it off' (PR 503).

Ricardo (1821 [1951–1955]) and later Robert Barro (1974) had argued that debt-financed public spending no more than replaces the private spending that had been taxed away. Total demand is unaffected by the transfer. The Ricardo-Barro fiscal equivalence theorem was anticipated by Malthus when in 1803 in the second *Essay* he said that the replacement demand would be the 'exact amount' (SE I 371). The conversion of private into public spending 'can have no tendency to diminish the general amount of demand' (SE I 371). He seems to be saying that tax and spend is cycle-neutral. Even in 1803, however, he was also identifying cases where it was not.

History shows that public spending puts the economy back on course. Writing in wartime, he shows that there has been a 'prodigious increase of produce and population' (SE I 372). The 'enormous amount of taxation' (SE I 372) had rather augmented than depleted the national wealth. The government had been recycling its revenues into defence-related services. It had been putting new demand into circulation. Taxing followed by spending had had a stimulatory effect on the economy. History proves it. It would not make sense to alleviate the burden in the downswing: 'The removal of taxes, however proper, and indeed absolutely necessary as a permanent measure, is certainly not the immediate and specific remedy' (SE I 373).

The costs can outweigh the benefits. Even so, there are economic and political limits beyond which the taxing authorities cannot go.

Economically, 'injudicious taxation' might 'stop the increase of wealth' (PR 480). It might 'almost prevent the possibility of accumulation' (PR 480). Taxation, 'if pushed to any considerable extent, can hardly fail of interfering with the powers of production' (PR 484). Private loses. Public gains. It is a risk. Public spending should not be 'so great that it cannot proceed without ruin' (PR 519).

Politically, there is slippage and bias: 'One should be extremely cautious of trusting to any government the means of making a different distribution of wealth, with a view to the general good' (PR 481). Government failure can shift the balance between saving and non-saving ever further from the 'just mean' (PR 516). Fine-tuning is hampered by ignorance. Taxes 'enhance the insecurity of property' (PR 485). They infringe on natural rights. They can be counterproductive. 'Bad laws or unwise exhortations' (PR 516) can be a brake on production. They can make a passing recession into a long-lasting trough. The cure can be worse than the disease.

Taxation, in short, is capable both of creating wealth and of diminishing it. Some taxation is 'absolutely necessary' (PR 477). Too much, however, crowds out private capital and misallocates resources. As usual, the optimum is the mix. It all 'depends upon proportions' (PR 482).

10.3.2 The National Debt

Hume and Smith had said that public spending financed not by taxation but by borrowing would be irresponsible and ruinous. Malthus believed that they had neglected the lagged benefit because of their concentration, myopic and doctrinaire, on the deadweight of the current cost: 'The main cause of their error was….not being able to see the vast increase of purchasing power to which the nation would subsequently attain' (PR 502). Like Hume and Smith, Malthus was in principle in favour of a balanced budget. Like Keynes, however, he felt that a budget deficit in a depressed economy would be preferable to an under-performance equilibrium.

Government debt drains resources from physical investment and wage capital into passive paper. Idle bonds on their own would clearly diminish the nation's wealth. As with taxation, however, Malthus refused to consider the withdrawals in isolation from the reinjections: 'The loans to government convert capital into revenue, and increase demand at the same time that they at first diminish the means of supply' (PR 373–374). The public sector spends what the private sector would have done. It is a straightforward transfer.

As always in economic life, public borrowing brings 'evils' (PR 507) in its train. Debt is 'very cumbersome' (PR 484). Carried to excess, it can be 'very dangerous' (PR 484). Debt must be serviced. The principal must be refunded. The taxes for interest and repayment 'may become suddenly so heavy as greatly to distress the productive classes' (PR 485).

So would an unanticipated change in prices. Inflation reduces the real burden on the State as borrower but simultaneously imposes an equivalent burden on fixed-interest coupon clippers. It is redistribution without consultation. It is not fair: 'In a country with a large public debt, there is no duty which ought to be held more sacred….than to prevent any variations of the currency' (PR 485). Confronted with an 'act of positive injustice', the creditors would be feeling 'unjustly deprived' (PR 485, 513). Money matters. The public debt is an argument for the convertibility of bank paper into gold.

Critics of deficit finance will argue for the permanent retirement of the national debt. Malthus saw no reason for the State to finance itself through current taxation alone. An excessive debt is 'fatal to production' but a moderate debt is not 'prejudicial to a state' (SE I 372).

In terms of effective demand, the interest-recipients are a spending estate: 'The incomes which are received and spent by the national creditors are....favourable to the demand for the great mass of manufactured products' (PR 484). Repayment of the debt would terminate the stream. It would provide a lump sum for rentiers who would lock away the funds in a new savings instrument. The retirement of the debt, through 'unfavorable distribution' (PR 488), might have an adverse effect on the level of total demand. It could 'more than counterbalance the increased power of production occasioned by the relief from taxation' (PR 488).

Much would depend on the taxes that had to be levied to fund the repayment. In the long run, the tax burden would decrease once the national debt had been extinguished. On paper, there would be a higher level of disposable income in the nation. In practice, the impact on total demand cannot be known *a priori*. Some taxes are paid disproportionately by the free-spending landlords but others fall mainly on the parsimonious capitalist class. The incidence of tax is a social *for whom* and not just a macroeconomic *how much*. A redistribution of disposable income could result in a 'diminution of effective demand' despite the stimulatory impact of 'the relief from taxation' (PR 488).

It is not certain. Effective demand is influenced by taxation and debt. The devil is in the detail. The result was that Malthus, always pragmatic and cautious, was reluctant to pass an unequivocal judgement. In the 1820 *Principles*, he suggested that the national debt, in the past so 'favourable to wealth' (PR 485), should in future be reduced or at best capped at its current level. In the 1836 *Principles*, less positive towards government borrowing (PR II 463), he warned that the payments to rentiers could 'occasion a distribution of property most unfavourable to production' (PR II 14). Effective demand could go either way. The sections on the positive effects—the debt had been 'favourable to wealth' (PR 485)—were considerably abridged in the second edition of the *Principles* (PR II 483). Included or not, Malthus knew that he was on shaky ground when he tried to predict the relationship between national debt and effective demand.

References

By T. R. Malthus

(1798 [1970]). *Essay on the Principle of Population, as It Affects the Future Improvement of Society, with Remarks on the Speculations of Mr. Godwin, M. Condorcet, and Other Writers* (abbreviated as FE), ed. by A. Flew. Harmondsworth: Penguin.

(1803 et seq. [1989]). *An Essay on the Principle of Population: Or a View of Its Past and Present Effects on Human Happiness, with an Inquiry into Our Prospects Respecting the Removal of the Evils Which It Occasions* (2nd edition, 1803; further editions in 1806, 1807, 1817, 1826) (abbreviated as SE I and SE II), 2 vols., ed. by P. James. Cambridge: Cambridge University Press.

(1820 [1989]). *The Principles of Political Economy* (abbreviated as PR), ed. by J. Pullen. Cambridge: Cambridge University Press.

(1827). Evidence to the Select Committee on Emigration (Third Report), in *Parliamentary Papers*. London: House of Commons, 5, 311–327.

(1836 [1989]). *The Principles of Political Economy: The Alterations to the First Edition* (abbreviated as PR II), ed. by J. Pullen. Cambridge: Cambridge University Press.

Secondary Literature

Barro, R. J. (1974). Are Government Bonds Net Worth? *Journal of Political Economy, 82,* 1095–1117.

Burke, E. (1790 [1968]). *Reflections on the Revolution in France* (C. C. O'Brien, Ed.). Harmondsworth: Penguin Books.

Galbraith, J. K. (1958 [1973]). *The Affluent Society*. Harmondsworth: Penguin Books.

Hume, D. (1752a [1955]). Of Commerce. In E. Rotwein (Ed.), *David Hume: Writings on Economics* (pp. 3–18). London: Nelson.

Hume, D. (1752b [1955]). Of Refinement in the Arts. In E. Rotwein (Ed.), *David Hume: Writings on Economics* (pp. 19–32). London: Nelson.

Keynes, J. M. (1930 [1972]). Economic Possibilities for Our Grandchildren. In D. Moggridge (Ed.), *The Collected Writings of John Maynard Keynes* (IX, pp. 321–332). London: Macmillan.

Marx, K., & Engels, F. (1848 [2011]). *The Communist Manifesto*. London: Penguin Books.

Ricardo, D. (1820 [1951–1955]. *Notes on Malthus's Principles of Political Economy*, in Ricardo, infra, II.

Ricardo, D. (1821 [1951–1955]. *Principles of Political Economy*, in Ricardo, infra, I.

Ricardo, D. (1951–1955). *The Works and Correspondence of David Ricardo* (abbreviated as Ricardo) (P. Sraffa & M. Dobb, Ed., 11 vols.). Cambridge: Cambridge University Press.

Smith, A. (1759 [1966]). *The Theory of Moral Sentiments*. New York: Augustus M. Kelley.

Smith, A. (1776 [1961]). *The Wealth of Nations* (E. Cannan, Ed., 2 vols.). London: Methuen.

Smith, A. (1795 [1967]). The History of Astronomy. In J. R. Lindgren (Ed.), *The Early Writings of Adam Smith*. New York: Augustus M. Kelley.

Wallace, R. (1753). *A Dissertation on the Numbers of Mankind in Ancient and Modern Times*. Edinburgh: G. Hamilton and J. Balfour.

Wallace, R. (1761). *Various Prospects of Mankind, Nature, and Providence*. London: William Hone.

11
Foreign Trade

Effective demand can be generated by the consumers, the businesses and the State. There is also the 'foreign vent' (PR 408) and the stimulus, albeit 'temporary' (PR 514), from fresh credit and currency. They are connected. Exports bring in bullion which, deposited in banks, makes possible an increase in loans. Like exports, new money adds to effective demand. Both exports and new money lean against a prevailing glut.

Neither trade nor money is, however, wealth. Money is an intermediary and a veil. Trade is a straightforward transfer of existing assets. Trade is a dyadic exchange of 'what is wanted less for what is wanted more' (PR 440). Subjectively speaking, the act of exchange must 'raise the value of both the products' (PR 440). In physical terms, it is nonetheless a sterile and unproductive quid pro quo in which the merchant is no more than a broker. The exchange of wine for textiles must not be confused with the wine and the textiles themselves. The need satisfaction is all in the mind. The trading partners feel 'better off than they were before' (PR 442). How they feel is closer to psychology than to statistics. In the sense of the national wealth, nothing has been created and nothing destroyed. Trade, like money, enables new value to be created. In terms of the increment itself, however, trade is simply not there.

D. Reisman, *Thomas Robert Malthus*, Great Thinkers in Economics,
https://doi.org/10.1007/978-3-030-01956-3_11

11.1 The Gains from Trade

Beggar-thy-neighbour mercantilism is as old as the tribal xenophobia of *Blut und Boden*: 'There is little reason to expect that individual states will ever consent to sacrifice the wealth within their own confines to the wealth of the world' (SE II 74). What is new is multilateral globalisation legitimated by the new economics of plus-sum gain. Mutual gain is, Malthus believed, an intellectual perspective whose time had come. The wars, the blockades, the harvest failures, the disrupted supplies were all fresh in people's mind when the classical liberals were looking forward to a century and more of peace and prosperity once the international flows had been liberated from trade-destroying controls.

Ricardo said that world allocative efficiency will be at its maximum when the national areas of specialisation track each country's comparative advantage. Full employment assured by Say's Law and flexible prices, the ideal for each partner will be to concentrate domestic production on the commodity where output per unit of input is at its peak relative to its next best alternative foregone. It should rely on international trade for the commodity in which it is relatively less productive (Ricardo 1821 [1951–1955]: 134–139).

Ricardo believed that each country should assess its strengths and weaknesses in terms of its domestic productivity alone. Adam Smith, more outward-looking, felt that true advantage was not comparative but rather absolute. The home nation should in the first instance scan the horizon. It should determine what it can do best relative not to itself but to its potential trading partners. Scotland has the capital for textiles, but not the soil for grapes. Because of the difference in the factor endowments, it would clearly be cost-effective for Scotland to import its grapes and to pay for them with woollens (Smith 1776 [1961]: I 480).

Comparative advantage and absolute advantage were the two choices open to a post-mercantilist who denied that trade is war. Malthus felt that absolute advantage made the most sense: 'If we were to make our own wines by means of hot-houses, they would altogether be worth much less money, and give encouragement to much less industry than at present' (PR 457). His illustration was the underdeveloped USA.

The USA, 'aided very greatly by foreign commerce' (PR 428), had grown at a rate matched by few other countries. The reason is that the Americans had been 'selling raw produce, obtained with little labour, for European commodities which have cost much labour' (PR 428). They had capitalised on their absolute advantage in primary produce to pay for imported manufactures in which the Europeans had the competitive edge.

Absolute advantage appeals to common sense. Comparative advantage is built on a distinctive theory of labour embodied which no one but the Ricardians regards as a reliable measure: 'The view of exchangeable value, which makes it depend exclusively upon the cost of production, is essentially incorrect, and utterly useless' (PR 450). A better standard than historic cost, and the standard which Malthus himself adopted, would have been subjective utility. It would return the discussion of free trade to the free market. It would replace the dogma of cost with the more familiar yardstick of the market clearing price.

One of the great gains from trade is a lower price. Malthus, while not denying the attraction, emphasises that there is more to trade than cheapness. Cheapness, he states, is 'only one half of its advantages, and…not the larger half' (PR 461). Tradeables are not all the same. Product differentiation and local monopoly can make a country the market leader in its own unique commodity. The real gain from trade might be that, irrespective of the price, the consumer's utility goes up in consequence of the revolutionary new choice set that comes in from abroad.

In Britain, the 'great mass' of imports are non-competing commodities like sherry, raisins, indigo, lemons and 'other articles peculiar to foreign climates' (PR 461). It would be 'perfectly preposterous' (PR 461) to estimate the benefits to the importer nation in terms of the quantity of labour and capital spared when, without trade, 'we should not have them at all' (PR 461).

Some endowments like scarce minerals are non-replicable. They are the quasi-physiocratic gift of a bountiful Providence. Other endowments evolve quantitatively and qualitatively in response to economic growth itself. Tomorrow's advantage will not be the same as today's.

The USA in its foundation years exchanged primary produce for European manufactures. Its strength in its early years lay in land rather than labour or capital. It will not always be so. The position would be very different once the geometrical ratio had multiplied the population and disposable income had made possible the accumulation of savings.

A threshold reached the emergent nations might be able to challenge the first movers in the manufacturing heartland itself. It need not mean a reversal of the roles. So long as the incomers are not 'successful competitors' in the same market niche, their betterment is Britain's betterment as well: 'Their increasing wealth must tend to increase the demand for its products' (PR II 13). The threat from hollowing-out would be greater if the newcomers moved to undercut the incumbents on a common battlefield (SE II 35). Malthus does not, apparently, regard mass-market textiles as such a battlefield.

What Britain is today, America or Poland could be tomorrow, Malthus's reaction to the catch-up, possibly over-confident and short-sighted, is that this 'very rarely happens' (PR 457). Even, moreover, if it did, the price competitiveness of the backward laggards might be bid away by the demand-diversion itself. Over time, prices in the newly developing economies would reach levels 'equal to what they bear in many of the countries of Europe' (PR 459). The law of one price takes away their advantage. The first movers have nothing to fear.

There may be enough demand in a growing global economy to accommodate both the incumbent and the challenger. Where there is not, 'yet the capital and labour, which in this case will be thrown out of employment, will generally, in enterprising and commercial countries, find other channels' (PR 457). Older countries will move up the value chain. Short-term dislocation will lead to subsequent reincarnation: 'It will rarely or never be found to fail' (PR 458).

The dynamic gains will make up for the losses in the transition. As trade expands, both the importer and the exporter nation will accumulate additional capital and employ additional labour. A portion of the mercantile profit will find investment outlets in home industry and agriculture (PR 457). The stimulus it gives to the real sector is 'one of the most desirable effects of foreign commerce' (PR 454). Even a transfer payment can unleash a sequence. In the long run, there will be a 'general and powerful tendency of foreign commerce, to raise the value of the national income' (PR 457).

British trade generates new demand both for British producers and for the foreign businesses that supply the imports: 'The increase in the value of foreign produce does not occasion a proportionate diminution in the value of home produce.... The demand for foreign and home commodities taken together decidedly increases' (PR 454). The tendency is towards trade creation rather than the trade diversion that made the mercantilists conceive of international business as a Hobbesian war. There is something for everyone when, 'instead of changing the channels of commerce, we are able to make large and distinct additions to them' (PR 510).

All the participants are made better off in their own estimation. All the partners must, however, be prepared to do their part. A foreign nation's wealth is our own nation's effective demand: 'It is impossible to sell very largely without being able to buy very largely' (SE II 247). Slow growth in our trading partners imposes a quasi-tax on ourselves. For Britain, 'the ignorance and indolence of others may not only be prejudicial, but fatal to its progress' (SE II 42). It is in Britain's self-interest, narrowly defined, that poor developing countries like the USA should grow rapidly into mature and high-spending customers: 'Their increasing wealth must tend to increase the demand for its products' (SE II 13).

Beggar-thy-neighbour is the downward spiral to trade destruction. Initiative and frugality, skill and equipment 'would be but of very short duration' (SE II 34) if the trading partners were to withdraw into protection and cut back on each other's exports. 'The division of labour is limited by the extent of the market' (Smith 1776 [1961]: I 21). If the world market were to shrink, the exporters would lose the economies of scale and scope that made them competitive.

The lesson is that each nation must spend in order that all nations might earn: 'The wealth of a particular nation is increased by the increasing wealth and prosperity of surrounding states' (PR II 13). Malthus does not directly address the problem of bad Samaritans, tempted to play the free rider on other nations' open borders while themselves building tariff walls to shelter their own constituents.

What one can do, all cannot. The hidden assumption seems to be that the general interest will spontaneously triumph over blinkered chauvinism precisely because one invisible hand washes another when both stand to reap a gain.

Malthus seems not to be looking forward to regional alliances and bilateral pacts to set the pace. Collective action had defeated Napoleon at Waterloo. Malthus does not state that it would work equally well in commerce. The Methuen Treaty of 1703 had shown that Britain and Portugal could agree on bilateral trade. The wartime coalition anticipated the multilateral World Trade Organisation. In spite of that Malthus is expecting a single-country solution. Unilateralism is the first step. Other countries will follow the leader when they see that free trade works.

One invisible hand washes another. As always, however, it is liberty within limits. Later generations have restricted trade in military hardware and advanced technology. Malthus more often than not was in favour of the Corn Laws and the bounties for grain. The rule is freedom. The exception is food.

Chapter 7 set out the British quandary. On the one hand, the corn trade is 'precarious', exposed to the 'accidents of time and chance', a threat to domestic supplies, a bargaining chip in the hands of blackmailing foreigners who might negotiate with food (SE I 384, 394, 395). Any interruption of primary supplies would upset the balance of internal trade upon which domestic industry in a dual economy is absolutely dependent. On the other hand, the nation needs free trade in grain because farmers abroad must earn income from our imports if they are to afford our exports in exchange (PR 494). Britain wants to make the foreigners rich. Britain also wants to protect its domestic producers and its home supplies of food. It is a quandary.

11.2 Home and Abroad

International trade came later. Internal trade came first. Gains from trade were being made long before the foreigner came on the scene. When a district with copper initiated trade with a district mining tin, 'a greater demand would take place, and a greater price be given both for tin and copper' (PR 441). The middlemen make a paper profit. Should their paper profit be reinvested in real capital, the result would be an expansion in physical quantities and national wealth. It is a good reason to buy and sell at home.

The export market builds on the home demand: 'There is no magic in foreign markets. The final demand and consumption must always be at home' (PR 411). Only later, when the home market becomes saturated, does an established industry have a need to grow new outlets abroad: 'If we could not export our cottons, it is quite certain that, though we might have the power, we should not have the will to consume them all in kind at home' (PR 411). Fair trade or dumping, the foreign market fills a gap left when the home market loses interest: 'It is specifically to overcome the want of eagerness to purchase domestic commodities that the merchant exchanges them for others more in request' (PR 442–443).

Foreign trade tops up the domestic demand. If the textiles or the tin could be entirely disposed of at home, 'foreign markets would be useless' (PR 412). Where they cannot be, foreign markets tank the overspill. They retard a contraction in a sector or a line of business. Absent that safety valve, 'there is every reason to fear that the exertions of industry would slacken' (PR 405).

Exports cushion output. In that way, they also protect jobs. Foreign trade reduces the volume of poverty and relief. It improves the living standards of the workers: 'I doubt if there has ever been an instance in any country of very great prosperity in foreign commerce, where the working classes have not had good money wages' (SE II 247). Good money wages mean a greater demand both for home-produced goods and for new imports from abroad: 'No country can buy very largely in which the working classes are not in such a state as to be able to purchase foreign commodities' (SE II 247). Foreigners buy more from us because we buy more from them. It is a win-win scenario in which the effective demand for the whole of our national wealth is underpinned from abroad.

James Mill was not convinced. Say's Law creates its own demand: 'A nation always has within itself a market equal to all the commodities of which it can possibly have to dispose' (Mill 1808: 96). There is no macroeconomic deficiency and no need for a White Knight. Ricardo agreed with Mill. There could never be a gap. Foreign commerce enhances our welfare. It does not top up a deficit in effective demand that in normal times will never occur.

It is a world away from Keynes's *General Theory*. Remembering the Pax Britannica that had been constructed on reciprocal trade, Keynes felt that the inadequacy of Say's Law and the observed market-stealing of the interwar period had been at the root of the world-wide slump. Keynes wanted to shift upward the average willingness to demand. He recognised that orderly trade was essential to restore full employment. Malthus had known it long before: 'No country with a very confined market, internal as well as external, has ever been able to accumulate a large capital' (PR 448). Like it or not, our businessmen will have to sell abroad.

References

By T. R. Malthus

(1803 et seq. [1989]). *An Essay on the Principle of Population: Or a View of Its Past and Present Effects on Human Happiness, with an Inquiry into Our Prospects Respecting the Removal of the Evils Which It Occasions* (2nd edition, 1803; further editions in 1806, 1807, 1817, 1826) (abbreviated as SE I and SE II), 2 vols., ed. by P. James. Cambridge: Cambridge University Press.

(1820 [1989]). *The Principles of Political Economy* (abbreviated as PR), ed. by J. Pullen. Cambridge: Cambridge University Press.

(1836 [1989]). *The Principles of Political Economy: The Alterations to the First Edition* (abbreviated as PR II), ed. by J. Pullen. Cambridge: Cambridge University Press.

Secondary Literature

Mill, J. (1808). *Commerce Defended.* London: C. and R. Baldwin.
Ricardo, D. (1821 [1951]). Principles of Political Economy and Taxation. In P. Sraffa & M. Dobb (Eds.), *The Works and Correspondence of David Ricardo* (Vol. I, 11 vols.). Cambridge: Cambridge University Press.
Smith, A. (1776 [1961]). *The Wealth of Nations* (E. Cannan, Ed., 2 vols.). London: Methuen.

12
Money

Money separates in time and space the act of buying from the act of selling. It also has an influence on the level of effective demand. Some thinkers had taken it on trust that money shapes the nominal variables of prices and wages, but that notes and coins have no direct impact on the real variables of employment and output. Other thinkers had said that even the 'classical dichotomy' (Patinkin 1966: 174) should be examined carefully to see if it really made sense to treat money as a veil. Malthus was one of the thinkers who after 1797 attempted to debate the functions of money in an open economy where full capacity operation could never be guaranteed.

12.1 The Economics of the Suspension

Paper money, issued by the commercial banks, had only recently come into general usage. Coins, minted by the State, had long been the accepted means of payment. Before 1797 paper notes, issued by the country banks or, in London, by the Bank of England, had been convertible by law into the precious metals. In 1797, the Bank Restriction

D. Reisman, *Thomas Robert Malthus*, Great Thinkers in Economics,
https://doi.org/10.1007/978-3-030-01956-3_12

Act suspended the redemption of paper for the duration of the hostilities. Paper replaced bullion in order to free up specie for the foreign war that had begun in 1793.

Between the suspension in 1797 and the restoration of convertibility in 1821, there was no explicit ceiling to the volume of fiduciary claims that the banking system could create. It was an open door. The country banks were deterred from over-issue by the ongoing convention that their currency remained convertible on demand into notes issued by the Bank of England. The Bank issue, however, was convertible into nothing but itself.

The Bank of England was first among equals. In fact, as Malthus pointed out, it was something more: 'We may fairly, therefore, consider an increase of Bank of England notes, in any particular proportion, as an increase of the whole currency of the country in the same proportion' (1811b [1963]: 115). Money-pull inflation could only originate in the Bank. When the Bank put new money into circulation through interest-bearing credit, the country banks regarded it as safe to expand their own loans. The country banks made a profit from such business. So did the Bank of England. Founded in 1694, only nationalised in 1946, the Bank of England was a private corporation. Despite the fact that it held the government's account, it was a commercial business like any other.

Prices were rising. It led to the suspicion that the bankers had been taking advantage of the suspension to feather their own nest. There were no reliable statistics to establish the truth. The result was the war of the pamphlets in which deduction and assertion were the only way of settling the debate.

12.1.1 The Bullionist Controversy

The suspension in 1797 unleashed the Bullionist Controversy: 'The participants were distinguished as bullionists and anti-bullionists according as they accepted or rejected the appearance of a premium on bullion as a demonstration of depreciation of bank notes and mismanagement of the currency' (Viner 1937 [1964]: 119n). Leading bullionists were Henry Thornton, Francis Horner, Walter Boyd, Lord King and

David Ricardo. Leading anti-bullionists were Henry Boase, Nicholas Vansittart, Coutts Trotter, J. C. Harries and Charles Bosanquet. Malthus, Jacob Viner says, adopted a 'moderate bullionist position' (Viner 1937 [1964]: 141). It is a polite way of saying that he had a foot in both schools.

The bullionists argued that home prices were rising and the international parity depreciating because paper claims had been over-issued relative to the quantity of money that would have circulated if Britain had remained on the specie standard: 'When we speak of an excess of bank-notes, we mean that portion of the amount of the issues of the Bank, which can now circulate, but could not, if the currency were of its bullion value' (Ricardo 1811b [1951–1955]: 230). The anti-bullionists denied that the Bank of England and the other banks had behaved irresponsibly. The banks had created no more claims than were justified by the needs of trade and underwritten by self-liquidating collateral. Inflation, the anti-bullionists maintained, had been the result of random exogeneities such as harvest failures. Money was not to blame. The bankers were not to blame.

The rhetoric was heated. Lord King condemned the 1797 suspension as a free pass to the Bank and its Directors. Abusing the spirit of contract and violating the public's trust, they were making 'an undue and improper use of the powers entrusted to them by Parliament' to share out 'larger profits among the Proprietors of their Stock': 'The bullion has not become dear; but the paper for which it is exchanged has been rendered cheap' (King 1804: 13, 29, 33). The venal had been putting private gain above the social interest. A return to convertibility was the only way to prevent them from papering the printing press.

Robert Mushet continued the attack. The Bank of England, he objected, had recklessly expanded credit 'in an undue proportion to the whole produce of the land' (Mushet 1810: 24). It had driven up the price-level 'exactly as the discovery of a gold or silver mine would do' (Mushet 1810: 24). It is all a question of supply and demand: 'The value of a commodity depends… on its scarcity or plenty' (Mushet 1810: 20). Once the 'salutary check' of convertibility had been removed, there was 'no possible obstacle' to over-issue but the 'prudence' of the Bank Directors (Mushet 1810: 41). Prices were rising. It proved his point. Their prudence had not been enough.

Ricardo too was quick to blame the banks for the 'too abundant quantity' of notes that had caused the price of bullion and other commodities to go up (Ricardo 1811a [1951–1955]: 78). Anticipating Milton Friedman's pronouncement that 'inflation is always and everywhere a monetary phenomenon' (Friedman 1970: 24, emphasis deleted), he said that money is not the effect but the cause of an increase in the nominal values of commodities. It is neither the effect nor the cause of a change in the real sector: 'However abundant may be the quantity of money or of bank-notes….nothing will be added to the real revenue and wealth of the country' (Ricardo 1811a [1951–1955]: 93). It is the classical dichotomy. Money matters for prices. Quantities are a thing apart.

The anti-bullionists felt that bullionists like Ricardo were excessively rigid in an ever-changing world. It was their reply to the bullionists that discretion performs better than rules if the lead is taken by philosopher-dentists who put the *bono publico* first. Medieval monarchs had recklessly debased the tokens. Honest bankers after 1797 had done no more than what was needed. The economy was growing. More transactions required more money. Gold was not available. Bank issues were topping up the circular flow.

The anti-bullionists had authority on their side. Adam Smith himself had denied the possibility of over-issue if, responsibly, 'a bank discounts to a merchant a real bill of exchange drawn by a real creditor upon a real debtor ….which, as soon as it becomes due, is really paid by that debtor' (Smith 1776 [1961]: I 323). Bosanquet was standing on the shoulders of greatness when he said that the banks in his experience were 'discounting only solid paper, given, as far as we can judge, for real transactions' (Bosanquet 1810: 50–51). If the discounts were solid, the bankers gentlemen and the debt repaid, there was no need for a return to gold. Paper was as good as gold: 'What would we gain?' (Bosanquet 1810: 107).

Money lent at interest is ultimately repaid. Not only is there no net expansion, the fact that the interest is added to the principal means that there is a moderate contraction. There can also be a premature reflux if borrowers find that they no longer have a need: 'The paper would revert to us if there were a redundancy in circulation' (Bosanquet 1810: 10). Short-term loans made on the security of real stock would not remain long enough in circulation to cause inflation. Bosanquet does not mention exchequer bills discounted to accommodate the State. There is no public choice in his economics. His message is a simple one. Money is always and everywhere the effect of inflation. It is never the cause.

12.1.2 Malthus and the Suspension

There were the bullionists and the anti-bullionists. Both schools asserted that there was a close correlation between money and prices. Neither school, however, could prove conclusively that it was the chicken or the egg that had led the series. Malthus, both as a Christian clergyman and a conviction liberal, was no stranger to propositions that were a leap in the dark. In spite of that, in the suspension period, he remained largely on the sidelines. He knew that the evidence was not robust.

Perhaps also he was intimidated by the quality of the contributors. Most were bankers, stockbrokers or Members of Parliament. Most had personal knowledge of the city. Malthus may, of course, had known more than he revealed. In his personal papers, there are almost a hundred pages of calculations on the speculative gain that can be made by buying gold in Amsterdam to resell in London (KG II 56–140). There is no evidence that he was actually in the market, or, still less, that he had discussed personal finance with his friend Ricardo who had a track record in dealing.

It may be because of his reservations that he never produced a dedicated tract on money. He declined an invitation from the *Edinburgh Review* in 1810 to review the *Bullion Report* that, authored by Thornton, Huskisson and Horner, had so great an influence in persuading Parliament to return to gold. He did, however, write a long review of six pamphlets under the title 'Depreciation of Paper Currency' in 1811. Later, also in 1811, he wrote 'Pamphlets on the Bullion Question' to survey a further five publications. The authors he assessed included, among others, Ricardo, Bosanquet, Huskisson and Blake. His reviews, in line with house practice unsigned, are idiosyncratic. He devotes more space to his own opinions than to the pamphlets themselves.

Before the *Edinburgh Review*, there had been the 1803 and the 1806 *Essay*. Later, in 1820, there was the *Principles* and, in 1823, a review in the *Quarterly Review* of Thomas Tooke. Malthus was not a monetary theorist in the sense of Ricardo. He was for all that an influential contributor to the debate on the quantity theory of money. Yet there was a problem. He seems more than once to have changed his mind.

In 1811, he indicated that the bullionist case was the stronger one: 'Every kind of circulating medium, as well as every other kind of commodity, is necessarily depreciated by excess, and raised in value by deficiency' (1811a [1963]: 73). Almost 15 years into the suspension, he wrote, the excess is even now upon us: 'All the circumstances attending the peculiar state of our currency, conspire to point clearly and unequivocally to an excessive issue of paper, as its main, and indeed almost sole, cause' (1811b [1963]: 108).

The cause was the currency. The effect was rising prices and a depreciating exchange. What was needed to correct the imbalance was a 'compression of the currency' (1811b [1963]: 110). What was happening instead was that there had been an expansion in the means of payment, and 'at the very moment when circumstances required it to be constricted' (1811b [1963]: 110). In 1811, it was pure bullionism. In 1823, however, in his review of Thomas Tooke, he was insisting that Tooke's statistics on price 'point out distinctly how this rise in prices may take place, even without an increase either of Bank of England paper or money' (1823b [1963]: 156). In 1823, it was pure anti-bullionism.

In 1811, he was asserting that, whether money or pins, an increase in the quantity supplied causes the market value to drop. This follows directly from 'the general principles of supply and demand, which are unquestionably the foundation on which the whole superstructure of political economy is built' (1811a [1963]: 73). In 1823, however, he was contending that money, passive and accommodating, can always be found to validate a previous rise: 'A general rise of bullion prices, including labour, seems to be at all times possible, even without any fresh importation of the precious metals' (1823a [1986]: 213).

In 1811, he was saying that money is the cause. In 1823, he was saying that money is the effect. In between the two *Reviews*, there was the *Principles*. In 1820 in the *Principles*, he was saying that money, like the philosopher, arrives *post festum*, after the deed is done: 'In the history of our paper transactions, it will be found that the abundance or scantiness of currency has followed and aggravated high or low prices, but seldom or never led them' (PR 514). Money is not the cause. It is simply a rubber ferret that accommodates itself to the needs of trade: 'Fresh paper may be issued without a fall in the rate of foreign exchanges, or a rise in the price of bullion and of goods' (PR 452). Money matters, but not very much.

Money in 1820 was the also-ran. Money in 1820 was not the prime mover. Even before 1811, however, there had been 1800. In 1800 in the *Investigation*, he had made clear that any increase in the money supply must be seen 'rather as the effect than the cause of the high price of provisions' (1800 [1986]: 24–25). Commodity prices had risen. More money had had to be created in order to validate a rise which had not been inherited from an even earlier new issue.

In 1803, there was the second *Essay*. It was all very clear. The bankers had conducted themselves well. The increase in the money supply had been 'rather a consequence than a cause of the high price of provisions' (SE I 354). Also in the second *Essay*, however, there was a footnote criticising Thornton for not having taken 'sufficient notice of the effects of the great paper issues of the country banks, in raising the price of commodities, and producing an unfavourable state of exchange with foreigners' (SE I 354n). The note said it was a cause. The text said it was a consequence. The note disappeared in 1806 in the third *Essay*. Possibly Malthus had become aware of the check exercised by the continuing convertibility of country bank currency into Bank of England issues.

Malthus could change his mind. Intellectually, it makes sense to be flexible. In terms of the primacy of specie it does not. Malthus was at heart a bullionist. He had to be a bullionist since it was the causal link between money and prices that underpinned his expectation of international monetary equilibrium in the post-fiduciary order. Prices and not parities would stabilise the balance of payments once the nations had reassumed the discipline of the specie standard. Malthus the anti-bullionist would have been no Malthus at all.

12.2 A Return to Specie

Malthus believed that there was no alternative: 'The moment we quit the precious metals as the constant standard of reference, there is no fancy so wild, respecting a paper circulation, which may not be indulged' (1811a [1963]: 90). Without a stable monetary constitution (Friedman 1962: 51–55) a nation's 'property and contracts' would forever be in 'a dreadfully critical state' (1811a [1963]: 90). Inflation would 'deprive individuals of half their fortunes' (1811a [1963]: 90).

12.2.1 The Quantity of Money

The suspension had to end. Paper once again had to be convertible on demand into gold and silver. There was no other way to keep the money supply on course: 'In no other way would it be *possible*...to regulate the quantity of bank notes' (1811a [1963]: 85, emphasis in original). The anti-bullionists had said that sensible bankers would know when to stop. Confidence in responsible lenders would not be misplaced. Arguing for rules and not discretion, Malthus objected that inperiod tinkering would be a hostage to 'the integrity of a few individuals, on which the great mass of the property of a country ought never to be made to depend' (1811a [1963]: 90). Good men do good things. Bad men do bad things. It does not inspire confidence: 'What security have we?' (1811a [1963]: 90).

Without the constraint of convertibility, the bankers would yield to temptation. The experience of the suspension years showed that they were not to be trusted. The Bank, lending excessively and on poor security, had become involved in 'profuse and unusual accommodations' (1811b [1963]: 117). The Directors had recklessly over-expanded into the sub-prime and the speculative in order to please their shareholders and 'for their own private fortunes' (1811a [1963]: 60). Paper had gone down relative to bullion. Prices had gone up. Self-regulation had failed: 'Even the assignats of France rested upon a better foundation' (1811a [1963]: 90). Fixed rules were the only way to prevent runaway money-making from debauching the monetary flow.

The Bank of England itself could not be trusted. It was the first among equals. For profit, it had nonetheless overstepped the limits of prudent lending. Its role had to be reappraised. Malthus experimented with two potential alternatives.

The first was market competition. Adam Smith, never comfortable with the claims of revealed religion, had suggested that convergence on a 'rational religion' could arguably be brought about if an established Church were broken up into 'two or three hundred, or perhaps into as many thousand small sects' (Smith 1776 [1961]: II 314). Smith was modelling his reformation through fission on the economic optimum of the market-clearing price under perfectly competitive powerlessness. Malthus, writing about a central bank, seems to be exploring a similar route. Substituting the Bank of England for Adam Smith's Catholic Church, he suggests that it might be desirable to pluralise the role of hegemon. 'One or more other banks' could come to duplicate the functions of an 'overgrown' Bank that had become 'a monstrous deformity in the state' (1811a [1963]: 102).

The second was State involvement. Malthus, in a letter to Ricardo, seems to be saying that convertibility is not enough to control the windfall gains being made by private lenders: 'Government ought to participate more largely in the profits of a paper circulation' (letter from Malthus to Ricardo, 1815, in Ricardo VI: 289). Malthus may have in mind the seignorage of the nationalised mint which had a monopoly in the manufacture of coin. Since he had as little confidence in the politicians as he did in the commercial bankers, the only way he could have taken this further would be through an independent monetary authority with operational autonomy and a mandate to maintain the stability of prices.

Even then, there would be not much that it could or should do. Because the money supply is linked to specie, a counter-cyclical monetary policy could not lean against the winds of slack. A 'sudden increase of currency' might 'give a temporary stimulus to trade', but that is all: 'It would be only temporary' (PR 514). It might even prolong the very downturn that it was seeking to reverse. Writing to Arthur Young in 1816, Malthus was cautioning that a stab in the dark could prove a stab too far: 'Too great a stimulus by means of a paper circulation would probably accentuate a glut and defeat itself' (letter from Malthus to Arthur Young, 1816, in Arthur Young Papers, ff.319). Monetary stimulus was always temporary and, probably, wrong-headed. Fiscal policy—'a large expenditure on the part of the government' (PR 514)—would be a more effective tool.

12.2.2 The International Standard

There has to be a common currency. There has to be a universal unit of account, store of value and means of payment if open economies are to settle their debts and balance their payments. It is a win-win solution for the international community. Their unanimity of consensus is proof that they as interdependent partners recognise the need for a social contract that would transcend the Hobbesian anarchy of trade-destruction and even of war.

Any asset is eligible to be the monetary standard provided that the players unanimously take it to be their rule. Treasure, historically, has been the most acceptable choice: 'The precious metals are the currency of the commercial world….All nations which have a mutual intercourse with each other, must partake of them' (1811a [1963]: 86). The dominant position of specie is derived from the 'common consent of society' (1811a [1963]: 83). It is not their intrinsic value per se that makes them money. Their moneyness is derived exclusively from the consent of all those who live subject to their law.

It is a good choice. The value of the gold and silver is 'known and remains constant' (PR II 95). Except in a price revolution such as follows the discovery of new mines, new flows are small relative to the stock (PR 112). The stability of the base ensures the stability of the *fiat* which is convertible into it. An unreliable money would cause swings in prices and redistribution of income. No trading partner wants that. Specie might in time be supplanted by a superior asset. For now, Malthus says, it is universally accepted as if it had been chosen by a constitutional convention.

The world supply of the precious metals is distributed in such a way as to harmonise the prices of the international tradeables: 'The precious metals are, on the whole, maintained in such proportions in the different countries of the commercial world, as, in reference to the commodities which form the subjects of their mutual intercourse, to be nearly of the same value in each' (1811a [1963]: 73). Moderate deviation from purchasing power parity may reflect the heuristic of inertia and the deterrence of transport. Excessive variation creates an imbalance. It will be corrected through successive price adjustments until in the end the 'equilibrium of the precious metals' (1811a [1963]: 75) will have been restored.

Since the national currencies are pegged to metal, the whole world in practice is trading with a single token. The jingo names of pounds and francs are just for show. Because the exchange rates are fixed, international imbalances may be settled in the short run through transfers of reserves, but in the long run can only be corrected through an adjustment in price. Prices must fall where there is a deficit and rise if there is a surplus. As David Hume describes it, 'money would soon sink in Europe, and rise in China, till it came nearly to a level in both places' (Hume 1752a [1955]: 65). The Government, Hume adds, need do nothing at all: 'Its money, it may safely trust to the course of human affairs' (Hume 1752a [1955]: 77).

So long as bank lending is linked to bullion flows, the price-levels in the partner nations will rise or fall with the inward or outward flux. Because of the self-stabilising specie flow mechanism, an international surplus or a deficit will automatically reverse itself. Money supply expands or contracts. Prices go up or go down. Exports and imports return to equilibrium. 'Natural inequalities' in the payments position of the respective nations, Malthus says, can 'never be of serious magnitude and continuance' (1811b [1963]: 127). Unless, that is, they are 'aggravated and prolonged' by the 'imprudent issues' of the Bank and of the banks (1811b [1963]: 127). Bad bankers ruin everything.

12.2.3 Modifications and Extensions

Malthus said that political economy, like life itself, has few straight lines: 'A desire to simplify, which has often led away the most scientific men, has induced you to ascribe to one cause phenomena that properly belong to two' (letter from Malthus to Ricardo, 1812, in Ricardo

VI: 82). Malthus was open to multicausality. It marked him out from the other participants in the monetary controversies, most of whom 'adhered to a single view of the question' (Pullen 2016: 353). If Malthus in places appears inconsistent, the reason may be that the evolving circumstances after 1797 were forcing him to think things out for himself. Even Adam Smith had not planned for a departure from gold. The exchange rate after 1797 was in free float. As much as he wanted a return to specie, Malthus knew that the game in the short run would be played by different rules.

Malthus worked through the stages. When exports exceed imports and gold flows in, the bankers would be in a position to increase their loans. The expansion in the money supply would tend to 'raise prices at home, and thus to shorten the duration of the favourable exchange' (1811a [1963]: 92). Between 1797 and 1811 the pound had slipped by 30%. Nothing could have produced this effect 'except an issue of notes not only insufficient to prevent that compression of the currency, which is at once the natural effect and natural remedy of an unfavourable exchange, but greatly to enlarge the medium of circulation, at the very moment when circumstances required it to be contracted' (1811b [1963]: 110).

Money causes a rise in prices at home. That, however, would not be the end of the sequence. Inflation makes British exports more expensive and British imports more competitive. The export surplus could not last. Even without a fixed parity, the price mechanism would 'increase the strength of the current in the opposite direction' (1811a [1963]: 92). Less money would be borrowed and circulated as the foreign demand for British output fell off. Prices would fall and would reverse the trend. Devaluation would join deflation in returning the balance of payments to equilibrium.

Devaluation would be especially attractive if the first-mover cause of inflation happened not to be the money supply at all. Ricardo, Malthus says, is 'particularly entitled to praise' (1811a [1963]: 73) for his demonstration that the deviation of bullion price from mint price *could have been* caused by 'a redundant or deficient currency' (1811a [1963]: 75). Then he comes to the point. It *could have been*. In the specific circumstances that Ricardo was describing it, however, *was not*.

Ricardo was blinkered by the narrow rigidity of his quantity theory of money. The result had been a 'partial view….of the causes which operate upon the course of Exchange' (1811a [1963]: 74). Ricardo had blotted out the *ceteris paribus* of bad harvests, remittances to allies, changes in tastes, wartime disruptions, all of which were likely to have had an effect on trade and exchange. Bullion might have been transferred abroad not because of a paper-glut at home but because of the 'unwillingness of the country to which the debt is owing' (1811a [1963]: 76) to receive British goods in exchange. Exports might be disrupted because overseas partners 'have not, at the moment, any other commodities that they can give' (1811a [1963]: 94).

Ricardo had oversimplified the multiplicity of potential causes. It left his account of the suspension period under-determined. An example would be the experience of 1808 when the fall in the exchanges was greater than 'could possibly be accounted for by the increase of notes that had been thrown into the circulation' (1811b [1963]: 113). Other forces had been at work. Malthus found Ricardo too focussed. Ricardo found Malthus too *ad hoc*.

Pragmatism has its downside. Multicausality can lead to indeterminacy. In an unpublished fragment dating from 1811 when he was at his most bullionist, Malthus concedes that inflation cost-pushed by scarce supplies of grain will 'require an extended rather than a diminished currency' (KG II 146). Sometimes even inflation must be accommodated and not stifled. Ricardo at least could give the policy-makers a single-valued reply.

Ricardo did not find the definition of money a problem. Thornton did. Bullionist, banker, Member of Parliament, Henry Thornton in his *Paper Credit* of 1802 had said that, alongside bank issues and coin, the census of spendable assets extended to bills of exchange, 'book debt' and an open-ended list of near-monies (Thornton 1802 [1962]: 91). Such money substitutes, although clearly not currency, were putting pressure on scarce consumables and pulling up the general price index. Endogenous and unregulated, quasi-money to Henry Thornton was a Pandora's Box.

Malthus does not say if his own definition of acceptable vouchers is narrow or open-ended. Probably a Ricardian in his definition of money, what is clear is that he was not a Ricardian in his attitude to speed. Ricardo denied that the number of times a monetary asset changes hands in a year is subject to extensive and unpredictable variation. Malthus said that turnover is a moveable feast. His recognition that velocity is a function of utility and expectations looks forward to the Keynesian precautionary and speculative motive (Keynes 1936 [1971]: 170). It has less in common with the fixed coefficients of Fisher's $MV = PT$ (Fisher 1911: 25–27). Money times constant velocity equals prices times constant quantity. Fisher's equation of exchange borders on a truism. Malthus was a dynamic thinker who was uncomfortable with invariant variables that refused to respond.

It was 'generally recognised at the time' (Viner 1937 [1964]: 130) that the velocity of money was not a constant. For Thornton, the 'rapidity of the circulation' (Thornton 1802 [1962]: 96) fluctuated with the news. Gold guineas were being hoarded as a hedge against a French invasion. Fiduciary paper was being run down lest the 'season of distrust' (Thornton 1802 [1962]: 97) culminate in a repudiation. Liquidity preference and the internal drain, Thornton advised, were entirely subjective and all around.

Malthus was convinced by the 'uncommon combination of extensive knowledge of detail with just principles, exhibited in the work of Mr. H. Thornton' (1811a [1963]: 72). Thornton had been right about the guineas: 'Gold may be said to be already quite banished from our circulation' (1811a [1963]: 100). Thornton had been right about the paper: a 'want of confidence' (1811a [1963]: 99) causes it to be spent without delay. One asset circulates more slowly. The other asset circulates more quickly. The outcome could be deflation rather than inflation.

The money supply could be contracting if coins were too rapidly being melted into ingots to capitalise on the higher market price (1811b [1963]: 112). Thornton, warning that the mix of velocities could in the end starve the nation of liquidity, turned to the Bank Directors to show discretion and make new loans (Thornton 1802 [1962]: 127). Thornton was a bullionist who diced with the anti-bullionists because a hard-line monetary constitution would be at variance with the needs of trade. Malthus departed from Thornton to the extent that he never trusted the Directors to manage a compensatory issue. Writing to the Chairman of the Bullion Committee in the year of the *Bullion Report*, Malthus told Horner that that the management of a currency requires 'great attention, great knowledge, and great disinterestedness'—qualities, pointedly, which the Bank Directors 'have not possessed in a sufficient degree' (letter to Horner, 1810, in KG I 111). On the issue of velocity, however, Malthus was at one with Thornton. Unstable velocity makes the relationship between money and prices difficult to predict.

In *The Measure of Value*, written two years after the return to gold, Malthus reiterates that monetary policy operates not through the stock of money per se so much as through the work that each unit of money will do. If there is a 'brisk demand', he says, it 'occasions a more rapid circulation of money, and enables the same quantity to perform a greater number of transactions' (1823a [1986]: 213). If the demand is 'brisk', he says in the *Principles*, 'a greater velocity is given to the circulation of the money actually in use' (PR 452). A high price of bullion can be caused not by an influx of treasure or by excessive new issue, but by a more intensive deployment of an existing or even a contracting asset stock. Velocity itself can force the effective exchange rate down.

Velocity is high-powered but unpredictable. Even a return to specie will not guarantee a return to proportionality. The gold standard may or may not ensure that the money supply creates precisely the quantity of demand that is required to keep the rise in prices in check.

12.3 Forced Saving

There is no forced saving where there is slack. An increase in money is met exclusively by a quantity response. Jeremy Bentham, whose theory of 'forced frugality' in 1843 was a part of the English verbal tradition as early as 1804 (Hayek 1932: 123), observed that new money, 'bringing into employment the quantity of capacity for labour as yet unemployed', would expand the volume of output, but 'would contribute nothing to the rise of prices' (Bentham 1952: II 330).

There is no forced saving where physical quantities are infinitely elastic. Nor is there forced saving where there is instantaneous adaptation without a lead or lag. The Walrasian *tâtonnement* assures a coordinated matrix without a time-dominated search. The pattern of demand is different where knowledge is imperfect, expectations are non-rational and recalibration takes time. In the interval between action and reaction, there is unplanned redistribution from one category of income-earners to another.

Forced saving occurs where a rise in the price of current output precedes the catch-up in the price of contracted input. In the transition to the new equilibrium, there is a shift in purchasing power from fixed-income to residual-income earners. Should the reallocation be from a spending to a saving estate, the profit-recipients will de facto have a greater pool of investible funds.

In the disequilibrium state, the classical dichotomy between the nominal and the real cannot hold. Malthus saw clearly what the lack of synchronicity and simultaneity would mean for output and employment in a dynamic economy where the money-supply was growing faster than things: 'The transfer of property occasioned by a rise of prices, has a tendency to give a stimulus to industry' (1811b [1963]: 119–120). Inflation, Malthus reasoned, could accelerate the process of economic growth effectively because the capitalists make a windfall while their workers are left behind: 'An influx of the precious metals has no doubt a great tendency to increase the demand for commodities, to raise profits, for a time, [and] leave less share of the produce to the labourer' (letter from Malthus to Prévost, 1822, in Zinke 1942: 186).

Labour is effectively co-funding the factories and the farms that make the capital grow. History shows that it can and does occur: 'The discovery of the mines of America, during the time that it raised the price of corn between three and five times, did not nearly so much as double the price of labour' (1814 [1986]: 93), Saving is necessary if investment is to grow. Since the wages fund is the capital that creates the additional openings, the quantity of employment compensates the working class for the fall in the average real wage.

Malthus knew that inflation could be an argument in the production function. He was, as Friedrich von Hayek says, not alone: 'The theory of "forced saving" was fairly widely known among monetary writers in the early nineteenth century' (Hayek 1932: 130). Henry Thornton was especially clear in identifying the way in which a fall from grace could be turned to advantage 'Provided we assume an excessive issue of paper to lift up, as it may for a time, the cost of goods though not the price of labour, some augmentation of stock will be the consequence; for the labourer, according to this supposition, may be forced by his necessity to consume fewer articles, though he may exercise the same industry' (Thornton 1802 [1962]: 239). Insider workers may feel aggrieved at the cut in their real wage. Not so the 'antecedently idle persons to whom we may suppose the new capital to give employ' (Thornton 1802 [1962]: 236). The money supply solves their problem. Prices and profits give them a job.

John Barton, in his unpublished commonplace book, documented the process through which nominal claims, by means of forced saving, can contribute to real wealth: 'An increased abundance of the precious metals raises the price of commodities in a greater proportion than the price of labour; it depresses the condition of the labourer, and at the same time increases the gains of his employer, who is thus induced to enlarge his circulating capital to the utmost of his ability, to have as many hands as he has the means to pay' (Barton, n.d.). Capacity is in surplus and sticky wages lag behind. While the forced saving survives, the real sector is converting the time-limited windfall into jobs and growth.

Malthus had read the *Paper Credit* even if he had not read Barton's notes. Most of all, he had drawn on 'the very just observations of Hume' (1811b [1963]: 120). Hume, in the mid-eighteenth century, had anticipated the stimulus that forced saving could provide: 'When any quantity of money is imported into a nation, it is not at first dispersed into many hands, but is confined to the coffers of a few persons, who immediately seek to employ it to advantage....They are thereby enabled to employ more workmen than formerly, who never dream of demanding higher wages' (Hume 1752b [1955]: 38). The bubble, Hume said, will eventually burst: 'In my opinion, it is only in this interval or intermediate situation, between the acquisition of money and the rise of prices, that the encreasing [sic] quantity of gold and silver is favourable to industry' (Hume 1752b [1955]: 38). In the long run, the wage gap will be closed. In the interim, the increase in the money supply will feed through into commodities and employment.

To Malthus, Hume's theory made sense. Money is not capital but it is, producing inflation, a mechanism through which capital can be created: 'All the industrious classes ....are, during the progressive rise of prices, making unusual profits' (1811a [1963]: 96). Their profits are being channelled into saving and investing. Overall, 'the produce of the country would be greatly augmented' (1811a [1963]: 96). It is not the money supply itself but the reallocation of demand that makes a nation rich. As it does: 'An increased issue of notes tends to increase the national capital' (1811a [1963]: 97).

The general counts. The specific counts as well. Sensible lenders will discriminate in favour of wealth-creating activity. New credit will not enhance material welfare if the money goes to 'the idle, and those who live upon fixed incomes' (1811a [1963]: 96). Nor will it make the nation more productive if the loans are wasted on petty speculators 'who may be said to gamble in trade' and 'in whose hands, therefore, the national accumulation is quite uncertain' (1811a [1963]: 97). Prudent bankers should steer well clear of wild men who make junk promises that are likely to result in a loss. Instead, they should direct their credits to 'the most respectable mercantile capitalists' (1811a [1963]: 97), to 'farmers, manufacturers and merchants', to social wealth-creators who 'mean to employ them in the prosecution and extension of a profitable business' (1811a [1963]: 96). Intelligent lending twists the composition of national expenditure towards the investing and away from the consuming estate.

Lenders will have to reduce their lending rate in order to grow their account-business to leverage their investment (1811a [1963]: 97). Malthus was groping towards the distinction that Knut Wicksell was later to make between the money rate and the natural rate of interest in an adjustment period when the lending community is seeking to run down its cash surplus (Wicksell 1898 [1936]: 102–121). So, interestingly, was David Ricardo, who in 1819 his evidence to the Lords Committee on the Resumption of Cash Payments had this to say about the short-run deviation: 'It is only during the Interval, that is, before the Prices are settled at the new Rate, that the Rate of Interest is either raised or lowered' (Ricardo 1819 [1951–1955]: 445).

In the event, Malthus did not develop what could have been a theory of 'forced interest' as a pendant to his theory of forced saving. Like

Ricardo, he believed that it was the profit on capital that ultimately determines the investors' willingness to borrow (Ricardo 1821 [1951–1955]: 297). Like Smith, he felt that it was the intersection of investment with saving that determines the interest rate: 'What can commonly be given for the use of money [is] necessarily regulated by what can commonly be made by the use of it' (Smith 1776 [1961]: I 378). That, however, is in the long run. There is also the short run. Malthus saw that the only way in which currency influences the rate of interest is through the disequilibrium effect of money on prices. He never found time to return to this important extension of his theory of forced saving.

Malthus saw that forced saving could contribute to economic growth. His advice to policy-makers was nonetheless that deliberate inflationism ought to be avoided. The 'grand and paramount objection' to economic stimulation through new money is that the engineered redistribution is 'a manifest injustice': 'Countries are often increasing in riches amidst an increasing quantity of individual misery' (1811a [1963]: 97). Inflation is a private tax, 'oppressive and unequal' (1811b [1963]: 119). It infringes the law of contract. It degrades 'the legal coin of the realm to whatever value in exchange a banking company may choose' (1811b [1963]: 123). Morally speaking, the meta-goal of growth 'cannot alter the foundations of right and wrong, or give the slightest sanction to unjust transfers of property' (1811a [1963]: 97). Parliament and the law courts 'must attend equally to the happiness of all classes of the community' (1811a [1963]: 104). All classes are not affected equally by inflation. Forced saving is not neutral, even handed or across the board. Even if it is economically beneficial, ethically it is always wrong. It is confiscation without consent. It is a violation of natural rights.

Inflation gives 'a most unfair advantage to the profuse debtor over the thrifty creditor' (1811b [1963]: 119). The landlord loses out in the short run, but will later be able to renegotiate his rents. The holder of the national debt has more reason to be 'most seriously alarmed' as the 'wide-wasting convulsion' (1811b [1963]: 125) steadily decimates his nest egg. It is what Keynes called the 'euthanasia of the rentier' (Keynes 1936 [1973]: 376). Fixed income or residual income, Malthus agrees with Hume that it cannot be just to expropriate decent people's honest claims: 'The most certain way of producing that poverty, beggary and sloth which he describes, is a profuse issue of bank paper' (1811b [1963]: 120).

The answer is a convertible currency which blocks the 'vain efforts to keep up prices by forcible issues of paper' (PR 515). The only way to keep bank money in line is by 'subjecting it to no other fluctuations than those which belong to the precious metals' (PR 515). Stable prices are pro-poor. Since wages lag behind, inflation 'must always bring more evil than good' (PR 522).

Speculative bubbles when they burst leave behind them a trail of 'ruined merchants', 'impoverished manufacturers' and a 'failure of confidence' (1811b [1963]: 120, 125). Manipulation of paper values is in the long run 'unfavourable to industry' (1811b [1963]: 120). The return to convertibility when it occurs will engender a crippling deflation. It cannot be regularly repeated. All things considered, 'the happiness of the great mass of society' (PR 522) is bound up with a stable currency. It is something that only the specie standard can ensure.

References

By T. R. Malthus

(1800 [1986]). *An Investigation of the Cause of the Present High Price of Provisions*, reprinted in *The Works of Thomas Robert Malthus*, ed. by E. A. Wrigley and D. Souden. London: Pickering and Chatto, 7, 5–18.

(1803 et seq. [1989]). *An Essay on the Principle of Population: Or a View of Its Past and Present Effects on Human Happiness, with an Inquiry into Our Prospects Respecting the Removal of the Evils Which It Occasions* (2nd edition, 1803; further editions in 1806, 1807, 1817, 1826) (abbreviated as SE I and SE II), 2 vols., ed. by P. James. Cambridge: Cambridge University Press.

(1811a [1963]). Depreciation of Paper Money. *Edinburgh Review, 34*, 1811, reprinted in *Occasional Papers of T.R. Malthus*, ed. by B. Semmel. New York: Bert Franklin, 71–104.

(1811b [1963]). Pamphlets on the Bullion Question. *Edinburgh Review, 36*, 1811, reprinted in *Occasional Papers of T.R. Malthus*, ed. by B. Semmel. New York: Bert Franklin, 105–127.

(1814 [1986]). *Observations on the Effects of the Corn Laws, and of a Rise or Fall in the Price of Corn on the Agriculture and General Wealth of the Country*, reprinted in *The Works of Thomas Robert Malthus*, ed. by E. A. Wrigley and D. Souden. London: Pickering and Chatto, 7, 87–109.
(1820 [1989]). *The Principles of Political Economy* (abbreviated as PR), ed. by J. Pullen. Cambridge: Cambridge University Press.
(1823a [1986]). *The Measure of Value Stated and Illustrated, with an Application of It to the Alterations in the Value of the English Currency Since 1790*, reprinted in *The Works of Thomas Robert Malthus*, ed. by E. A. Wrigley and D. Souden. London: Pickering and Chatto, 7, 179–221.
(1823b [1963]). 'Tooke—On High and Low Prices', review of Thomas Tooke's *Thoughts and Details on the High and Low Prices of the Last Thirty Years*', *Quarterly Review*, 1823, reprinted in *Occasional Papers of T.R. Malthus*, ed. by B. Semmel. New York: Bert Franklin, 145–170.
Zinke, G. W. (1942). Six letters from Malthus to Pierre Prévost. *Journal of Economic History, 2*, 174–189.
T.R. Malthus: Unpublished Papers in the Collection of Kanto Gakuen University, Vols. I (1997) and II (2004), (abbreviated as KG), ed. by J. Pullen and T. Hughes Parry. Cambridge: Cambridge University Press.
Arthur Young Papers, British Library, Additional Manuscript Collection, 3. 35.133.

Secondary Literature

Barton, J. (n.d.). Unpublished Commonplace-Book, Archives Section, British Library of Economic and Political Science, R (SR) 1088.
Bentham, J. (1952). *Jeremy Bentham's Economic Writings* (W. Stark, Ed., 2 vols.). London: George Allen & Unwin.
Bosanquet, C. (1810). *Practical Observations on the Report of the Bullion-Committee*. London: Richardson.
Fisher, I. (1911). *The Purchasing Power of Money*. New York: Macmillan.
Friedman, M. (1962). *Capitalism and Freedom*. Chicago: University of Chicago Press.
Friedman, M. (1970). *The Counter-Revolution in Monetary Theory*. London: Institute of Economic Affairs.
Hayek, F. A. (1932). A Note on the Development of the Doctrine of "Forced Savings". *Quarterly Journal of Economics, 47*, 123–133.

Hume, D. (1752a [1955]). Of the Balance of Trade. In E. Rotwein (Ed.), *David Hume: Writings on Economics* (pp. 60–77). London: Nelson.
Hume, D. (1752b [1955]). Of Money. In E. Rotwein (Ed.), *David Hume: Writings on Economics* (pp. 33–46). London: Nelson.
Keynes, J. M. (1936 [1973]). *The General Theory of Employment, Interest and Money*. In *The Collected Writings of John Maynard Keynes*. London: Macmillan.
King, P. (1804). *Thoughts on the Effects of the Bank Restrictions* (2nd ed.). London: Cadell and Davies.
Mushet, R. (1810). *An Inquiry into the Effects Produced on the National Currency and Rates of Exchange by the Bank Restriction Bill*. London: C. and R. Baldwin.
Patinkin, D. (1966). *Money, Interest, and Prices: An Integration of Monetary and Value Theory* (2nd ed.). New York: Harper & Row.
Pullen, J. R. (2016). Malthus on Causality. *European Journal of History of Economic Thought, 23*, 349–377.
Ricardo, D. (1811a [1951–1955]). *The High Price of Bullion, A Proof of the Depreciation of Bank Notes* (4th ed.), in Ricardo, infra, III 47–127.
Ricardo, D. (1811b [1951–1955]). *Reply to Mr. Bosanquet's Practical Observations on the Subject of the Bullion Committee*, in Ricardo, infra, III 155–256.
Ricardo, D. (1819 [1951–1955]). *Evidence to the Lord Committee on the Resumption of Cash Payments*, in Ricardo, infra, V 416–457.
Ricardo, D. (1821 [1951–1955]). *Principles of Political Economy*, in Ricardo, infra, I.
Ricardo, D. (1951–1955). *The Works and Correspondence of David Ricardo* (abbreviated as Ricardo) (P. Sraffa & M. Dobb, Eds., 11 vols.). Cambridge: Cambridge University Press.
Smith, A. (1776 [1961]). *The Wealth of Nations* (E. Cannan, Ed., 2 vols.). London: Methuen.
Thornton, H. (1802 [1962]). *An Enquiry into the Nature and Effects of the Paper Credit of Great Britain* (F. A. v. Hayek, Ed.). London: Cass.
Viner, J. (1937 [1964]). *Studies in the Theory of International Trade*. London: George Allen & Unwin.
Wicksell, K. (1898 [1936]). *Interest and Prices* (R. F. Kahn, Trans.). London: Macmillan.

13

God's Design

The Reverend Malthus was an ordained clergyman in the Church of England. As a parson in Okewood and Walesby, he had signed the Thirty-Nine Articles of the Faith and preached his sermons from the Bible. Malthus was also a utilitarian philosopher who believed that 'the happiness of a society is.... the legitimate end even of its wealth, power, and population' (SE II 70). Clergyman and utilitarian, Malthus was in the tradition of Adam Smith's great mentor, the 'never-to-be-forgotten' Francis Hutcheson (quoted in Scott 1937: 31).

Francis Hutcheson was Professor of Moral Philosophy in the University of Glasgow. He was also an ordained minister in the Church of Scotland. Francis Hutcheson declared, almost a century before the Benthamite radicals, that the supreme end of earthly endeavour was the maximisation of total utility: 'That *Action is Best*, which procures the *greatest Happiness* for the *greatest Numbers*' (Hutcheson 1725: 181, emphasis in original). Such a credo was not to the taste of the dour Presbytery. God's will, they said, could not be reduced to eating, drinking and the theatre which was forbidden because it was sinful self-indulgence.

D. Reisman, *Thomas Robert Malthus*, Great Thinkers in Economics,
https://doi.org/10.1007/978-3-030-01956-3_13

Adam Smith had himself trained, on a Snell Scholarship at Oxford, to become a clergyman. David Hume's *Treatise on Human Nature* made him question the revealed dogmas which in his published work he references less than Shakespeare's Scottish play. David Hume, unable to secure an academic appointment because his empiricism was tainted with agnosticism, had never advanced beyond the post of Librarian to the Faculty of Advocates. Smith never ascended with Hutcheson into the Church but never descended with Hume into the Advocates.

The Enlightenment was the Age of Reason. Many intellectuals were drawn to a God of Nature who shunned self-appointed prophets and unverifiable scriptures. Privately, Adam Smith may have been a non-denominational deist like the others. A former student once wrote to him 'Oh, venerable and worthy man, why was you not a Christian?' (quoted in Rae 1895 [1965]: 130). All that is known with certainty is that Smith followed Hutcheson to the Chair and not Hume to the Library.

Malthus was standing on the shoulders of giants when, an ordained clergyman seeking to reconcile pestilence and famine with the benevolence of an omniscient Creator, he was drawn to political economy because he hoped that it would unlock the secret. In the concluding Chapters 18 and 19 of the first *Essay on Population*, Malthus wrestled with the theodicity of evil and the teleology of the divine. Starvation and smallpox, perfection and faith, he sought to grasp what Job could not.

William Empson saw that Chapters 18 and 19 were crucial for an understanding of Malthus's world view: 'They contain….the principle of the answer which he continued to give, as often as he was applied to for a philosophical solution of the problem of human life' (Empson 1837 [1963]: 262). John Pullen regards the chapters on God's design as the missing link: 'The position of this discussion at the end of the *Essay* suggests that Malthus saw it as the culmination of the argument….These theological ideas provide the essential logical framework for the *Essay* and introduce a consistency into what otherwise might appear to be contradictory aspects of the principle of population' (Pullen 1981: 47).

'Philosophical solution', 'essential logical framework', the fact is that by the second *Essay* in 1803 the two chapters were gone. The argument became more secular, more policy-orientated. God's design went into hiding. It never went away.

13.1 Mind and Matter

God created the earthly order. The 'finger of God is, indeed, visible in every blade of grass that we see' (FE 205). Ivory-tower cogitation is as nothing compared with the microscopes and the telescopes that give access to the 'immortal mind': 'It seems absolutely necessary that we should reason from nature to nature's God and not presume to reason from God to nature' (FE 201). Malthus's manifesto is in the spirit of the *Essay on Man* where Pope had cut the Gordian knot: 'Know, then, thyself, presume not God to scan/The proper study of mankind is man' (Pope 1732–1734 [1891]: Epistle II).

Physics comes in and metaphysics goes out. It is only in 'the book of nature' that man can 'read God as he is' (FE 201). The Architect's purpose can only be inferred from the Architect's build. Relying on the verifiable authority of deeds rather than on the unauthenticated testimony of words, scientific investigation is the way in which questioning humanity can penetrate the veil. There is no other way: 'Can we judge of the Creator but from his creation?' (FE 201).

Malthus is all but saying outright that the 'mighty process of God' is encoded not in the parables and the miracles but in 'the world', 'this life' and 'the laws of nature' (FE 202, 205). Empiricism is exegesis. To understand the arcane, it is necessary not so much to pour over the handed-down classics as to get to know the physical properties of real existing reality. Only people suffering from 'crude and puerile conceptions' venture into 'unfounded ideas and 'extravagant dreams of fancy' (FE 201). There is no proof that the stories in the Bible are true.

The Creator acts through natural laws which even the Great Lawmaker is obliged to obey. God is a constitution-maker who knows that mental and physical equilibrium is contingent upon relatively constant goalposts that do not vacillate inperiod: 'The Supreme Being should act always according to general laws. The constancy of the laws of nature, or the certainty with which we may expect the same effects from the same causes, is the foundation of the faculty of reason' (FE 205).

A stable environment is 'the foundation of the industry and foresight of the husbandman', of 'the skillful researches of the physician' (FE 205). Were God frequently to alter his imputed purpose, human activity would relapse into torpor. Even 'the bodily wants of mankind would cease to stimulate them to exertion' (FE 205). There would be no work ethic if there were no reasonable hope of success. There are things that even the Author of Nature dare not and cannot do.

Pain and death are endemic to the rule of rules. There is no *deus ex machina* to conjure up a wonder drug or rescue a named child swept out to sea. It would be a serious mistake to 'exalt the power of God at the expence of his goodness' (FE 201). Yet the goodness is there and it is embodied in the rules. The evidence from nature speaks for itself. God himself has respected the rule of proportion: 'There is no more evil in the world than what is absolutely necessary' (FE 216). In designing the world, the Great Designer ensured that there should not be *too little* or *too much*.

God's build is stable but it is not immutable. The world was not created in six days. It is still a work in progress: 'Mind in this world is in a state of formation' (FE 210). Mind in motion is the most eternal of eternal truths. The creation of the world is not finished yet. The Deity planned it that way: 'A certain process may be necessary, a certain time....may be requisite, in order to form beings with those exalted qualities of mind which will fit them for his high purpose' (FE 201).

Mind is in motion. Matter is in motion. It is an unfolding skein in which God works through man to create the institutions that are the best suited to nature's 'high purpose': 'God is *constantly* occupied in forming mind out of matter' (FE 202, emphasis added). God is the first mover who endows naked Adam with the *ab initio* potential that, bursting into 'excitements and impressions', shocks inert man out of his 'sluggish existence' (FE 202). God is the original engineer who puts in train a process which tends to 'purify, exalt, and improve the human mind' (FE 216). God is good. Perfectibility, because of God, is taking its course. The Invisible Hand, in its infinite wisdom, is luring man into the development of his reason, industry and intellect. Without God, these 'exalted qualities' would have been lost to the sterility of 'torpor and corruption', drunkenness and debauchery (FE 201, 202).

It is the pilgrim's progress from the 'miry Slough' of Despond towards Doubting Castle and then, free from 'the lusts, pleasures, and profits of this world', to the Paradise of God (Bunyan 1678 [2008]: 18, 38).

It is Abraham Maslow on the newborn's evolution from passive consumption to active fulfilment and meaningful integration (Maslow 1954: 100). It is G. W. F. Hegel on the World Spirit which, proceeding through the dialectic of opposites—'to produce is also to destroy'—ultimately 'finds itself in producing itself', in 'the Becoming of ourselves and of our own knowledge' (1840 [1894]: I 4, 5, 51). What it is not is the Church of England. It is an idiosyncratic theology in which evil bears witness to the beneficence of God but where man plays an active part in the transcendence of the soul.

13.2 Activity

The human essence has many facets. Emile Durkheim singled out sociability (Durkheim 1893 [1984]: 399). Thomas Hobbes emphasised conflict (Hobbes 1651 [1968]: 186). Malthus focused on sloth. While not denying that there were other dimensions to human nature, Malthus concentrated on the gravitational pull of somnolence and leisure: 'A state of sloth, and not of restlessness and activity, seems evidently to be the natural state of man' (SE I 60). The 'natural indolence of man' (SE I 102) is a core axiom in all six editions of the *Essay*. It is a cause for concern. Consumers demand necessaries. Producers are too lazy to supply.

God is a Creator who delights in his craftsmanship. Man is a passenger who has no innate drive to achieve. Marx imputes to man a de-alienated 'species being' that is only fully itself when it externalises its promise in excellence (Marx 1844 [1973]: 113). Thorstein Veblen estimates that alongside the instinct for emulation there exists an 'instinct of workmanship' so intense that it all but equals the 'parental bent' (Veblen 1914 [1990]: 25–27, 91). Malthus, in contrast, denies that man is by nature a *homo faber*. The Creator, in Malthus's assessment, did not incorporate either Marx's fulfilment or Veblen's artisanship into his build. Instead of intrinsic satisfaction, it was the sound of the dinner bell that would force the under-motivated ever further along their upward-sloping supply curve: 'The savage would slumber forever under his tree unless he were roused from his torpor by the cravings of hunger or the pinchings of cold' (FE 203).

God created evil. It was part of his design. God created the discomfort of hunger and cold in order that the weak-willed fatalist might 'form and keep in motion his faculties, which otherwise would sink into listless inactivity' (FE 203). God put obstacles in man's way because, in the words of the Archbishop of Canterbury, 'trial, severe trial, is absolutely requisite to purify and establish the human character' (Sumner 1816: II 210). God has displayed his 'comprehensive wisdom', the Archbishop said, through the invention of the population multiplier which compels men to 'exert and improve their powers': 'The quick multiplication of the species enables the arts to be carried on, and all the labourers in them to be supported, with a far less proportion of real evil, and a much greater share of advantage, than any hypothetical change of system could provide' (Sumner 1816: II 132, 134, 147).

John Bird Sumner had seen clearly that the axial principle which powers human improvement was the great driver that had been enunciated in Malthus's *Essay*. Malthus returned the compliment in his fifth edition when he said that 'I fully agree with Mr. Sumner' ('a masterly development') (SE II 250) that evil caused by the pressure of population had the unexpected consequence of personal and social improvement. Evil is not bad. Hunger is good.

The 'happiness of man was consulted by his Creator' (Sumner 1816: II 186), the Archbishop declared, when he raised up hurdles that would challenge his children to mature. It was the basis of the theology of enforced activity that Sumner shared with Malthus. Evil, Malthus had said, is a negation that negates itself: 'Evil exists in the world not to create despair, but activity. We are not patently to submit to it, but to exert ourselves to avoid it' (FE 217). The more we succeed, the more we add flesh to 'the great designs of the Creator' (FE 206).

Without evil, there would be no economics. Without 'the strong goad of necessity' (SE I 60), the greater part of humankind would 'sink into listless inactivity' until ultimately they would fall to 'the level of the brutes' (FE 203). Rousseau's Noble Savage would never reach his production possibility curve. It is not a lifestyle choice that he is in a position to make. The population is increasing in a geometrical ratio. The supply of subsistence is increasing in an arithmetical ratio. Sooner or later the checks will set in.

'Partial evils' are needed in order that greater evils may be avoided. They do not obstruct but advance 'the high purpose of the creation' (FE 206). Material challenge keeps man from relapsing into his natural apathy: 'Had population and food increased in the same ratio, it is probable that man might never have emerged from the savage state' (FE 206). A family man has no choice but to add value. Without children, the celibate would slumber forever under a tree.

There is more. Alongside the economic benefit, there is also the social spillover. Hard times have a welcome tendency 'to soften and humanize the heart, to awaken social sympathy, to generate all the Christian virtues' (FE 209). Hard times foster communities: 'The heart that has never known sorrow itself will seldom be feelingly alive to the pains and pleasures, the wants and wishes, of its fellow beings' (FE 209). Hard times can be good times. Richard Titmuss traces the origins of the British Welfare State to the Dunkirk evacuation and the London Blitz. War had made one nation of Buckingham Palace and the impoverished East End (Titmuss 1950: 347).

Adversity shared is good fellowship among friends. If so, then the return to good times might be socially divisive: 'The general tendency of an uniform course of prosperity is rather to degrade, than exalt the character' (FE 209). If you have never had it so good, and if your neighbours have never had it so good, then there might be a general consensus that mutual aid no longer has a function to fulfil. It was not an argument for the school of hard knocks and positive checks with which Malthus was ever comfortable. Shared or not, distress was a social evil that had to be alleviated. Irresponsible procreation was the tiger in everyone's path.

The world must be populated. It says so in *Genesis*. God was not a prude. What Malthus calls 'the sex' is not a synonym for deplorable fornication but rather a part of God's grand design. For 'the sex' to be sustainable, however, the food supply must increase in proportion. The Supreme Being could have provided an inexhaustible buffet. He chose not to do so because of the need to 'rouse man into action, and firm his mind to reason' (FE 204). An easy life is a ticking time bomb. It is destructive of 'all the germs of future improvement' (FE 204).

Necessity is the mother of invention: 'The difficulties of life contribute to generate talents' (FE 208). Faculties which in good times have lain dormant are pressed into service: 'Some of the noblest exertions of the human mind have been set in motion by the necessity of satisfying the wants of the body' (FE 203). God planned it that way.

The body has the lexicographic primacy: 'The first great awakeners of the mind seem to be the wants of the body' (FE 203). Yet the wants of the body are not the only wants. There is also 'intellectual activity' and 'the thirst of knowledge' (FE 212) that have their material embodiment in Stephenson's locomotive and Jenner's cowpox. The dissatisfied mind stumbles upon 'new and original combinations' that furnish 'endless food for speculation' and stimulate still further the 'thinking faculty' (FE 212, 213).

The unintended outcome may be welfare-enhancing discovery but the 'high purpose of the creation' (FE 212) had initially been to restore mental tranquillity. Malthus's image of science as mental gymnastics is similar to the divine discontentment of Veblen's 'idle curiosity' (Veblen 1914 [1990]: 85–87). The chord resolved, the mind experiences the 'superior enjoyment' (FE 202) of having put right a nagging imbalance.

The mind has a God-given propensity to probe. It keeps the body alive. All plants and animals are trapped in a struggle for survival. Lacking sustenance and territory, forever exposed to 'becoming the prey of others' (FE 76), their future is on the line. Human beings at least have a 'peculiar and distinctive superiority' (SV 268) over the other species. They are 'capable of reason' (SE II 107) even as they are swayed by passion. Deferred propagation and calculated investment, unique to the *homo sapiens*, give the naked ape a head start in the race for natural selection.

In that race, self-interest is a more dependable driver than benevolence. The 'dispensations of Providence', acting as if by an invisible hand, direct man into 'that line of conduct which is essential to the preservation of the human race' (SE II 213, 220). It is a second-best incentive structure but God is nobody's fool: 'Perfect virtue is indeed absolutely necessary….But whoever expected perfect virtue on earth?' (SE II 221). In the absence of self-denying altruism, there is purposive activity in the economic market. It gets the job done.

13.3 Utility

Activity is the means to the end. The end is need-satisfaction, self-perceived. In the first instance, the appeal must be to 'the interest and happiness of each individual' (SE II 105). Only the unique one-off can say if the shoe is too tight and by how much. The discrete consulted, the data can then be aggregated to quantify the total utility of the collective: 'The happiness of the whole is to be the result of the happiness of individuals' (SE II 105). Evil is disutility. Good is utility. Ethics or economics, it is the utilitarian calculus wherever you look: 'To avoid evil and to pursue good seem to be the great duty and business of man' (FE 204).

Duty is non-negotiable commitment. Business, however, is profit and pleasure. A strict deontologist would insist that they are two kingdoms apart. Focusing on the motives and not on the outcomes, the deontologist would say that rightness and *oughtness* are constitutional absolutes that cannot be swapped at the margin for a mess of pottage. An open-minded consequentialist would, however, reply that the rose cannot be rejected merely because its beauty is inseparable from its thorns. Other-regarding intentions are not necessary to maximise the mutually beneficial deliverables: 'It is not from the benevolence of the butcher, the brewer, or the baker that we expect our dinner, but from their regard to their own interest' (Smith 1776 [1961]: I 18). Good ham comes from filthy pigs. Thorns and filth are not a problem so long as the greatest happiness of the greatest number is the unintended outcome. The *Essay on Man* knew that there was nothing to fear: 'Thus God and Nature linked the general frame\And bade self love and social be the same' (Pope 1732–1734 [1891]: Epistle III).

One would have expected the Reverend Malthus to have preached the gospel of right relationships and uncompromising truth. One would have been surprised. Malthus situated himself, together with Hutcheson, Hume, Paley, Sumner and Adam Smith, among the 'friends of human happiness' (SV 267). Smith, conducting 'an examination of the works of Nature', decided that the Great Utilitarian had 'intended to promote happiness, and to guard against misery' (Smith 1759 [1966]: 235). If Great Books do not produce the greatest happiness, then ethics dictates that purposive search should have the last word. The laws of nature are 'calculated to promote the general good' (SV 268). It is enough. God is not inscrutable. Nature is God's design. Nature is as good as God.

Utility is the selective standard. It is the guiding light in the marketplace for pins. It is the rational choice in the marketplace for right and wrong. Utility is 'the great foundation of morals' (SE II 104). It is the gold standard of any passion, 'the test by which alone we can know whether it ought or ought not to be indulged' (SE II 157). Utility is the universal equilibrium on which all the lines of force converge: 'All the moral codes which have inculcated the subjection of the passions have been, as I conceive, really built upon this foundation, whether the promulgators of them were aware of it or not' (SE II 158). The Creator is there. The 'heathen moralists' (SE II 96) are there. Hume and Smith are there. It is the only place to be.

Virtue is built on utility: 'Our virtue, therefore, as reasonable beings, evidently consists in educing, from the general materials which the Creator has placed under our guidance, the greatest sum of human happiness' (SE II 93). Happiness is the endstate that makes informed consent so easy to win. God's will is encrypted in pleasure and pain. Vice is vicious because misery is disutility. Moral restraint is moral because it keeps the positive checks at bay. Saving is a virtue because it fructifies a happiness differential. Morality seems to be the philosophical name for what ordinary people call the balance of advantage. Malthus condemns actions that are not cost-effective relative to the happiness differential that is billed to the payback.

The payback legitimates the social distance. Mobility fosters collective happiness because meritocracy adds to value. Progress would come to a stand 'if no man could hope to rise or fear to fall, in society, if industry did not bring with it rewards and idleness its punishment' (FE 207). A society cannot afford to waste scarce potential or sacrifice tolerable inequalities to the jealousy of the mob. The proper balance between *too much* and *too little* should be determined by the test of utility. The population is going up. The supply of subsistence must go up as well.

Outcomes shape ethics. Utility is the reason why affordable procreation is in keeping with the natural law. Premature marriage without the ability to support a family 'clearly offends against the will of God' (SE II 102). Later marriage when the breadwinner is better able to provide 'would rather tend to increase than diminish individual happiness' (SE II 102). The theology is the calculus of sensation: 'It is the apparent object of the Creator to deter us from vice by the pains which accompany it, and to lead us to virtue by the happiness that it produces' (SE II 103). The Creator is on the side of happiness. Even without the Deity, however, the same outcome would be produced by ordinary common sense: 'This duty is intelligible to the humblest capacity' (SE II 105). Christian or heathen, no one wants to starve.

The Bible is averse to fornication. Yet nature and reason are just as much on the side of self-control. Sex-seeking couples see that 'a promiscuous intercourse' will weaken 'the best affections of the heart' (SE II 97). They calculate that the short-run utility will be inferior to the deferred alternative. Seeking to maximise 'the sum of pleasurable sensations', they therefore opt for 'regulated indulgence of the passions' (SE II 100, 105). Premarital intercourse is bad effectively because married couples have more fun. It is carnal utility and not purely the sacred edicts that Malthus has in mind when he states that 'the law of chastity cannot be violated without producing evil' (SE II 97).

13.4 The Dilemma of Utility

Nature is the university. Utility is the lesson. The moral sentiments must pass 'the test of utility' (SE II 157). The student must acquire the habit of gratifying his 'natural passions.... only in that way which, being unattended with evil, will clearly add to the sum of human happiness' (SE II 157). It is the best possible education. Learning by living that utility is the sole selective standard, the graduate will then be well equipped to 'fulfill the apparent purpose of the Creator' (SE II 157).

Ethics is built on utility and legitimated by outcome. Malthus knew it was easier said than done. Virtue, he concedes, may be a maze. Sometimes even a utilitarian might not know which turning to take.

One dilemma is the choice of utilities. On the surface, it looks like a trade-off gone wrong: 'It so frequently happens that the excess of one check is balanced by the defect of some other' (SE I 146). Carefully considered, the problem is more complex. Later marriage blocks off the great disutility of the positive checks. Yet preventive checks create great disutility of their own in the form of repression, frustration and an evening meal consumed alone. Unmarried people are abstaining from their 'fatal extravagances' at precisely that stage in their life cycle 'when the passions most strongly prompt to it' (SV 264). The stifling of their natural impulses may be taking its toll both on their happiness and on their productivity at work. A post-Freudian generation, more attuned to disturbing neurosis, might wish to press for vice in forms such as contraception and prostitution. As Anthony Flew says, 'in so far as such vice and misery are alternatives, it follows that to indulge in....vice must be to reduce misery' (Flew 1970: 48). To indulge in vice might be to maximise utility. Vice is natural. Vice is good.

Prostitution can be 'a most powerful check to population' (SE I 55). 'Irregular gratifications' may be the answer. Malthus, however, says that they are the problem: 'In whatever light we view the situation of man, on earth, he can never be justified in recurring to vice in order to avoid misery' (quoted in Rashid 1984: 136). Malthus assumes that disutility has a positive rather than a negative impact on industry. Because misery is a necessary stimulus to assiduity, vice, clearly, can never be a virtue. It can never be right to rank fleeting pleasure above sustainable progress that would in time produce the greater total utility. If Ulysses had succumbed to the Sirens' song, he and his crew would never have completed their trip. A life is too much to pay for a song.

Time is also at the centre of the second dilemma. The maximisation of utility presupposes that economic actors have a scientist's knowledge of their means and ends. The future, however, is a non-rational country. Fear casts a long shadow before.

The moral choice might not, behind the veil of unknowledge, be the actuarial expectation. The reason is that, in terms of the mental calculus, pleasure and pain are not equal and opposite along the frequency distribution. The asymmetry between the objective and the subjective magnitudes, identified by authors such as John Locke (1690 [1967]), Daniel Bernoulli (1738 [1954]) and James Buchanan (1975), lies at the root of the disposition to minimax. Man is driven more by his anxieties than by his aspirations: 'The endeavour to avoid pain rather than the pursuit of pleasure is the great stimulus to action in life' (FE 204). Insecurity is all around. Private insurance and social security are the utilitarian response.

The default position in Malthus's economics is an underdeveloped country in which basic subsistence is a major concern. His sensitivity to *less* and not just to *more* looks forward to the veil of ignorance and the 'difference principle' in the thought-experiment of John Rawls (1971: 154). It leads him to an unexpected proposal for 'exercising our charity' in such a way that, 'when brought to the test of utility, will appear to be the most beneficial to the poor' (SE II 158).

The future is unknown and unknowable. Distinction is precarious. Profit can sour into loss. In a draft sermon delivered between 1789 and 1800, Malthus warned the 'great & fortunate' that even they might 'one day be numbered among the least & lowest of mankind': 'This uncertainty may furnish a prudential motive to conduct ourselves with that equity & benevolence to our fellow creatures in one station of life, which we woud [sic] desire and expect from them in another' (KG II 6). It is a gamble and an investment. We forgive them their trespasses in the unenforceable expectation that they will one day volunteer to forgive us our own. The Golden Rule is a gigantic neighbourhood watch pact. Kant's Categorical Imperative (Kant 1785 [1961]: 96) is an n-period Prisoner's Dilemma.

It was God's design that human beings should plan for the worst even as they hoped for the best. The risk-aversion and the endowment effect remain hard-wired into their economic psychology even after they have advanced beyond the stage of elemental survival. It is the well-to-do and not just the destitute whose anticipated utility is amplified by the safety net of welfare.

13.5 Compulsion by Consent

At one extreme, there is revelation. The Great Legislator has set out his irrefutable absolutes in his Commandments and in his Gospels. At the other extreme, there is license. Even murder is moral if it raises the entrepreneur to a higher plane of utility, self-perceived. In the middle, there is

Malthus, who was uncomfortable both with the dominance of Great Books and with libertines like Bernard Mandeville who believed that the one-off shopper will always pursue his own *summum bonum*: 'Let me not be supposed to give the slightest sanction to the system of morals inculcated in the *Fable of the Bees*, a system which I consider as absolutely false, and directly contrary to the just definition of virtue' (SE II 214n).

Malthus was in favour of morals by consent but not in favour of norms which forever fluctuate with evanescent interest and passion. Inperiod pleasure-seeking must be situated within the framework of multiperiod rules which define what each player can and cannot do. The maximisation of each individual's utility will degenerate into the war of each against all unless relatively constant constants can be identified and social actors disciplined into self-control. It is compulsion by consent. Thinking citizens sign up to the rules that will maximise their multiperiod happiness while protecting them from external diswelfares. Only then do they have the coordinates they require to play the game.

Authority is easy. Evaluation is hard. For the sentiments to be moral, each decision-maker must understand the contract that he is signing. Passive conformity is not enough: 'A being with only good placed in view may be justly said to be impelled by a blind necessity' (FE 210). Freedom of choice is the benchmark if the sovereign citizen is bottom-up to rank the alternatives and assess the options: 'The being that has seen moral evil and felt disapprobation and disgust at it is essentially different from the being that has seen only good' (FE 210).

Freedom of choice is an essential part of the great design. God in constituting the natural order was clearly taking a risk. The Author of Nature cannot be said to be all-powerful if he expects each face in the crowd to give his informed consent to one crossroads selected from a slateful of scenarios. Even God cannot 'foreknow with certainty' (FE 210) the road that ant-like monad will take. The Deity could have simplified the process by creating fully grown oaks. Instead, he created greenfield seeds that had to make their own luck through the floods and the predators. God left it to humankind to do its best in a material world where there is not enough to go round: 'Moral evil is absolutely necessary to the production of moral excellence' (FE 210). What happens then is out of the hands of God. Children have a will of their own.

Free will is the logic of market economics and political democracy. It underlies the radical liberalism of ethics by acclamation. If there were a single choice, the normative constraint would entail no more than the rubber-stamping of a predetermined script. It would 'in all probability tend to repress future exertion and to damp the soaring wings of intellect' (FE 213). Stonewall fundamentalism and knee-jerk dogmatism make under-informed followers of people who do what they are told. Dwelling in the darkness of the Book, 'it is difficult to conceive how human beings could be formed to a detestation of moral evil, and a love and admiration of God' (FE 214).

Even if an imposed catechism could arrest the practice of vice, it would never promote a love of virtue: 'Virtuous conduct would be no indication of virtuous disposition' (FE 214). Only thinking and understanding can do that. A 'universal overpowering conviction' would stifle the 'endless motives to intellectual activity': 'The finest minds seem to be formed rather by efforts at original thinking….than by passively receiving the impressions of other men's ideas' (FE 212, 213, 214). Malthus in the circumstances welcomes the 'doubts and difficulties' (FE 213) in the scriptures. The Supreme Being deliberately made his divine meaning obscure. Ambiguity would keep the detectives on their toes.

Yet there is ambiguity too in Malthus's own text. It relates to the moral status of a normative code which relies on threats and promises to purchase allegiance. Malthus says that religion's pie-in-the-sky is no more ethical a bargain than is the mugger's your-money-or-your-life: 'Few, I think, would call an action really virtuous which was performed simply and solely from the dread of a very great punishment or the expectation of a very great reward' (FE 214). The problem is that not just religion but the whole of the utilitarian world view is built upon the *quid pro quo*. Strictly speaking, the entry into Heaven in exchange for an unblemished record on earth is on a par with any other voluntary transaction. Either way, it is the means to an end.

13.6 From Nature to Revelation

Utility is utility even if the Deity is not hands-on with advice. We do not need to be told to eat when we are hungry. Later marriage itself is the message not just of 'religion' but of 'nature' and of 'reason'

(SE II 205). It is a triple whammy. Even one whammy would be enough. Like tradeables in the economic market, virtues are produced in the quantity for which the need is the greatest. Function is all. An anxious God has built in a plethora of reinforcements. If belt fails, then braces will take over.

There is Shaftesbury's innate 'moral sense' (Shaftesbury 1711: 42): 'A sense of virtue and vice is ....closely interwoven in our frame' (KG II 8–9). The existence of an 'internal sense', of a 'directing principle within', Malthus says, is 'evident beyond question' (KG II 9). The sixth sense of right and wrong is an innate stabiliser. We know vice when we see vice. We were born that way.

There is Adam Smith's 'impartial spectator' (Smith 1759 [1966]: 429): 'Nothing can be more pleasurable to the mind than to reflect that our conduct has been such as reason and conscience have approved' (KG II 10). Human beings choose right and eschew wrong because they desire 'self-congratulations' and 'self-approval' (KG II 9, 10). The alternative is to be 'self-condemned' (KG II 9). There is always one witness when I drop litter or tell a lie. Cheating to Malthus is not a free good: 'My heart shall reproach me so long as I live' (KG II 9). Spoiled identity does not maximise an individual's utility. Before committing a street mugging, it is prudent self-interest to 'invert the case & place ourselves in our neighbours situation' (KG II 7).

There is Smith's 'real spectator' (Smith 1759 [1966]: 162): 'Do we not suppose that our complaints will be thought well grounded and that the publick [sic] voice will concur with our own in condemning it?' (KG II 5). Social sanctions are 'the means of pointing out & prompting us to acts of honesty, humanity & justice' (KG II 4). No one wants to be hated or ostracised. No one wants to be made subject to the 'the impressions of disapprobation which arise from the spectacle of moral evil' (FE 210).

Last but not least, there is revelation. The 'injunctions of the Gospels' make clear that the 'author of our being' has taken as his objective 'the common happiness of mankind' (KG II 6, 7, 9). The Supreme Creator is a God of love but he is also an examiner. In a sermon dating from 1789 to 1793, Malthus invokes 'the judge of the whole earth', 'the gate to immortality', who may be expected to pronounce 'a gracious sentence at the final judgment' on all who have lived 'in conformity to the laws of our maker' (KG II 9, 10, 11).

'Eternal filicity [sic] thro [sic] all eternity' (KG II 10) is a prize worth having. It is, however, already in the bag. The moral sense, the impartial spectator and the real spectator are in agreement that the Golden Rule is the golden road to the utility peak. Malthus says that it all comes back to the Gospels: 'Our Saviour was the first who taught this comprehensive principle' (KG I 7). What Malthus demonstrates is that it does not. High road or low road, the destination is the same. Even heathens and pagans will get there in the end.

It is reason. It is nature. Last but not least, it is revelation: 'The Christian religion places our present as well as future happiness in the exercise of those virtues which tend to fit us for a state of superior enjoyment' (SE II 96). It may be Christian morals but it is natural law as well: 'Nature will not, nor cannot, be defeated in her purposes' (SE II 116). Man lives in an over-determined universe where virtuous conduct is 'dictated to him by the light of nature, *and* sanctioned by revealed religion' (SV 272, emphasis added). It is a very eloquent *and*. If nature will not and cannot be defeated, then the Author of Nature may be said to have no further role to play. His job is done.

13.7 The Shadow of Paley

William Paley's *Principles*, published while Malthus was a serious-minded undergraduate, paved the way. Malthus mentions Paley by name in the unpublished *Crisis* and in the 1817 *Essay* (SE II 101, 107, 193). In the 1798 *Essay*, he says of the ideal of reason, revelation and happiness that Paley 'very justly expresses it' (FE 147).

Malthus was drawn both to religion and to utility. Paley had shown that they were the same: 'God Almighty wills and wishes the happiness of his creatures, and consequently....those actions which promote that will and wish' (Paley 1785: I 76). Happiness, self-perceived, is the supreme test: 'The obligation of every law depends upon its ultimate utility' (Paley 1785: II 436). Utility streams right from wrong.

God's will has been made explicit in the revelations and the scriptures. It has also been made flesh in the external reality that the utilitarian Creator has so expertly crafted. God could have designed the teeth to ache. Instead, he designed the teeth to chew. God's works bear witness to God's will. 'Contrivance proves design' (Paley 1785: I 69). The blueprint is an open book: 'Private happiness is our motive, and the will of God our rule' (Paley 1785: I 69). It is quite literally a pleasure to serve a supreme leader like that.

Paley was a clergyman as well as a social philosopher. He saw in the Christian religion the same exchange nexus that he had admired so greatly in the butcher, the brewer and the baker: 'Every sect and modification of Christianity holds out the happiness and misery of another life, as depending chiefly upon the practice of virtue or of vice in this' (Paley 1785: I 352). Paley saw the Christian religion as an esoteric amplification of the shopkeeper pleasures and pains that are the custodian of superior outcomes. Maximising the pleasures of everlasting paradise, minimising the pains of eternal damnation, the calculative Christian will hold back from violating a general rule. The short-term gain will not be worthwhile when discounted against the ultimate price.

The rules in themselves are the functional precondition for individual utility: 'A state of happiness is not to be expected by those, who are conscious of no moral or religious rule' (Paley 1785: I 56). Order is good. Directionless *anomie* is not. Civil war is not. Narrow opportunism is not. Discipline per se is important. Equally important, however, is the content of the rules.

The rules that sink the deepest roots and command the greatest allegiance are those which are the most 'consistent with the will of God' (Paley 1785: I 95). They are the norms that are most easily generalised from the interest of one to the benefit of all: 'The obligation to perform promises may be deduced from the necessity of such a conduct to the well being, or existence indeed, of human society' (Paley 1785: I 143). Promise-keeping is the cake and not the icing: 'Confidence therefore in promises is essential to the intercourse of human life' (Paley 1785: I 144). It is social functions and not holy absolutes that determine the patterns that are the most likely to be codified into custom.

All roads, sacred and secular, lead to utility. It is a law of nature: 'Who....would labour, if his necessities could be supplied with equal certainty by prayer?' (Paley 1785: II 41). The 'Supreme Proprietor' has designed the great system with one supreme end in mind: 'There is one end of civil government peculiar to a good constitution, namely the happiness of the subjects' (Paley 1785: II 212). God acts through the incentive structure of the discrete and the devolved. Revealed preference may or may not be a true measure of 'real happiness'. The crucial point is that it is 'the best measure we have' (Paley 1785: I 36–37).

Malthus was inspired by Paley's theology of nature, induction, expediency, personal autonomy, normative regulation and the utilitarian calculus: 'The final view of all rational politics is to produce the greatest quantity of happiness' (Paley 1785: II 367). Paley assigned a greater role to Heaven and Hell and also to top-down Christianity. The similarities were stronger than the differences. Paley's utilitarianism focused on the invisible hand of attraction and aversion. Paley was the bridge. He demonstrated that nature, reason and revelation could be one and the same. It is all in Paley.

13.8 Was Malthus a Christian?

The Reverend Malthus was an ordained clergyman in the Church of England. He knew that the opinions he expressed in Chapters 18 and 19 were not what his fellow clergymen were expecting to hear: 'I hope I shall be pardoned if I attempt to give a view in some degree different of the situation of man on earth' (FE 200).

Idiosyncrasy is not always held in high esteem in the Church. While the sections on scientific demography were welcomed and debated, the chapters on God's design were regarded as a striking deviation from mainstream Christianity. Too close to nature and reason, too far from the revealed truth, one author was speaking for many when he called the first *Essay* 'a libel against the Almighty himself' (quoted in James 1979: 117).

By 1803, the controversial chapters had been expunged. It was 'in deference', Bishop Otter says, 'to some distinguished persons in our Church' (Otter 1836 [1964]: lii). The prelates aside, the chapters were 'unsatisfactory to some of his private friends' (Empson 1837 [1963]: 262). There is no reason to think that they were unsatisfactory to the author himself. Squeezed into isolated paragraphs, never again allocated a full chapter on its own, the conversation between nature, reason and God remained a lifetime concern.

Malthus knew that orthodox Christians were suspecting him of revisionist tendencies. He addressed their doubts with qualifying clauses. In 1803, he said that 'no stone can fall, or plant rise, without the immediate agency of divine power' (SE I 301). In 1817, he specified that the test of utility had to be 'confirmed and sanctioned by revelation' (SE II 96). The law of population is no exception. 'The scriptures most clearly point it out to us as our duty, to restrain our passions within the bounds of reason' (SE II 100).

In 1830, 32 years after the first *Essay*, Malthus was declaring that 'moral discipline and probation' were in line with 'the letter and spirit of revelation' (SV 271). Even the ratios had been explained clearly by the Great Economist who had dictated the Testament: 'The principle of population, instead of being inconsistent with revelation, must be considered as affording strong additional proofs of its truth' (SV 272). The Great Books had got it right. So had nature and reason.

Malthus invokes scripture to validate propositions which he elsewhere derives from the natural order of things. The 'moral code of Christianity' is all but demoted to the status of an external examiner who 'confirmed and sanctioned' (SE II 96) the script that nature and reason had already handed in. In some cases, he seems deliberately to be borrowing the clothes of the Sunday traditionalists to market a secular theory that is logically watertight 'independently of the revealed will of God' (SE II 157n).

One instance, in the first *Essay*, is his rebranding as 'Christian virtues' (FE 209) the moral sentiments of kindliness, sympathy, compassion, good fellowship and brotherly love that Shaftesbury and Smith had made the unintended consequence of the 'social state of our nature' (KG II 6). Malthus, multiplying unnecessarily his explanatory variables, looks vertically to the Invisible Hand when the same convergence could be derived by looking horizontally to his neighbours and friends: 'A soul possessed of these amiable qualities....seems to hold a nearer commerce with the skies than mere acuteness of intellect' (FE 210).

A similar instance, in the fifth *Essay*, is his insistence that the principle of utility is divinely inspired. God, he reveals, is the custodian of pleasure and pain: 'It is the apparent object of the Creator to deter us from vice by the pains which accompany it, and to lead us to virtue by the happiness that it produces' (SE II 103). God the Philosopher is clearly a consequentialist who will accept most motives so long as the outcomes are good. God is a utilitarian. Life on earth is not a vale of tears. East of Eden dwells Hutcheson's 'greatest happiness' that human beings can render even happier through economic progress and moral restraint.

It is an assertion. It is not a proof. God might equally well be regarded as a deontologist who puts conformity to eternal absolutes above all else. 'Thou shalt not' might mean what it says. Strict constructionists, reading Malthus, will have accused him of imputing his own 'Apparent Purpose' to the Supreme Lawmaker. They will have said that Malthus was putting words into God's mouth in order to recreate God's purpose in his own preferred image.

Traditional Christians criticised Malthus for the inference that God's will coincided miraculously with his own; for his use of weasel-words like 'evidently', 'acknowledged' and 'apparent'; and for his almost total failure to underline the uniqueness of Jesus Christ or to give number and verse from the Bible. On the rare occasions when he does open the Book, Malthus reinterprets the text until its meaning is in tatters. The preacher's 'If a man will not work, neither shall he eat' is softened into the professor's 'if he marry without being able to support a family, he must expect severe want' and then relaxed still further into 'without a reasonable prospect of supporting a family' (SE II 161, 161n). It is 'the spirit' of revelation but not 'the letter' (SV 271). Compromise and casuistry are taking the place of the holy writ. St. Paul is being downsized into a 'reasonable prospect', a rational expectation.

The hard-hearted questioned whether it was right to downsize St. Paul in a way that St. Paul had never intended. The inescapably charitable, on the other hand, objected that Malthus's proposal to phase out poor relief was not in keeping with the witness of the loaves, the fishes and the wine. Even those least fitted to survive were created in God's image. Even sinners who repent must be forgiven.

Orthodox Christians felt that Malthus's obsession with the containment of births was at variance with God's commandment to 'be fruitful and multiply'. They saw it as sacrilege to limit family size. They regarded it as an insult to the Bible to treat later marriage as an investment in social mobility.

Mainstream Christians did not share Malthus's reinvention of original sin as indolence and sloth: 'The original sin of man is the torpor and corruption of the chaotic matter in which he may be said to be born' (FE 202). The Bible conveys the message that the historic Fall had been caused by the moral dereliction of Adam and Eve. Malthus describes the Fall not as innate but transitory. Even the Irish crofter can acquire a work ethic. When he does so, his sluggishness will wither away. Economic growth will triumph over original sin. It was not what the children were being taught in their Sunday school.

Fundamentalist Evangelicals, taking the Word of God literally, felt that Malthus was trivialising the writ. Original sin reinvented as the savage slumbering under a tree seemed to be cutting the Bible down to size. So was Malthus's reinterpretation of man's duty to propagate the species as man's duty to 'propagate virtue and happiness' (SE II 148). It was too clever by half. It was not what God had said. Jesus came to save man from sin and not from idleness. Jesus showed no interest in the geometrical ratio or the wealth of nations.

Devout Christians often viewed man's life on earth as a state of trial. Good conduct was taken to be merit-making that would yield its return in the life after death. Malthus did not share their view of ethics as an investment. This worldly activity, he stated, is a process of human betterment that is an end in itself. God's purpose is 'to awaken inert, chaotic matter, into spirit, to sublimate the dust of the earth into soul, to elicit an aethereal spark from the clod of clay' (FE 202). Life on earth is 'soul', 'spirit' and 'spark'. The 'mighty process of God' was put in motion 'not for the trial, but for the creation and formation of mind' (FE 202).

Life is creation and self-creation. It more than the struggle for an entry-ticket into the Paradise beyond: 'Life is, generally speaking, a blessing independent of a future state' (FE 215). That said, life is also the anteroom to the afterlife, and God is ever-vigilant to keep the score: 'We must all one day appear at the awful tribunal of heaven' (KG II 7). Malthus describes the population multiplier as 'a law peculiarly suited to a state of discipline and trial' (SE II 250). He is not denying the reality of the probation and the assessment. Simply, he is leavening the inevitability of the final examination with an insistence that God is simultaneously improvement and acceptance. A 'truly Christian life', he states, is motivated 'more by love than by pure unmixed fear' (FE 215).

At the end of life, there is death. Traditional Christians were the ultimate consequentialists in that they held out the prize of heaven and the terrors of hell. They were not satisfied with Malthus's account of salvation and destruction. Sinners presumably would like it more. Heaven exists. Hell does not.

Malthus likens human life on earth to a 'mighty creative furnace' (FE 215). Those vessels which come out of the furnace 'in lovely and beautiful shapes' will be 'crowned with immortality' (FE 215). They will be placed in the presence of God. Those which emerge from the process 'misshapen' or mentally 'not suited to a purer and happier state of existence' (FE 215) will be scrapped and discarded. They will perish. They will return to 'their original clay', 'their original insensibility' (FE 215).

The wages of sin are not eternal suffering but 'eternal death' (FE 210). Malthus refuses to accept that the Great Potter would ever condemn any of his creatures to perpetual weeping, wailing or the gnashing of teeth: 'Could we once accept such an idea, all our natural conceptions of goodness and justice would be completely overthrown, and we could no longer look up to God as a merciful and righteous Being' (FE 215). The very notion of hellfire is not consonant with the ideal of a beneficent Deity. Annihilationism is a more palatable proposition. The sinful, unable to demonstrate 'their fitness for some superior state', will be thrown aside as useless (FE 201). Punishment will no longer be an option. Their body and soul will have ceased to exist.

God is forever. Satan is not. Malthus said it was confirmed by 'both reason and revelation' (FE 210). The Bible Belt said it was confirmed by neither and was simply not true. Mainstream churchmen were wondering if Malthus really was a Christian. Once Chapters 18 and 19 were withdrawn they lost interest in a war that they thought they had won. In fact, it was Malthus that had won. It was Hutcheson and Paley that had won. Christian or deist is unlikely that his theology of nature ever changed very much.

References

By T. R. Malthus

(1798 [1970]). *Essay on the Principle of Population, as It Affects the Future Improvement of Society, with Remarks on the Speculations of Mr. Godwin, M. Condorcet, and Other Writers* (abbreviated as FE), ed. by A. Flew, Harmondsworth: Penguin.

(1803 et seq. [1989]). *An Essay on the Principle of Population: Or a View of Its Past and Present Effects on Human Happiness, with an Inquiry into Our Prospects Respecting the Removal of the Evils Which It Occasions* (2nd edition, 1803; further editions in 1806, 1807, 1817, 1826) (abbreviated as SE I and SE II), 2 vols., ed. by P. James. Cambridge: Cambridge University Press.

(1830). *A Summary View of the Principle of Population* (abbreviated as SV), in FE, supra.

T.R. Malthus: Unpublished Papers in the Collection of Kanto Gakuen University, Vols. I (1997) and II (2004), (abbreviated as KG), eds. by J. Pullen and T. Hughes Parry. Cambridge: Cambridge University Press.

Secondary Literature

Bernoulli, D. (1738 [1954]). Exposition of a New Theory on the Measurement of Risk (L. Sommer, Trans.). *Econometrica, 11*, 22–36.

Buchanan, J. M. (1975). *The Limits of Liberty*. Chicago: University of Chicago Press.

Bunyan, J. (1678 [2008]). *The Pilgrim's Progress* (R. Pooley, Ed.). London: Penguin Books.

Durkheim, E. (1893 [1984]). *The Division of Labor in Society* (W. D. Halls, Trans.). New York: The Free Press.

Empson, W. (1837 [1963]). Life, Writings, and Character of Mr. Malthus. *Edinburgh Review*, 64 (Reprinted in *Occasional Papers of T.R. Malthus*, pp. 231–268, by B. Semmel, Ed., New York: Bert Franklin).

Flew, A. (1970). Introduction, in FE, supra, 7–56.

Hegel, G. W. F. (1840 [1894]). *Lectures on the History of Philosophy* (3 vols.). London: Kegan, Paul, Trench, Trübner and Co.

Hobbes, T. (1651 [1968]). *Leviathan* (C. B. Macpherson, Ed.). Harmondsworth: Penguin Books.

Hutcheson, F. (1725). *An Inquiry into the Original* [sic] *of Our Ideas of Beauty and Virtue*. London: D. Midwinter and Sons.

James, P. (1979). *Population Malthus: His Life and Times*. London: Routledge and Kegan Paul.

Kant, I. (1785 [1961]). *Groundwork of the Metaphysic of Morals*. In H. J. Paton (Ed.), *The Moral Law*. London: Hutchinson.

Locke, J. (1690 [1967]). *Essay Concerning Human Understanding*. Oxford: Clarendon Press.

Marx, K. (1844 [1973]). *Economic and Philosophic Manuscripts of 1844*. London: Lawrence & Wishart.

Maslow, A. H. (1954). *Motivation and Personality* (2nd ed.). New York: Harper and Row.

Otter, W. (1836 [1964]). Memoir of Robert Malthus. In T. R. Malthus (Ed.), *Principles of Political Economy*, (2nd ed., pp. xiii–lix). New York: Augustus M. Kelley.

Paley, W. (1785). *Principles of Moral and Political Philosophy* (2 vols.). Dublin: Exshaw, White and others.

Pope, A. (1732–1734 [1891]). *An Essay on Man*. London: Cassell.

Pullen, J. R. (1981). Malthus' Theological Ideas and Their Influence on His Principle of Population. *History of Political Economy, 13*, 39–54.

Rae, J. (1895 [1965]). *Life of Adam Smith*. New York: Augustus M. Kelley.

Rashid, S. (1984). Malthus' Theology: An Overlooked Letter and Some Comments. *History of Political Economy, 16*, 135–138.

Rawls, J. (1971). *A Theory of Justice*. Oxford: Oxford University Press.

Scott, W. R. (1937). *Adam Smith as Student and Professor*. Glasgow: Jackson, Son, & Co.

Smith, A. (1759 [1966]). *The Theory of Moral Sentiments*. New York: Augustus M. Kelley.

Smith, A. (1776 [1961]). *The Wealth of Nations* (E. Cannan, Ed., 2 vols.). London: Methuen.

Sumner, J. B. (1816). *A Treatise on the Records of the Creation and the Moral Attributes of the Creator* (2 vols.). London: J. Hatchard.

Third Earl of Shaftesbury. (1711). *An Inquiry Concerning Virtue and Merit.* London: John Darby.

Titmuss, R. M. (1950). *Problems of Social Policy.* London: His Majesty's Stationery Office and Longmans, Green and Co.

Veblen, T. (1914 [1990]). *The Instinct of Workmanship and the State of the Industrial Arts*. New Brunswick: Transaction Books.

14

Malthus's Legacy: A System of Ideas

The name itself opens and closes the debate. Malthus said that the population increases more rapidly than the supply of food. Famine and disease thin out the numbers. Later marriage and social upgrading struggle to keep down the births. The poor are being sacrificed by the law of nature to vice and misery. The future will be Malthusian in tooth and claw. There it is: Malthusian. Like Marxian and Keynesian one word says it all.

Except that it does not. Malthus was not a curmudgeonly ideologue who did no more than accuse the common people of procreating themselves into extreme deprivation. Rather, he was a late Enlightenment man of letters who wanted to use economics to improve the physical and spiritual well-being of all the social classes. Like Adam Smith, like Alfred Marshall, Malthus was a missionary who believed that individual and collective betterment was the supreme objective and that the wealth of nations was the precondition for social progress.

Yet the truth is elusive and the doctors disagree. A Cameralist is not a Mercantilist. A Physiocrat is not a Ricardian. Surrounded by conflicting opinions and determined to do good, Malthus had no choice but to be careful and scholarly. 'Partial facts' were no substitute for the

D. Reisman, *Thomas Robert Malthus*, Great Thinkers in Economics,
https://doi.org/10.1007/978-3-030-01956-3_14

deductions and inductions that slowly and laboriously document the 'modifications, limitations, and exceptions' (PR 7) of which real-world multi-causality is made. Malthus believed that the 'principal cause of error' among the schools of political economy had been 'a precipitate tendency to simplify and generalize' (PR 6). William Empson remembered him as a man of caution who knew enough not to leap to conclusions: 'Mr. Malthus himself frequently observed, that in political economy we must be content for the most part with approximations' (Empson 1837 [1963]: 232). Things change. Ideas change. Malthus's enviable prose conceals the many inconsistencies and internal contradictions in his technical economics. It is not an accident. Malthus knew that he had to move with the times.

Malthus saw himself as an impartial social scientist who wanted to track, extrapolate and explain. He also believed that as a teacher and a preacher he had a social obligation to comment on current affairs with a view to influencing the thrust of public policy. He must have anticipated that his conclusions would attract opprobrium as well as acceptance. It went with the territory: 'The opportunity of being useful was excitement enough; and his spirits rose with the occasion' (Empson 1837 [1963]: 258).

Malthus wanted to be taken seriously both by his peers in the Political Economy Club and by the politicians and intellectuals who were shaping public policy. In spite of that he has entered into the popular imagination as a hate-figure who warned that even the standing room had gone. The saloon-bar stereotype of Population Malthus is irresponsible gratification, starving children, feckless paupers, depleted resources, dust-bowl exhaustion. It is not an accurate or a complete picture of a social philosopher who ranged so widely over so many topics. There is more to Malthus than the debatable ratios and the dubious checks.

Malthus was a man of vision. He knew that he needed an encompassing system in order to situate the isolated parts in an integrated whole. That is just the problem. Malthus never unified his grand theory into an all-embracing text like Smith's *Wealth of Nations*. His most comprehensive synthesis, the *Principles of Political Economy* in 1820, is not so much a guided tour around his world view as it is an encyclopedia of essays without a connecting link. It is not the missing book that Malthus never wrote.

Patricia James attributes what she calls his 'failure as an economist' to his ability to 'throw spot-lights but not illuminate a whole scene' (James 1979: 321). Morton Paglin shares her view that Malthus in the end is bits and pieces without a home. The disparate insights, valuable as each on its own may be, 'cannot be considered as a unified system of thought': 'Malthus did not have a system in the sense that Ricardo possessed one' (Paglin 1961: 14, 116).

Ricardo had followers like James Mill and J. R. McCulloch. His economic theories inspired Karl Marx. Marshall at the end of the century reinterpreted Ricardo as a misunderstood neoclassical (Marshall 1890 [1949]: 670–676). Malthus in contrast had friends but no disciples. Richard Jones, his successor at Haileybury, shared his interest in evidence but was too literal-minded a historicist to speculate on tendencies to come (PR II 156n). William Whewell was a physical scientist who never saw the value of economic theory. Malthus might have attracted more disciples if he had made clear to his contemporaries what it was that he was trying to achieve. In the end, there was no *Wealth of Nations* to rally the troops.

The two great classics, the *Essay* in 1798 and the *Principles* in 1820, barely acknowledge each other's core concerns despite the fact that the final revision of the *Essay* appeared in 1826, mid-way between the first and the second editions of the *Principles*. In the *Essay*, the dismal prediction is that the population tends to multiply to the limits of subsistence. In the *Principles*, the dismal prediction is that aggregate supply tends to increase more rapidly than effective demand. Whichever way you look at it, the future is dismal. It is dismal for two different reasons. They are free-standing. They are not related.

The two reasons seem to dwell on different planets. The implication seems to be that not one but two solutions will have to be found if the nation is to be rescued from decline and fall. It is a major challenge for the policymaker. As Paglin says: 'The crux of the matter is that it makes a great deal of difference to Malthus's argument in terms of policy whether poverty is due to one cause rather than the other' (Paglin 1961: 149).

If widespread poverty is being caused by overpopulation, the solution will be fewer births and tight-fisted relief. If, however, the principal cause is excessive saving, then what is needed will be public works and unproductive consumption. The policies might be contradictory: demand-management in a recession would suggest not strict but open-handed welfare. The policies might be unconnected: deferred marriage is only tangentially linked to menial servants. There is a third possibility. The policies might be linked but the interconnecting relationships might be hidden. Malthus's *Wealth of Nations* might be there but it might be buried beneath the words.

That was the assessment of Joseph Spengler. Spengler felt that the implicit synthesis could be reconstructed from the stand-alone parts. What Malthus *meant* was greater than the sum of what Malthus had *said*. Readers who had failed to probe, Spengler said, had 'missed his *total* population theory' (Spengler 1945: 83, emphasis in original). They had seen only the tip of the iceberg. They had not seen enough.

Different readers will find different icebergs. This book has indicated that the connecting link is the self-sustaining dynamic of growth. Malthus, like his great mentor Smith, believed that mind and matter are continually in motion. Progress is not assured. *Decline and Fall* is always ready and waiting. Malthus in the final analysis was, however, an optimist. The greatest happiness of the greatest number is all but inevitable if population, subsistence and effective demand settle into their proper proportions.

Investment both in fixed capital and in the wages fund will be the effect and cause of the change in wealth: 'The faster the value of the annual produce increases, the greater will be the power of purchasing fresh labour, and the more will be wanted every year' (PR 261). Wealth and numbers advance together. The derived demand for labour impacts upon the level of wages and the volume of employment. More people with more money augment the effective demand for final output. Demand makes the supply go round.

A fresh worker is a fresh consumer. Input, output, purchase, sale, Spengler hazards the guess that Malthus's macroeconomics 'probably evolved out of his consideration of the population question.... Malthus apparently came to recognize the importance of the role of the effectual demand for labour in consequence of his initial concern with the checks to population growth' (Spengler 1945: 84, 100). Spengler says that the demand side of the circular flow was 'vaguely foreshadowed in the first edition' (Spengler 1945: 86). It was developed further in the fifth. Spengler sees it as a hidden bridge between the *Essay* and the *Principles.*

Accumulation creates jobs: 'What is mainly necessary to a rapid increase of population, is a great and continued demand for labour' (PR 261). A tight labour market empowers the marginal grades to marry and to multiply. It reproduces the mill-hands and the farmworkers who will reproduce the things. One hand washes the other. All classes together climb the ladder of sustained economic advance.

It is not guaranteed. Investment can be inadequate if the saving classes lack the hunger or the opportunity to better their condition. Investment can be excessive if home and foreign consumers do not take up the unsaleable stock. Oscillations and even stagnation can be the result of the mismatch. Business economics is not a tidy mathematical proof. A dynamic market by its very nature never gets its equilibrium right.

There is also technology. Should the composition of capital evolve in the direction of the inanimate input, the consequence will be that growth is sustained but living labour displaced. Especially if the changeover is sudden, it could be the robots and not the instincts that queer the pitch: 'If the substitution of fixed capital were to take place very rapidly….a slack demand for labour and great distress among the labouring classes of society would be universally felt' (PR 265). Vice and misery could result even if family size were small. Malthus did not think it very likely. In a growing economy, the absolute increase in both the fixed and the wage capital was likely to exceed any change in their relative coefficients.

Agriculture is different. The geometrical ratio will forever experience positive and preventive checks so long as the food supply lags behind. A Hell on earth seems to have been a part of the Supreme Utilitarian's original design. Malthus, while accepting the niggardly inexorability of diminishing returns, nonetheless denies that the stationary state is in sight. Improvements in yield per acre and the free importation of grain from abroad are shifting outward the margin of nutrition. Moral restraint and fewer children are containing the pressure on the land. The ratios and the checks are tendencies but not extrapolations. Manure, rotation, upward mobility and emulative *embourgeoisement* could mean that all the bets are off.

Affluence is the product of spontaneous interaction. Yet public policy too is needed to complement the utility and the profits. Food security should be ring-fenced by the Corn Laws in violation of the freedom of absolute advantage. Social traditions and political stability should be safeguarded through a restricted suffrage, the law of primogeniture and the enforcement of property rights. There should be countercyclical public works and moderate budgetary imbalance to steady the level of aggregate demand. There should be a non-fiduciary money supply tied to foreign currencies by a fixed rate of exchange to block off the temptations open to self-seeking bankers. There should be the fallback of state paternalism through a modicum of outdoor relief.

There has to be a cultural valuation of assiduity, frugality and success. There has to be social mobility based on merit, education and achievement. There has to be God: 'Of the various aspects of his radical theology, it is his growth-of-mind thesis which has the most relevance for his principle of population, transforming it from a principle of demographic pessimism (as it is still popularly interpreted) to one of moderate optimism for the progress of mankind' (Pullen 1987: 139). God is nature and nature is utility. God is on the side of economic growth.

It is not a ragbag of bits and pieces. All the parts fit into a single whole. The name of Malthus conjures up a dystopia of vice and misery. The headline image has concealed the underlying message. Like Adam Smith, it was not the poverty of the residuum so much as the happiness of the whole that gives unity to the multiple dimensions of Malthus's economic thought.

References

By T. R. Malthus

(1820 [1989]). *The Principles of Political Economy* (abbreviated as PR), ed. by J. Pullen. Cambridge: Cambridge University Press.

(1836 [1989]). *The Principles of Political Economy: The Alterations to the First Edition* (abbreviated as PR II), ed. by J. Pullen. Cambridge: Cambridge University Press.

Secondary Literature

Empson, W. (1837 [1963]). Life, Writings, and Character of Mr. Malthus. *Edinburgh Review*, 64 (Reprinted in *Occasional Papers of T. R. Malthus*, pp. 231–268, by B. Semmel, Ed., New York: Bert Franklin).

James, P. (1979). *Population Malthus: His Life and Times*. London: Routledge and Kegan Paul.

Marshall, A. (1890 [1949]). *Principles of Economics*. London: Macmillan.

Paglin, M. (1961). *Malthus and Lauderdale: The Anti-Ricardian Tradition*. New York: Augustus M. Kelley.

Pullen, J. R. (1987). New Information on the Rev. T. R. Malthus. *History of Political Economy, 19*, 127–140.

Spengler, J. J. (1945). Malthus's Total Population Theory: A Restatement and Reappraisal. *Canadian Journal of Economic and Political Science, 11*, 83–110 and 234.

Index

D. Reisman, *Thomas Robert Malthus*, Great Thinkers in Economics,
https://doi.org/10.1007/978-3-030-01956-3